ABSOLUTE POWER

ABSOLUTE POWER

The Legacy of
Corruption in the
Clinton-Reno
Justice Department

David Limbaugh

Since 1947
**REGNERY
PUBLISHING, INC.**
An Eagle Publishing Company • Washington, DC

Library of Congress Cataloging-in-Publication Data

Limbaugh, David.
    Absolute power / David Limbaugh.
       p. cm.
    Includes bibliographical references.
    ISBN 0-89526-237-1 (alk. paper)
       1. United States. Dept. of Justice—Corrupt practices. 2. Justice, Administration of—Corrupt practices—United States—History. 3. Political corruption—United States—History. I. Title.

KF5107 .L56 2001
345.73'02323—dc21   2001018581

Published in the United States by
Regnery Publishing, Inc.
An Eagle Publishing Company
One Massachusetts Avenue, NW
Washington, DC 20001

Visit us at www.regnery.com

Distributed to the trade by
National Book Network
4720-A Boston Way
Lanham, MD 20706

Printed on acid-free paper
Manufactured in the United States of America

10 9 8 7 6 5 4 3 2 1

BOOK DESIGN BY KASHKA KISZTELINSKA
SET IN JANSON

Books are available in quantity for promotional or premium use. Write to Director of Special Sales, Regnery Publishing, Inc., One Massachusetts Avenue, NW, Washington, DC 20001, for information on discounts and terms or call (202) 216–0600.

To Lisa and the girls,
Christen, Courtney, and Caitlyn.

Contents

	Introduction	ix
One	Waco	1
Two	Tobacco Wars	39
Three	A Genuine Conspiracy	65
Four	Investigating the Investigator	93
Five	"A Substantive, Savvy, and Experienced Professional"	139
Six	Presidential Privilege	157
Seven	The Mother of All Scandals	169
Eight	The Mother of All Scandals Moves to Congress	203
Nine	The Mother of All Scandals and the Justice Department	231
Ten	Bill Lann Lee: Quota King	275
Eleven	Treating with Terrorists	293
Twelve	Elian	307
	Afterword	333
	Notes	337
	Acknowledgments	367
	Index	369

Introduction

This book is about the consummate corruption and politicization of the Clinton-Reno Justice Department. It examines how this enforcement arm of the executive branch was used as both a sword and shield for the Clinton-Gore administration's innumerable crimes and abuses of constitutional power.

Much lip service was paid to the "rule of law" during the Clinton years, primarily to distract attention from how often it was undermined. "The rule of law" is the very core of our constitutional system. It is a maxim holding that we are a government of laws, not men. This means that no man is above the law and that the law restrains government itself. As James Madison wrote in Federalist No. 51: "In framing a government which is to be administered by men over men, the great difficulty lies in this: You must first enable the government to control the governed; and in the next place oblige it to control itself."

The law is not an end in itself, but a necessary means to preserve our liberties. The framers' solution was to incorporate into the Constitution a scheme of governmental powers and limitations. The powers would be divided between the federal and state governments and among the three branches in each. A complex system of checks and balances would help to prevent each branch from becoming too powerful at the expense of individual liberties.

But the framers understood that no constitution, regardless of how brilliantly crafted, could completely prevent abuses. John Adams said, "Our Constitution was made only for a moral and religious people. It is wholly inadequate to the government of any other."

If, for example, the president happens not to be a man of virtue and one or both of the other branches of government fail to restrain him, he has a green light to wield his executive power arbitrarily and capriciously. But even then, there are further checks within the executive department itself, such as the Justice Department, provided that honorable people control that department.

This book examines the record of the Clinton-Gore administration in light of our constitutional history, focusing on President Clinton's executive abuses—in particular, those involving the complicity of the Justice Department. The Clinton-Gore administration's rampant corruption and trampling of the rule of law permeated the entire executive branch. Whether conscious conspirator or unwitting puppet, Janet Reno dedicated the awesome enforcement power of the Justice Department to protect and defend President Clinton's multiple crimes and abuses of power. She prostituted Justice into a base political arm of the administration.

In 1993, shortly after she was installed as attorney general, Janet Reno sent an unmistakable signal that her Justice Department would primarily serve the political ends of Bill

Clinton rather than the ends of justice. At once, she fired all ninety-three of the country's United States attorneys. According to no less an authority than Ted Olson, President George Bush's chief post-election attorney, Reno's move was extreme and unprecedented. "In order to maintain continuity in thousands of pending prosecutions, and as a statement to the public that elections do not influence routine law enforcement, the nation's top prosecutors are traditionally replaced only after their successors have been located, appointed, and confirmed by the Senate. On instructions from the White House (she claimed it was a 'joint' decision; no one believes that), Reno ordered all 93 to leave in ten days. There could not have been a clearer signal that the Clinton campaign war room had taken over law enforcement in America."[1]

The firings were only the beginning. Throughout Clinton's two terms, the Clinton-Reno Justice Department, instead of dispassionately enforcing the law, waged war against the administration's political and legal enemies.

When President Clinton wanted to practice character assassination on the White House Travel Office staff, Ken Starr, or Linda Tripp, he relied on the Justice Department for logistical support. When frustrated by a recalcitrant Republican Congress, President Clinton used Janet Reno to orchestrate end runs around the legislative branch—misusing the judicial system to usurp legislative prerogatives, such as with their wholesale war on the tobacco industry.

When Clinton ducked responsibility for his excesses, as at Waco, the buck stopped with Janet Reno rather than the president. But if the polls swung in her favor, he swooped in to take personal credit. When the president became embroiled in a personal lawsuit, he enlisted the aid of Reno's department to file briefs on his behalf. When he was at legal war with the independent counsel,

Reno joined forces with the president rather than the independent counsel whom she was legally obliged to assist. Throughout the Clinton-Gore administration, Reno was complicit in the assertion of phony legal privileges and disruptions of the judicial process.

When congressional and independent counsel investigations struck close to the administration, Reno conveniently assumed jurisdiction over the investigation and became the president's surrogate stonewaller. While pretending to conduct investigations, she blocked Congress, denying it access to critical information and stalled long enough to stifle whatever momentum and progress investigators had achieved. Just as Clinton failed to maintain a wall of separation between his private and public lives, he misappropriated Justice to do his private dirty work and refused to keep his private attorneys separate from the Justice Department.

Even when matters as serious as national security and illegal foreign campaign contributions were involved, Reno, instead of performing her constitutional duty to enforce and uphold the law, used her office to insulate the Clinton-Gore administration from scrutiny and resulting accountability. When Charles La Bella, the Special Task Force attorney she appointed to investigate the campaign finance scandal, recommended the appointment of an independent counsel, she brazenly ignored the request and denied Congress access to La Bella's recommending memo.

Indeed, just as this book is going to press, *New York Times* columnist William Safire is reporting that on December 20, 2000, soon after Al Gore's concession, three top Justice Department aides, including an assistant attorney general, ordered one of the last remaining independent counsels, David Barrett, to stop his grand jury investigation. Barrett refused and Justice is apparently in a panic, especially with the prospect that the "incorruptible"

John Ashcroft, if confirmed, will be taking the helm at Justice. Barrett is reportedly investigating allegations that the Justice Department pressured the Internal Revenue Service not to cooperate with his investigation into where disgraced Clinton appointee Henry Cisneros got the money to pay his former mistress—payments that led to Cisneros's prosecution and resignation. Justice allegedly told the IRS not to allow Barrett to see all of Cisneros's tax returns. So, as Safire asks, "Was Justice colluding with the IRS in protecting any Clinton appointees or heavy contributors from charges of tax fraud?" "Equal justice," Safire reminds us, "demands the law to move in, not to 'move on.'"

The Clinton-Reno Justice Department, from Waco to Elian—with Travelgate, Chinagate, Monicagate, and the illegal war against tobacco in between—was one continuous, perfidious scandal factory. The republic cannot long endure such corruption and abuses of power.

While there have been numerous books about the Clinton administration and its multitudinous scandals, there has been no comprehensive case-by-case critique of the Clinton Justice Department. All of the sordid details must be exposed and articulated in a way that is accessible and intelligible to the average reader. If we can't succeed in bringing the late administration to account for its misdeeds, at least we can attempt to deter future administrations from such illegality by publicly exposing the abuses of the Clinton-Reno Justice Department.

Chapter One

Waco

On February 28, 1993, the United States government launched an unprecedented military-style raid on the Mount Carmel compound of David Koresh and his Branch Davidian followers near Waco, Texas. While the government's ostensible purpose was to serve a search warrant and an arrest warrant, its agents didn't bother to announce their arrival and demanded entry. The evidence suggests that they intended a dynamic entry, and a consensual search would not have fit into their plans. With congressional appropriations hearings scheduled for just a few weeks later, the Bureau of Alcohol, Tobacco, and Firearms (ATF) needed to demonstrate its worthiness for additional funding.

The government's "Showtime" raid—"Showtime" was the ATF agents' code name for the operation—didn't go as planned and four ATF agents were killed as well as six Branch Davidians. After a cease-fire was negotiated, a fifty-one-day standoff ensued during which the government tried to save face and resurrect what it could of its botched plan. On April 19, 1993, the government grew impatient and stormed the residence again. A fire broke out and consumed the compound and all but nine of its remaining eighty-plus Davidian inhabitants.

The Waco tragedy exposed a government all too willing to pursue extreme measures against its own citizens. However deplorable the behavior of David Koresh, did it really require a shootout, a siege, and the death of nearly one hundred people to bring David Koresh to justice?

To understand what went wrong, we have to learn something about the life and theology of Branch Davidian leader Vernon Howell, a.k.a. David Koresh. Had the government done its homework about his beliefs, the Waco nightmare might have been averted.

So, who was David Koresh and what did he and his followers believe?

Seventh-Day Adventism and the Branch Davidians

The Branch Davidians at Mount Carmel were an offshoot of the Seventh-Day Adventist Church (SDA). Of the seventy-two adults living there, all but seven had been members or in some way involved with the SDA Church.

The foundations for "Adventism" were laid by William Miller of New York. He thought he had calculated the exact date for the Advent—the Second Coming of Christ—to be October 22, 1844, despite the fact that Christ Himself had said that "No one knows about that day or hour, not even the angels in heaven, nor the Son, but only the Father.... Be on guard! Be alert! You do not know when that time will come."[1]

Miller, whose beliefs came to be known as "Millerism," developed a substantial following. Great numbers of Millerites met on hillsides wearing white robes to meet Christ on the date Miller had predicted for His return. When Christ did not appear, the Millerites were devastated. One of them, Hiram Edson, resourcefully overcame this Great Disappointment, as it came to be called. He claimed that God told him in a vision that Christ had done something very important on the predicted day, but He had done it in heaven. He would return to earth in the very near future to begin His judgment.[2]

One of Millerism's most distinguished devotees was Ellen G. White, a prolific theological writer whose most famous work was *The Great Controversy* (1888). White adopted Edson's revisions to Millerism. She further augmented the theology by borrowing from her friend Joseph Bates the notion that the Fourth Commandment—that the Sabbath should be kept holy—meant setting aside the period from Friday at sundown until sundown on Saturday as the day of religious worship; Sunday worship was a pagan construct. With the Sabbath being restored to the seventh day of the week, White's followers organized as the General Conference of Seventh-Day Adventists in 1863. There are about three million in the United States today.

Christ warned that Christians would be persecuted. Ellen White taught that only SDAs would be persecuted because they were the only true believers. She prophesied that they would be pursued by the wicked who "would enter the houses of the saints with a sword. They raised the sword to kill us, but it broke, and fell as powerless as a straw." Koresh and his followers believed that White's prophecy had been fulfilled in the February 28 raid on Mount Carmel.

White taught that God had imparted His truth to man incrementally in history, through progressive revelation. Unlike mainstream evangelical Christians who believe that God has sent no other prophets or apostles since the end of the New Testament period in the first century A.D., Ellen White taught that revelation was continuing and that she was just the latest in the line of prophets through whom God chose to reveal Himself.

According to White, there were Seven Angels (or Messengers) referred to in Revelation 14, and Miller was the spokesman for the first two, while she was the Third Messenger. She taught—and this is important—that only these anointed messengers were qualified to understand and explain Scripture. This belief would be made to order for Koresh who later claimed to be the Seventh (and final) Messenger. It would help to solidify his authority and virtually immunize him from criticism regardless of his conduct. The Branch Davidians, even the very intelligent ones, believed that they were wholly dependent on Koresh for insight into the Bible.

Victor Houteff, a Bulgarian immigrant, claimed to be the Fourth Messenger of Revelation. He had been officially expelled from the SDA Church for heresy. His major sin was that he deviated from Ellen White's teaching that the Kingdom of God would be established in heaven as a spiritual phenomenon. Houteff taught instead that the Kingdom of God was to be established physically on earth where Christ would literally occupy King David's throne, which was the more traditional evangelical view. When Houteff was expelled from the mother church he organized the Davidian Seventh-Day Adventist movement. The name "Davidian" obviously came from his teachings about the establishment of the "Davidic" throne.[3] In 1935, the Davidians migrated to Texas and founded the first Mount Carmel center close to Waco.

Houteff became ill and when he was in the hospital his wife, Florence, asked him to reveal when Christ would return and establish His Davidic Kingdom in Palestine. He told her that she would have the answer "tomorrow." When he died unexpectedly later that day, Florence and the Houteffs' close associates were perplexed. Why had he died without giving them the answer? Eventually, they concluded that he *had* told them. By saying "tomorrow," he surely meant that the forty-two-month period preceding Christ's return (foretold in the books of Daniel and Revelation) would begin "tomorrow." Christ would return on April 22, 1959, exactly forty-two months from "tomorrow," the day following Victor Houteff's death.

The group moved to a new location not far away on a tract that would later be called the New Mount Carmel. This remained the Davidians' home through Koresh's reign. Florence Houteff began to spread the word that her deceased husband, Victor, would be resurrected on April 22, 1959, to herald the return of Christ. Just like the Millerites in 1844, the group gathered in anticipation of the big event. When it failed to materialize the group split and most of the people followed Ben Roden, who would later establish himself as the Fifth Messenger.[4]

Roden's group remained at Mount Carmel and began referring to themselves as Branch Davidians because Roden fancied himself to be the messianic "Branch" foretold in Zechariah (3:8; 6:12). He also considered his followers to be "Branches" based on Jesus' statement to his disciples: "I am the vine, you are the branches."[5] When Roden died in 1978, his wife Lois replaced him, becoming the Sixth Messenger of Revelation. Lois Roden would pave the way for the Seventh Messenger, Vernon Howell (David Koresh), who would stand at the center of the Waco tragedy.

Vernon Howell

Howell was born in 1959, the illegitimate son of fourteen-year-old Bonnie Clark and Bobby Howell. He was so hyperactive as a child that they nicknamed him "Sputnik," after the Soviet satellite. Vernon was transferred back and forth from his mother to his maternal grandparents during his early years. His stepfather repeatedly beat him and held his feet to a hot furnace grating. Howell later revealed that between the ages of five and nine he was often raped by one of his mother's male relatives.

Howell was fascinated with religion from an early age. His mother was raised in the SDA Church, and she raised Vernon in it as well. She often took him to church. He was mesmerized by radio and television preachers and memorized large sections of the Bible, mostly prophecy.

As he grew in the Adventist faith he decided that the church had deviated from Scripture and from its particular mission. He was troubled that following the 1915 death of SDA prophet Ellen White, there were no living prophets to carry forth the sect's message. He began praying tirelessly to God to send another prophet.

He started attending an SDA church in Tyler, Texas, in 1979. He became further interested in prophecy there and particularly the prophecy about the Second Coming and the end of the world ("End Time") prophecy. A fellow member of the Tyler congregation told him about the Branch Davidian Community in Mount Carmel outside of Waco, Texas. He was intrigued as he learned of Mount Carmel's living prophet, Lois Roden, and especially by her teaching concerning the femininity of the Holy Spirit. He began making trips to Mount Carmel in 1981 and was drawn to its theology. For a few years Howell traveled back and forth between Tyler and Mount Carmel. As he straddled the two congregations his allegiance was divided. In 1983, his dilemma was solved because he was expelled from the Tyler congregation for reasons that included a sexual interest in the pastor's daughter.

When Howell began living at Mount Carmel he was viewed as obnoxious and arrogant. In an effort to humble him, Lois Roden assigned him undesirable rooms and demeaning tasks.

Howell shrewdly worked his way into the leadership hierarchy by developing a relationship with Lois Roden. Initially, their relationship was platonic, and they often discussed theology. Lois, perhaps unwittingly, legitimized Howell among the group by chiding Davidians not to dismiss him and to listen to what he had to say. After a time, Howell and Roden, then in her sixties, began a sexual relationship. Roden believed that she would miraculously conceive a child with Howell just as the Bible tells that Sarah gave birth to Isaac when in her nineties.

In 1984, Howell married resident Rachel Jones, which drove Lois Roden to public fits of jealousy. Eventually, her behavior caused Davidians to lose faith in her and she fell from power. This void in leadership led to a split in the group with some following Howell and others George Roden, the son of Ben and Lois Roden. It is interesting that Lois Roden had earlier prophesied about a seven-year period that would begin in 1977. She had predicted that two major events would take place, one in 1981 and the other in 1984. Koresh's arrival in 1981 and the group's split in 1984 legitimized Roden's prophecies and thus Koresh's authenticity.

Howell took his group and set up a makeshift community near Palestine, Texas. Meanwhile, George Roden turned to crime, setting up a methamphetamine lab. He also began collecting weapons. The next few years witnessed a power struggle between Roden and Howell for possession of the Waco property, involving a series of bizarre incidents.

Roden challenged Howell to a contest to determine who was really God's chosen leader. He dug up the body of a deceased

Davidian who had been buried on the property twenty years before and said that whoever could raise her from the dead was the rightful leader. Howell declined the challenge.

Howell had devised an easier way to dethrone Roden. He decided to turn him in to the authorities for his grave-digging escapade. In an effort to obtain photos of the disinterred body to incriminate Roden, Howell led a group of his followers onto the Mount Carmel property with paramilitary garb and weapons. A shootout ensued and Howell and his troops were arrested, charged, and tried for attempted murder. They were eventually acquitted.

Around the same time, Roden was jailed for contempt of court and lost possession of the compound. Howell's group acquired possession of the property and soon disassembled the methamphetamine lab and turned the equipment and manuals over to the sheriff. The ATF would later use this same defunct drug lab to petition for U.S. military assistance in the "Showtime" raid (Congress had authorized the use of American military forces in the so-called "drug war"). Authorities told Howell that in order to perfect title to the property his group would have to remain in continuous possession of it for five years. The five-year period was scheduled to end on March 22, 1993, which was three and-a-half weeks after the initial government raid on the property on February 28, 1993. Reportedly, the Branch Davidians were very reluctant to surrender possession during the siege because of their fear of losing the property.

Not long after he assumed control of the group Howell changed his name to David Koresh, which was to signify a number of things. "David" was derived from the Biblical King David, the greatest king of the Jews. As noted above, Jesus was to establish the throne of David on earth at his Second Coming.

"Koresh" was the Hebrew name for King Cyrus of Persia, who was called God's anointed. Koresh declared himself to be the Seventh Messenger of Revelation.

Koresh modified his theology to accommodate his sexual proclivities. He described himself as "the sinful messiah" because, unlike Jesus, he was sinful and was therefore uniquely positioned to fulfill Biblical prophecies that required a human sinner.[6]

Branch Davidian Theology Regarding the Seven Seals

The Book of Revelation talks about a scroll locked with Seven Seals. Only the Lamb of God, Jesus Christ, can open the Seven Seals and unlock the scroll. Most evangelical Biblical scholars interpret the Seven Seals to constitute a yet unfulfilled prophecy about the end times preceding Christ's return (His Second Coming) when God will pour out His judgment on the earth. Revelation describes the opening of each of the seals in succession and with it the unleashing of an event of judgment. Many Bible scholars believe the events to be ushered in by the Seven Seals will occur during the second half of the last seven years (the forty-two month period referred to above) preceding Christ's return—the period of the Great Tribulation.

Evangelical author Warren Wiersbe explains the reason for the Biblical reference to a scroll locked with seals. He says that in Rome during Biblical times a person's "will was sealed with seven seals; this scroll is the will, or testament, giving Christ the right to claim creation by virtue of His sacrifice."[7] Bible scholar Charles Ryrie suggests that "the scroll seems to contain the story of humanity's losing its lordship over creation and the regaining of that authority by the man Christ Jesus. The scroll might be titled the 'Book of Redemption' since it contains the story of redemption to its final consummation."[8] Koresh's interpretation was characteristically convoluted and self-serving. He read the text to mean that the scroll secured by the Seven Seals represented the entire Bible. Where most Christians believe the "Lamb" mentioned in the Book of Revelation to be Jesus Christ alone, Koresh claimed to be the Lamb.[9] Koresh, being the Lamb, was the only one who could open the seals and interpret the Bible. It's important to clarify that Koresh didn't claim to be the historical Jesus. He claimed to be another Christ,[10] as he believed that God had designated him, the Lamb, actively to bring about the fulfillment of End Time prophecy.[11] He was supposed to make it happen. This would be extremely relevant as the Waco incident unfolded.

Investigation

After he returned from Israel in 1985, Koresh became sexually active with women—in some cases underage girls—at Mount Carmel. He said that in a vision on Mount Zion, God ordered him to procreate with Michele Jones, his wife Rachel's eleven-year-old sister. Though Rachel was initially devastated, she later had a dream that convinced her that Koresh had to obey God's command.[12] Koresh began to have relations with many young girls, some underage, and to have children with them. Koresh claimed that he was divinely required to perpetuate his genes; and according to Davidian survivor David Thibodeau, Koresh viewed these relations as constituting Biblical marriage. Before he died he had sired seventeen children with eleven different women.[13] He would later refer to his many wives as the "House of David."

Prior to August 5, 1989, Howell made advances only on single women. After that, he began to teach that all women, including married women, belonged to him. All children that he sired were to acquire a special status in the coming Kingdom of God. These teachings emanated from his "New Light" revelation.[14]

This outrageous announcement may have marked the beginning of the end for Koresh because it greatly alienated his close confidant Marc Breault, who broke from Koresh and returned to Australia.[15] Breault, as we shall see, later became Koresh's fiercest opponent and caused the investigations of Koresh to begin.

Among Koresh's sexual conquests were more than ten underage women. Thibodeau seemed perplexed that Koresh chose to violate the civil law (statutory rape) when he could have had any number of women who were of lawful age. Thibodeau, still an avowed supporter of Koresh, admitted that Koresh "was guilty on multiple charges [of statutory rape] that could have sent him to prison for a very long time, perhaps for life."[16] In view of this, Thibodeau speculated as to whether Koresh had a death wish of sorts, "inviting his own apocalypse," but concluded that the answer was unclear.

While previous leaders of Mount Carmel, such as Houteff and the Rodens, preached End Time prophecy, they didn't see their role as actively bringing about those events that would usher in the end of the world. This was markedly different from Koresh, the Seventh Messenger, who would be God's final Word to the world.[17] In fact, Koresh had a ten-year plan for the world to come to an end, beginning in 1985 with his vision on Mount Zion.[18]

Just as candidly as Thibodeau admits Koresh's egregious violation of the statutory rape laws of Texas, he adamantly denies that Koresh otherwise abused Branch Davidian children. Koresh treated the children with delicate care, according to Thibodeau, contrary to the ATF's charge that "women and children to him [Koresh] are expendable items."[19] Thibodeau's assessment may not be entirely accurate in that Koresh and the Davidians report-edly employed a policy of aggressive corporal punishment toward their children. Janet Reno testified at the congressional hearings about an incident in 1988 where Koresh allegedly had spanked an eight-month-old child for more than a half hour for refusing to sit on his lap.

This is where disaffected member Marc Breault came in. He is the one who initiated the child-abuse charges. He and some other Davidians in Australia hired a private investigator to follow up on these allegations. After nosing around, federal authorities declined to prosecute because no federal laws had been broken.[20]

Breault was persistent and managed to interest an Australian television network to do a special on Koresh and the Branch Davidians for *A Current Affair*. The one-hour special reported that Koresh beat children, punished them through grueling phys-ical exercises, and deprived them of food and water. Thibodeau related that Koresh was very upset with the show. "How could they lie like this?"[21]

Breault also continued to prod the sheriff's department into taking action against Koresh, and in early 1992 the sheriff called in the Texas Department of Child Protective Services (CPS). The CPS formally closed its investigation on April 30, 1992, because none of the allegations could be verified. Whatever evidence there may have been of physical child abuse in the past, the CPS deter-mined that there was no evidence of abuse in 1992.

On June 9, 1992, the ATF in Austin opened a formal investi-gation of the Branch Davidians based on a call they had received a month before from the McLennan County Sheriff's Department. The sheriff had been called by the UPS because some dummy hand grenades were discovered in an accidentally broken package that was scheduled for delivery to the Mount Carmel compound.

When the ATF began investigating, they found that Koresh had recently purchased powdered aluminum and black gunpowder. While there are lawful uses for these items, they can also be used as the explosive components of grenades. Grenades constitute destructive devices whose ownership is prohibited by federal law.

The ATF also discovered that the Davidians had bought more than $40,000 worth of arms, including more than a hundred "upper receivers" for AR-15 rifles.[22] The ATF suspected that the Davidians planned to combine those upper receivers with lower receivers to convert the semiautomatic AR-15 weapons into machine guns.[23]

The AR-15 rifles are semiautomatic, meaning they will only fire one shot with a pull of the trigger but will automatically reload. AR-15s can be converted to M-16 machine guns with special kits, but the ATF never found proof that the Davidians had acquired all the necessary parts to complete such a conversion.[24]

Semiautomatic AR-15s can also be converted to M-16 machine guns by another, more difficult method. This involves manufacturing the necessary parts with lathes and milling machines. The Davidians did possess some of this equipment, but so do hundreds of thousands of other Americans. There are many lawful and innocuous purposes for such machinery.[25]

Even the Treasury Department's investigative report included an opinion from a firearms specialist who admitted that "None of the many pieces of information available to me is sufficient, by itself, to answer the question as to whether Koresh and his followers inside the compound were engaged in assembling automatic weapons in violation of the National Firearms Act."[26]

Federal law does not prohibit ownership or possession of machine guns but does impose a registration requirement and a fee of $200 per weapon. So even if it were true that Koresh had converted some semiautomatic weapons to machine guns (which he may have, according to testimony during the 1994 trial of eleven Davidians), his crime was not possession but possession without registration and paying the tax, which is hardly a capital offense. Political correctness aside, there is no law against stockpiling weapons.[27]

It would later be learned that the Davidians acquired guns both for protection and investment purposes. In fact they bought and sold weapons and paraphernalia at gun shows throughout the state. They also sold vests made by Davidian women who spruced them up by sewing dummy grenades into them.[28]

Warrant

The ATF sought and obtained an arrest warrant for David Koresh and a search warrant for the Davidian compound. The Treasury Department in its internal report on Waco concluded that probable cause had been established for the arrest and search as of November 1992.[29]

The joint congressional subcommittees investigating Waco agreed that the ATF had probable cause but strongly criticized the ATF for the numerous misstatements contained in the affidavit used to procure the warrants.[30] The errors included matters of fact as well as law. Many of the allegations contained in the warrant applications were based on stale information, involving activities that occurred between 1988 and June 1992.[31]

Some errors were admittedly minor, though they could have been problematic if the case had been brought to court. For instance, the arrest warrant application mistakenly cited the statute defining "destructive device" rather than the statute that makes it illegal to manufacture or possess a destructive device.[32]

The factual errors in the affidavit were worse. The affidavit alleged that Koresh had obtained kits to convert semiautomatic guns to machine guns, when, in fact, there was no such evidence. Some authors have argued that the powdered aluminum and black gunpowder could have been acquired to build explosives to help excavate the ground for a swimming pool the Davidians were building at the time.[33]

The affidavit also alleged that the Davidians possessed "*Shotgun News* and other related clandestine magazines." But *Shotgun News* is hardly clandestine. At the time, it reported a subscription base of well over 100,000 people. Its Web site boasts that *Shotgun News* is the world's largest gun sales publication.[34]

Further, the affidavit contained allegations about Koresh's sexual abuse of minors, a subject outside the jurisdiction of the federal government. The affidavit did not reveal that the Texas Department of Child Protective Services had concluded that the child-abuse charges could not be substantiated.

The statement that the ATF had established probable cause for arrest warrants by the end of 1992 is contradicted by Koresh nemesis Marc Breault, who conceded that ATF agent Davy Aguilera had told him in December 1992 that he could not do anything about Koresh because he lacked direct evidence.[35] Likewise, ATF director Stephen Higgins, in testimony before the subcommittees, confirmed that the ATF lacked probable cause as of December 1992.

Because it felt it lacked probable cause, the agency started an undercover operation by setting up surveillance cameras in a rental home across the road from the compound. When the cameras yielded no fruit, it sent in an undercover agent, Robert Rodriguez. Though Rodriguez was unable to obtain any additional evidence to support the warrant application, the ATF pressed forward to pursue a warrant anyway. On February 25, 1993, it obtained an arrest warrant for Koresh for possession of destructive devices and a search warrant that covered, among other things, machine guns and destructive devices.[36]

There is no question that the government had accumulated certain suspicious tidbits concerning Koresh. Unfortunately, the agents may have allowed their imaginations to run out of control when they also found that Koresh was in possession of grenade casings and harbored a powerful distrust for the government.

Earlier, when the government had an opportunity to investigate more deeply into Koresh's weapons ownership, it declined. ATF investigators were questioning Koresh's main arms dealer, Henry McMahon, on July 30, 1992, when McMahon stepped out of the room and secretly called Koresh to tell him about the investigators. Koresh told McMahon to invite the agents out for a look-see. While Koresh was still on the line, McMahon conveyed the offer, but Special Agent Aguilera nervously declined.[37]

The Dawning of the Raid

The *Waco Tribune-Herald* began a series on Koresh's "cult" on February 27, 1993, the day before the fateful raid. The story mobilized public opinion against the Mount Carmel residents.

But the Davidians weren't the only ones under the media spotlight. A month earlier the CBS show *60 Minutes* had featured a story on sexual harassment allegations against the ATF by some of its female agents. This story couldn't have aired at a more inopportune time given that congressional budget hearings were scheduled for March 10, 1993.

We will never know for sure whether ATF superiors were considering the potential impact on congressional funding when they were planning the raid, but there are certain things we do know.

We know that ATF special agent Sharon Wheeler, a public information officer, was in charge of videotaping the agency's raid preparation and the raid itself, as well as handling the media that arrived. We also know that when she testified before Congress, Wheeler confessed, "You want to promote your agency in a good light, and ATF hired public information officers over the last two years to do that, to show the agency in a good light."[38]

While the official name for the February 28 raid was "Operation Trojan Horse," the agents themselves code-named it "Showtime." It's hard to conceive that the agency wasn't hoping to score big points with its Hollywood-style assault. In fact, the subcommittees concluded that the ATF had a variety of options at its disposal to serve the arrest and search warrants.[39] Koresh was seen many times off the Mount Carmel premises, jogging, shopping, and frequenting restaurants in town. They could have arrested him any of those times.

Plus, had the ATF truly wanted to nab him without fanfare, it missed a golden opportunity. The ATF's official records indicate that just nine days before the raid, certain ATF undercover agents went to the compound and fired weapons with Koresh, using Koresh's ammunition. The ATF could have arrested him on that occasion.

The ATF also could have approached him nonviolently and asked him to consent to a search. You will recall that he had invited agents to come out the previous summer to inspect his weapons, but they refused. In all his other brushes with the law, Koresh had been cooperative with law enforcement authorities.

Instead, as the subcommittees noted, "The ATF chose the dynamic entry raid, the most hazardous of the options, despite its recognition that a violent confrontation was predictable."[40] Koresh's violent reaction was predictable because he viewed the government as the evil "Babylon" and believed that Babylon would ultimately try to take him out. By its every action the government reinforced Koresh's theological views.

The agency's predisposition to theatrics was also shown by the fact that it proceeded with the raid even though it knew on the morning of the raid that the element of surprise had been lost. Let me repeat this outrageous truth. The ATF knew immediately before the raid that Koresh had been tipped off that it was coming, but it went forward anyway. Two agents later denied this, but as we shall see, the subcommittees found that their denials were lies. The subcommittees concluded that the ATF's reckless decision to proceed with the raid, despite having lost the element of surprise, "more than any other factor, led to the deaths of the four ATF agents killed on February 28, 1993."

Koresh was warned of the upcoming raid through an unlikely event. When a local TV cameraman got lost looking for the compound that morning, he sought directions from a mailman who happened to be a Branch Davidian. After letter carrier David Jones pointed out the compound to the cameraman, the cameraman told him that a raid was likely going to take place that day and "that there may be a shooting."[41] After the cameraman left, Jones rushed back to the compound to warn his father, Perry Jones, who in turn warned Koresh.

Perry Jones had to interrupt Koresh to give him the news. Koresh was in the middle of a conversation with ATF undercover agent Robert Rodriguez at the time. Rodriguez reported that when Koresh returned from talking to Perry Jones, he was "extremely agitated" and told him, "They're coming, Robert, the time has come. They're coming, Robert, they're coming." Even more ominously, Koresh added, "Neither the ATF nor the National Guard will ever get me. They got me once and they'll never get me again."[42]

When Rodriguez discovered that Koresh knew the raid was going down all he could think about was getting out of there and alerting his superiors so that they would call off the raid. He was also worried that Koresh was on to him and might hold him as a hostage. As it turned out, Koresh let him go and bid him good luck.

Rodriguez rushed back to the undercover house across the road and informed James Cavanaugh, ATF's deputy tactical coordinator for the ATF operation, that Koresh knew they were coming. Apparently unfazed by the news, Cavanaugh asked Rodriguez only whether he had seen any guns. When Rodriguez said he hadn't, Cavanaugh told him to report the news to Chuck Sarabyn, the tactical coordinator for "Showtime."[43]

When Rodriguez phoned Sarabyn with the news, the superior's response was not to cancel the raid but to ask the same questions as Cavanaugh. Had he seen any guns? What were the Davidians wearing? And so forth. Sarabyn then met with Phillip Chojnacki, his immediate superior. Chojnacki asked Sarabyn whether he thought they should go forward. Sarabyn said yes, "if they hurried."[44]

Rodriguez testified to the subcommittees that Sarabyn hung up so fast that he didn't have time to ask him to cancel the raid. "That's why I quickly left the undercover house to go talk to him at the command post because I wanted to have a more—more of a lengthy conversation with him about the events."[45]

Rodriguez hurriedly drove to the command post, but Sarabyn had already left. Rodriguez testified, "At that time, I started yelling and I said, 'Why, why, why? They know we're coming.'" Rodriguez then walked outside and started to weep.[46]

Here's where it gets interesting. When he testified to the subcommittees, Sarabyn denied that Koresh really believed the raid was going down. He admitted that Rodriguez told him Koresh was expecting the raid but that he (Sarabyn) didn't think Koresh really meant it. Agent Chojnacki, in his testimony before the subcommittees, backed up Sarabyn's version that Koresh didn't really believe they were coming.

But the Treasury report makes it clear that as soon as Sarabyn got the call from Rodriguez, he rushed to the staging center for the raid. He excitedly told the agents, "Get ready to go, they know we are coming... they know ATF and the National Guard are coming. We are going to hit them now."[47]

Also, Rodriguez directly contradicted Sarabyn and Chojnacki and challenged their veracity. "Those two men know—know what I told them and they knew exactly what I meant. And instead of coming up and admitting to the American people right after the raid that they had made a mistake... they lied to the public and in doing so they just about destroyed a very great agency."[48] Other ATF agents also testified that Sarabyn had told them that Koresh knew they were coming.[49] The subcommittees concluded that, contrary to his denials, Sarabyn knew that the Davidians were tipped off and would be lying in wait for the ATF agents to arrive.[50] The subcommittees also concluded that the Clinton administration attempted to absolve itself by asserting that it had issued a directive to cancel the raid if the element of surprise had been lost. In fact, there had been no such order by the Treasury Department to the ATF, nor by the ATF to its agents in Waco.[51]

Despite having lost the element of surprise, the ATF invaded the Davidian compound with seventy-six agents. In the brutal gunfight that followed, six Davidians and four ATF agents were killed with many others wounded on both sides. It appears that two primary factors contributed to the ATF's decision to press forward. One was that the ATF only knew one speed. Its history militated in favor of lightning-like, dynamic entries. It is used to dealing with drug dealers who generally realize they are overwhelmed and quickly surrender.[52] This pragmatic mentality was not shared by the Davidians, who believed it was their sacred duty to resist the evil Babylon.

The second factor contributing to the violent assault was that the ATF had collaborated with the military in preparation for the raid and was in a warlike mode. This civilian use of the military is a controversial practice and one that has been historically disfavored by Congress and the courts.

In 1878 Congress passed the Posse Comitatus Act to restrict the military's involvement in civilian law enforcement. The rationale for the statute was that the military is trained to fight and kill foreign enemies, whereas civilian law enforcement's primary purpose is not to win wars but to enforce the law and, in the process, not to trample on the constitutional rights of citizens.

After many judicial rulings and further congressional enactments, the scope of the Posse Comitatus law is not crystal clear. As it stands, the law forbids the military from taking an active role in civilian law enforcement but permits passive assistance.[53] In 1989, Congress carved out an exception for the active role prohibition. In situations where drugs are involved, the military may participate directly. One of the consequences of this exception is that when the ATF or other law enforcement agencies call on military assistance, they are not required to reimburse the military if drug issues are involved. In the case of the Waco raid, the ATF mentioned allegations only of gun violations by the Davidians when initially requesting military helicopters. Just a few days later, the ATF disingenuously amended its request to establish the "drug nexus." The drug connection was bogus. The only evidence connecting Davidians to drugs was the old dismantled methamphetamine lab of Koresh's predecessor, George Roden—which Koresh had personally reported to the sheriff in 1988—and suspicions that some Davidians had been involved in drugs in the past. One, indeed, had been convicted.[54]

The Raid

One of the most controversial mysteries surrounding the Waco ordeal is the question of who fired first. The Davidians claimed that the ATF fired first and that they responded, while the government insists that the Davidians opened fire through the steel front door. Several possibilities have been suggested.

Both sides seem to agree that as the agents approached the compound Koresh opened the front door, but what happened next is disputed. The Davidians' version is that Koresh exclaimed that women and children were inside and was immediately shot and wounded. The government says that Koresh just smiled an eerie smile, closed the door, and the Davidians began firing through it.

Helicopters were also hovering over the property and some say that the first shots were exchanged between the Davidians and the airborne agents, with each side claiming the other fired first. Finally, some believe that the ATF fired accidentally or shot the Davidians' guard dogs, prompting the Davidians to return fire.[55] The subcommittees concluded that although there was no decisive proof, it is more likely that the Davidians fired first.[56]

Dick DeGuerin, Koresh's lawyer, and Jack Zimmerman, attorney for Koresh's lieutenant, Steve Schneider, both examined the door when they visited their clients during the siege. Both swore that their examination of the front door led them to believe that the bullet holes were fired from the outside rather than the inside. David Kopel and Paul Blackman, in their book No More Wacos, relate that the Davidians introduced photographs taken by the

Waco Herald-Tribune at their 1994 criminal trial. The photographs supposedly show the ATF firing at the compound at a time when there were no bullet holes yet in the door. This would tend to disprove the ATF's version that Koresh fired first. "The prosecutor argued that there was no way of telling when the photographs involving the door were taken. But if ATF had opened fire at any time before a bullet hole appeared in the front door, then ATF's story of an opening fusillade through the front door could not have been correct."[57]

Roland Ballesteros, the ATF agent leading the charge to the front door, claims he saw an unarmed Koresh standing in the open doorway and loudly announced, "Police! Search warrant! Lay [sic] down!" He says that Koresh then closed the door and shots were immediately fired from the inside through the front door. [58]

Had the Davidians been lying in ambush for the ATF agents, as the government later claimed, the Davidians would have mowed the agents down as they emerged from the ATF cattle trailers. The agents would have been sitting ducks. Even the FBI's Waco commander, Jeffrey Jamar, admitted as much.[59] Instead, Koresh opened the door in plain view and unarmed. The most likely scenario, as some ATF agents later admitted, is that the first shots might have been fired by agents shooting the guard dogs,[60] leading to a general gunfight because each side believed the other had initiated gunfire.

Perhaps as important as the question of who shot first is the government's plan of "attack." The ATF was oriented solely toward a "dynamic entry"-style raid. They had trained exclusively for a violent confrontation and apparently had no contingency plan if something were to go wrong with the dynamic entry.[61]

Another curious aspect of the raid is that the ATF had arranged for no telephone contact to be established with the

Davidians in the event the raid didn't go as planned. When Davidian Douglas Wayne Martin, a lawyer, called 911 desperately trying to get the government to cease firing, he was hooked up with Larry Lynch, a sheriff's deputy. Lynch tried fruitlessly for more than thirty minutes to reach the ATF and only after thirty-eight minutes did he reach someone at the ATF command team. But even after that line of communication was opened there was no direct communication between the ATF and the Davidians. They had to communicate through Lynch.

Shortly after the February 28 raid and during the standoff, the government started to investigate itself. The ATF began its review almost immediately. No sooner had it started than it was ordered to back off by its parent, the Treasury Department. Treasury was yielding to a request from its sister, the Justice Department, to curtail the internal investigation. Justice was concerned that the investigation would produce evidence that would be exculpatory to defendants in the inevitable Waco criminal trial. In criminal cases, the government, under what is known as the Brady rule, is required to disclose evidence that might point to the defendant's innocence. Rather than risk that, the government preferred to halt the investigation in its tracks.[62]

Apparently the government was concerned about more than just losing criminal cases. It was also worried about the embarrassing and damning evidence that was being uncovered. A September 17, 1993, confidential Treasury Department memo to Assistant Treasury Secretary Ron Noble stated that on March 1, the Bureau of Alcohol, Tobacco, and Firearms initiated a shooting review and "immediately determined that these stories [by the agents involved] did not add up." The memo continued that a Justice attorney "at this point advised [ATF supervisor Dan]

Hartnett to stop the ATF shooting review because ATF was creating exculpatory material that might undermine the government prosecution of the Davidians."[63]

It is troubling that the government would delay and therefore irreparably damage an investigation into the truth for fear that the truth might undermine a future case against potential criminal defendants. Besides, the government, as a matter of law and ethics, should not have suppressed a review that could lead to exculpatory materials. Contrary to a Justice Department PR memo that was being circulated during congressional hearings into Waco, this practice of withholding evidence is not customary, or "Prosecution 101," as the memo referred to it. There is a well-recognized exception to the rule that American jurisprudence is adversarial. Prosecutors in every jurisdiction—federal and state—are honor bound to pursue truth and justice, as corny as that may sound, and let the chips fall. Their primary charge is not to win convictions.[64] It is unconscionable that the government deviated from this rule and then brazenly defended the propriety of its actions. So much for the rule of law.

When its investigation finally resumed, the Treasury Department did find fault with the conduct of certain agents and took some remedial action. Phillip Chojnacki and Charles Sarabyn, the two ATF commanders who made the decision to proceed with the raid despite being aware that the element of surprise had been lost, were fired. Later, however, they were reinstated and awarded retroactive salary payments. Some other ATF officials involved were forced to resign or were suspended.

In their book *No More Wacos*, Kopel and Blackman took exception to the prevailing media opinion that the Treasury report was hard-hitting. They agreed that the report would help to improve future ATF attacks but noted that it totally failed to address why the assault was necessary in the first place.[65] Dr. Alan Stone, an independent reviewer of the government's conduct at Waco, similarly rejected the notion that the Treasury report was sufficiently critical of its own bureau, the ATF. He said the report was written so as to give the ATF agents the benefit of every doubt.[66]

The Siege and Its Aftermath

Just a few hours after a cease-fire was achieved, the ATF called in the FBI to assist it in bringing the confrontation to a close. FBI agent Jeff Jamar was designated as the agent in charge. According to some sources, the FBI agents involved had never heard of the Branch Davidians or of David Koresh prior to being called.[67]

Initially, the FBI intended to take all the time it needed to reach a peaceful solution. But the FBI negotiators were baffled by the peculiar Davidian theology and were unwilling to engage outside religious experts to assist them with this highly unusual situation. The subcommittees noted the negotiators' resistance to expert assistance and criticized them for failing to try to understand Koresh's theology.

Religious scholars Philip Arnold and James Tabor were pressing the FBI to allow them to assist in the negotiations. They were convinced that Koresh had to be approached from a theological perspective. Arnold had earned the respect of Koresh when he expounded on the Seven Seals and offered his assistance on a radio show during the siege. Though Koresh and his lieutenant Steve Schneider often asked to talk to Arnold, neither Arnold nor James Tabor was permitted to participate in the negotiations with Koresh.

James Tabor later wrote that the FBI's approach was flawed from the beginning. While the FBI treated the standoff as a hostage/barricade situation, the Davidians didn't perceive it that way at all. Koresh was not holding any of his people hostage.[68] In fact, during the first week of the siege, twenty-three people left the compound. Koresh had ordered most of the children who were not his biological offspring to leave the premises shortly after the raid ended.[69] Post-raid government reports conceded that the Davidian adults wanted to remain inside. Koresh, unlike most hostage takers, was making no demands and setting no deadlines.[70]

Professor Nancy Ammerman, one of twelve law enforcement and scientific experts selected by the Justice Department after the tragedy to evaluate the department's handling of the crisis, echoed this criticism of the FBI negotiators. She wrote that she and her fellow experts came to the disturbing conclusion that the FBI almost totally dismissed the religious beliefs of the Branch Davidians.[71] Ammerman also seemed mystified by the fact that the FBI negotiators and tactical commanders felt they had done nothing wrong in their approach to the Davidians. The FBI's self-absolution didn't square with Ammerman's observation that she had yet to meet "a single sociologist or religious studies scholar who has the slightest doubt that the strategies adopted by the FBI were destined for tragic failure."[72]

Early into the standoff, conflict developed between the FBI's tactical teams and its negotiators. The tactical teams were action oriented and didn't want to wait for tedious talks. Soon the tactical commanders were ordering activities that had the effect of undermining the negotiations.

As the siege continued and government frustration swelled, the FBI launched psychological warfare and adopted numerous harassing tactics against the Davidians, including cutting off their electricity, shining blinding spotlights at night to prevent them from sleeping, harassing them with cacophonous music, and taunting them with derisive remarks. They ridiculed Steve Schneider for letting Koresh "marry" his wife.[73]

Reportedly, one of the times that the FBI's Hostage Rescue Team cut off electricity was not to aid its negotiations but to boost the morale of its own people who were "out and cold and away from home."[74] Considering that the government's ostensible aim was to protect the children and other innocents, some of its tactics can only be described as reprehensible.

The government also bargained in bad faith in certain instances. After some of the Davidian mothers stopped lactating due to stress, the FBI agreed to send in milk (paid for by the Davidians) in exchange for several "hostages." When the hostages were sent out, the FBI reneged and demanded the release of more children before it would send in the milk.[75]

None of these tactics worked. So the government upped the ante and began using tanks to destroy Davidian property outside the compound, including children's toys, adults' vehicles, and a mobile home.[76] The negotiators were unable to restrain the itchy tactical commanders. The result of all this was to strengthen the resolve of the Davidians and diminish the chances of a peaceful resolution of the conflict.

Throughout the siege some FBI behavioral science experts were urging caution, but the tactical commanders ignored their warnings.[77] The tactical teams went so far as to pressure some of the FBI experts to recommend action to end the standoff. One such expert, Peter Americk, of the Bureau's Behavioral Science Center, had cowritten a series of memos urging the FBI to proceed carefully. He then reluctantly changed his recommendation.

Americk denied that anyone from the FBI directly ordered him to alter his position but said he certainly felt pressure to that effect. "No one at FBI headquarters, at any time, told me or directed me that, hey, write different memos. But... we all have a tendency of wanting to please our supervisors. And I believe what I did subconsciously is to tone down my memo... to more or less fall in line with what they would want to hear."[78]

The FBI squandered one final and genuine opportunity to end the siege when it chose to ignore Koresh's pledge to surrender when he completed work on his written exposition of the Seven Seals. On April 14, Koresh sent a letter to his lawyer, Dick DeGuerin. God, Koresh wrote, had told him that he would be "given over into the hands of man." Koresh said that after he finished his commentary on the Seven Seals, he would "stand before man to answer any and all questions regarding his actions."[79] In the letter Koresh even asked how he could maintain contact with DeGuerin once he was in prison. Steve Schneider offered to provide the FBI some of Koresh's work in progress to convince the government that he was sincere.

Davidian survivor David Thibodeau later wrote, "The significance of the letter was huge." Koresh, he explained, had never written down his message because he hadn't received permission from God. At last, that permission was granted.[80] Thibodeau said that it was remarkable how different the Davidians' view from the inside was from the FBI's on the outside. With Koresh's feverish work on the seals, the residents were actually beginning to anticipate a peaceful resolution, but "the feds were lurching toward violence."[81]

The subcommittees confirmed the Davidians' dramatic change in outlook accompanying Koresh's writing. The report quotes surviving Davidians as saying, "We were so joyful that weekend because we knew we were coming out, that finally David had got his word of how to do this legally... and theologically in terms of his system."[82]

Tragically, the FBI interpreted the letter as another stalling tactic. DeGuerin said that when he told the FBI that the Davidians would surrender upon Koresh's completion of the writing, Agent Bob Ricks was contemptuous. A few days after the assault, FBI agent Jeff Jamar said the FBI discounted Koresh's surrender promise because they had "absolute certain intelligence" that it was a sham. This intelligence has never surfaced.[83] Probably influencing their attitude was the fact that Koresh had sent hostile letters in the preceding weeks, threatening violence against the FBI. Also, Koresh had earlier reneged on a promise to surrender, saying that God had told him to wait.[84]

During the final week before the April 19, 1993, climax, the FBI had to win approval from newly appointed attorney general Janet Reno for the plan to end the standoff with debilitating CS gas and tanks. Reno, to her credit, initially opposed the plan. Properly, she asked the pivotal question: "Why now?" In response, the FBI gave Reno three main reasons: 1) there was no reason to believe Koresh would come out voluntarily; 2) the health and safety of the children were in jeopardy; and 3) the Hostage Rescue Team was getting fatigued.[85]

But, in fact, there was a very strong reason to believe Koresh would come out voluntarily. Negotiators believed they had achieved a breakthrough with Koresh regarding his work on the Seven Seals. Religious experts who examined Koresh's work have estimated that it would have taken him just two to three weeks longer to complete it. On April 16—just three days before the tank assault—Koresh told FBI negotiators that he did not intend "to die in this place." Many of the religious experts believe that Koresh was sincere.

As to the health and safety of the children, there was no indication that the children were in any danger from Koresh during the siege. The only danger they faced was from an overeager government assault. Reno later insisted that she was told, though she couldn't remember by whom, that they were being beaten during the siege. There was no evidence to support that unattributed claim.

Finally, the fatigue of the Hostage Rescue Team certainly shouldn't have militated in favor of accelerating the conflict to a violent conclusion. The FBI could have procured replacements or let the team stand down for a while. There was no urgency.

The FBI finally convinced Reno that CS gas presented no health risk to the women and children and that the gas would be administered gradually, over a forty-eight-hour period. So just a few days before April 19, Reno approved the FBI's assault on the compound. Reportedly, Reno was never told of Koresh's surrender letter, for fear it might cause her to deny permission for the attack.[86]

The plan was to spray gas into the compound gradually and get the Davidians to evacuate. While the stated objective was to save the children, the FBI had to know that there were no gas masks available to fit the children. There is no question that the children suffered horribly. Even worse, FBI tanks blocked the residents' access to the one place in the compound where they could safely seek refuge, an "underground bus"—a bus that had been buried to serve as a tornado shelter.[87]

As it turns out, there was never a realistic possibility that the assault would be gradual, as Reno had been promised. Even the agent in charge, Jeff Jamar, admitted there was a 99 percent likelihood that the Davidians would respond to the gas with gunfire.[88] As some critics have accurately observed, the plan for a gradual assault was doomed from the beginning. It was inevitable that the "gradual" assault would accelerate into a full-blown operation almost immediately after it began. In this case, "immediately" was no exaggeration. It took less than ten minutes from the initial injection of gas into the compound at about 6 A.M. for the government tanks to start demolishing the compound.[89]

Shortly after noon, fires began in different parts of the building and within minutes the compound and all but nine of its remaining inhabitants were incinerated. FBI transcripts reveal that when the fires were breaking out, FBI broadcasters on the scene uttered words over the loudspeakers such as, "David, you have had your fifteen minutes of fame" and "Vernon is finished. He's no longer the Messiah." Perhaps the most despicable government action occurred shortly after the fires had consumed the buildings. The flames were so hot that they burned Mount Carmel's flag some twenty-five feet away from the building. In its place, someone had hoisted the flag of the ATF.[90] That act did more to illustrate the government's warlike attitude toward its own citizens than any words could ever convey. Complete conquest had been achieved.

Some Davidians claimed that the government started the fire when the force from a tank knocked over kerosene lamps. Government surveillance tapes, however, revealed that Davidians did start and spread the fires. Later government investigations concluded that nothing the government did contributed to the cause of the fires.

Following the immolation, Janet Reno offered to resign, stating she accepted full responsibility. While this sounded noble on the surface, she did not admit to any fault herself or on the part of the FBI or the Department of Justice. Indeed, Reno's Justice

Department, not long after the tragedy, conducted its own internal investigation. It found no fault with the FBI in its handling of the Waco affair. It concluded that from beginning to end, everything was David Koresh's fault.

Another member of the group of twelve experts commissioned by the Justice Department to review the affair was Dr. Alan Stone, a Harvard law and psychiatry professor. Dr. Stone characterized the Justice Department's self-investigation as a "total whitewash." "The Department," wrote Stone, "proclaimed the Waco operation a success even though all the patients died."

In the formal report that Dr. Stone submitted to the Justice Department, he was quite critical of the FBI, making it clear that he disagreed with the conclusion that "nothing the FBI did or could have done would have changed the outcome." He said that the FBI "embarked on a misguided and punishing law enforcement strategy that contributed to the tragic ending at Waco." The FBI tactical officers, according to Dr. Stone, did not understand unconventional religious groups, lacked an expert who knew the Davidians, and decided to show Mr. Koresh "who was the boss." "I am also now convinced that the FBI's noose-tightening tactics may well have precipitated Koresh's decision to commit himself and his followers to this course of mass suicide." Stone's point was that because Koresh and his followers were expecting an apocalyptic ending as part of their religious beliefs, the government should have known that they would not submit to tactical pressure. Indeed, the ATF, the FBI, and the Justice Department, would have known that had they not stubbornly refused to use outside religious experts.

Dr. Stone, by the way, is no friend of the right wing. He later wrote about the reaction to his criticism of the government: "I have been taken up by right-wing fanatics, pilloried by the liberal

Democrats to whose campaigns I contribute, and assured by knowledgeable colleagues that my services will never again be needed in Washington."

There is simply no question but that the ATF, the FBI, the Justice Department, and Attorney General Reno bear some responsibility for the tragic outcome of Waco. The buck stops at the top, so ultimately President Clinton, too, is culpable. Clinton's first concern with Waco was not ascertaining the truth but protecting himself politically. Clinton hid behind Janet Reno when public opinion looked in doubt, then jumped on her bandwagon when public opinion supported the raid. Authors Edward Timperlake and William Triplett wrote, "As might be expected, the White House was a busy place that afternoon [April 19, 1993], and the president was preoccupied. Bill Clinton was not too distracted, however, to chat with his leading contributors—James Riady, John Huang, and Mark Grobmeyer—in his little study off the Oval Office. Riady later told Indonesian diplomats that, during their chat, a television in the corner showed the Waco compound burning over and over as CNN repeated its coverage. Clinton even took time to show his visitors the White House Situation Room, then on full alert. White House entry logs confirm that Riady and his companions were in the presidential offices [West Wing] of the White House that day.... How many other presidents, in the middle of such a tragedy, would have spent their time giving major donors a White House tour?"[91]

The Danforth Investigation

In 1999 an audiotape surfaced that included an FBI commander authorizing the use of pyrotechnic teargas canisters on April 19, 1993. Because the FBI had been denying the use of such incendiary devices for six years, Janet Reno was furious and humiliated. Deeply concerned about her own credibility, in September 1999 Reno appointed former Missouri senator John Danforth as special counsel to reopen an investigation into the Waco incident. Reno charged Danforth with resolving five "dark questions"—whether the government: 1) started or contributed to the April 19, 1993, fire; 2) fired at the Davidians on that day; 3) used incendiary devices on that day; 4) illegally used the military; and 5) engaged in a massive cover-up.

After a ten-month investigation, Danforth revealed his preliminary findings on July 21, 2000. "I can say that the conclusion that I have reached in this report was reached to my satisfaction with 100 percent certainty. There is no doubt in my mind," said Danforth. As to four of the five questions, he found the government to be blameless. He concluded that the government did not start the fires and did not fire any shots at the Davidians on April 19, 1993. It did not illegally use the military and did not engage in a massive cover-up. As to the use of incendiary devices Danforth found that incendiary teargas canisters were launched on April 19, 1993, but not into the Davidian compound. Nor did they contribute to causing the fire. Moreover, while he found no massive cover-up involving agents and lawyers regarding the use of pyrotechnic devices, he was still investigating whether any criminal acts occurred.

Danforth did report, however, that the Justice Department was at times very uncooperative with his investigation and was improperly asserting control over it. He detailed repeated instances of "substantial resistance" and nondisclosure by the Justice Department and other federal agencies. He described the interaction between the Justice Department and the special counsel—the first special counsel appointed following the repeal of the Independent Counsel Act—as a turf battle. The department, according to the report, "resisted the production of notes and records of its attorneys."

Danforth revealed that Justice Department employees tried to maintain a certain degree of control over the conduct of the investigation. They tried to deny his office "access to internal documents... and resisted the production of important e-mail as being too burdensome." Both the Justice Department and the FBI resisted the production of documents. At one point, Danforth asked FBI Director Louis Freeh to intervene to assist in obtaining FBI documents.

Though Danforth alleged no deceit by the department, the pattern of resistance described in the report seems to suggest a marked absence of candor. For example, the report states that the "Office of Special Counsel repeatedly received assurances from the Department of Justice that [it] had produced all hard copy documents, yet witnesses told the Office that certain categories of documents had not been turned over to the Office. Similarly, individual witnesses arrived at interviews with notes, videos, and diaries that the Department of Justice had never asked them to provide to the Office of Special Counsel."

Senator Danforth's integrity is above reproach, but his investigative scope was so narrowly drawn that it cannot be seen to absolve the government of all wrongdoing. He was not charged with examining the initial ATF raid on February 28, 1993. He was not called to investigate whether the government exercised bad judgment that led the Branch Davidians to set fire to their own buildings. It is that action—the Davidians' deliberate suicidal arson—that Danforth ultimately relied on for his conclusion that "the United States government is not responsible for the tragedy at Waco on April 19, 1993." But, as we have seen, the climactic inferno might have been avoided if the ATF, the FBI, and Reno had behaved differently.

Conclusion

The Waco tragedy has caused as much distrust and polarization between the government and many of its citizens as any other event in recent memory. In some cases advocates on both sides have become entrenched and, in some cases, taken extreme positions relative to the other. One extreme says the government did very little wrong and that Koresh murdered his own people rather than letting them flee the compound during the gas and tank assault. The other extreme has gone so far as to say that the government murdered the Davidians in retaliation for their killing of the four ATF agents.

Many have fallen into the trap of concluding that the culpability of the Branch Davidians and the culpability of the federal government are mutually exclusive propositions. It is not that simple.

David Koresh and some of his assistants were guilty, in some cases, of egregious misconduct. But the Davidians did nothing to precipitate the violent ATF raid of February 28 or the FBI assault on April 19. The government forced the action in both instances.

The only way to prevent further tragedies like Waco is for the government to come clean with its mistakes. But there has been no expression of regret from Reno or Clinton and no admission of faulty judgment. Reno said, "There is much to be angry about when we talk about Waco, and the government's conduct is not the reason. David Koresh is the reason."[92] Clinton's assessment was even more self-serving: "I do not think the United States government is responsible for the fact that a bunch of religious fanatics decided to kill themselves."

No, but the government surely is responsible for taking military action against its own citizens without due cause, without pursuing peaceful alternatives, and without anticipating and being accountable for the inevitable casualties.

Chapter Two

Tobacco Wars

The Clinton-Gore administration believed the ends justified the means. For President Clinton, using—or more accurately, abusing—the power of the federal government in furtherance of certain causes was an end in itself. The Clinton Justice Department's war against the tobacco companies is a perfect illustration of how the administration was willing to use any means to attempt to bring a targeted, private, legal industry to its knees without regard to law, fairness, or the long-term implications for American freedom.

Opening Shots

In January 1994 a raft of colleagues, supporters, and health groups began urging President Clinton to take action against the tobacco industry. Bill Clinton's surgeon general, Joycelyn Elders, declared that tobacco remains "the leading cause of preventable death and disease in America. Any form of tobacco—whether smoked, chewed, spit or inhaled—is lethal," said Elders in a press conference. Former president Jimmy Carter sent a letter to Clinton encouraging him to raise the cigarette tax by $2 a pack to protect adults and children. The American Heart Association, the American Lung Association, and the American Cancer Society pressed Clinton to institute aggressive regulation on cigarette advertising and sales and pushed for higher cigarette taxes, as well as mandatory smoke-free schools, workplaces, and public buildings.[1]

Anti-tobacco lobbyists criticized the Federal Trade Commission for not clamping down on deceptive advertising. They also criticized the Justice Department for not bringing any suits against big tobacco. Elders revealed that the "next battleground" would be children "victimized" by the tobacco companies. The Federal Trade Commission was pressured to specifically target "Joe Camel" for extinction because the promotional character allegedly enticed children to smoke. The anti-tobacco groups also wanted Congress to give the Food and Drug Administration authority to regulate the sale, distribution, and advertising of tobacco products.[2]

By May 1994, Democratic politicians, such as Congressman Henry Waxman of California, upped the ante, calling for criminal investigations of the industry. Congressman Martin Meehan and several of his colleagues sent a letter to Attorney General Janet Reno, charging that the tobacco companies might have engaged in mail and wire fraud, obstructed Congress, restrained trade, and defrauded the public, and should be subject to a federal criminal investigation.

The Justice Department announced that it was beginning an "inquiry" into possible criminal charges. The charges were based on the congressional testimony of seven tobacco industry executives in April 1994. Attorney General Reno said, "We are looking at all the allegations, all the comments, all the information that we have received to determine what would be the appropriate action by the Justice Department in terms of a variety of issues." Reno made clear that she was not only considering criminal remedies, but civil action as well, including antitrust.

In the meantime, states were also taking action against the tobacco companies. Mississippi attorney general Michael Moore filed a civil lawsuit seeking reimbursement for his state for Medicaid expenses due to smoking-related illnesses. Florida considered a similar suit, and Moore lobbied the Justice Department to follow his lead and bring a federal Medicare reimbursement action against tobacco firms.[3]

The anti-tobacco congressmen were relentless. Not seeing any action by the Justice Department, Congressman Meehan wrote another letter to Janet Reno accusing tobacco executives of perjury in their congressional testimony and reissuing his call for a criminal investigation. Unable to muster a majority to take congressional action against the tobacco industry, the Democratic legislators wanted to revert to the executive branch—where President Clinton was an eager ally—and the courts. Said Meehan, "Given the groundbreaking work of Waxman and the information that's been uncovered in the last year, it warrants additional investigation and follow-up."[4]

By mid-1995 the Justice Department graduated its "inquiry" to a formal investigation to look into charges that tobacco executives had committed perjury when they denied before Congress that their companies "spiked" products with higher levels of nicotine to make them more addictive.

The Regulatory Hammer

To crack down on the tobacco companies, President Clinton weighed two options. One was to allow the Food and Drug

Administration (FDA) to classify tobacco as a drug, which would make it subject to federal regulation. The other was to use the mere threat of regulation as leverage to compel the industry to cut back on its advertising and make it more difficult for minors to acquire cigarettes. The FDA wanted regulation, with FDA commissioner David Kessler labeling nicotine addiction a "pediatric disease."[5]

The regulators got a boost when three former Philip Morris employees (two scientists and a production official) presented affidavits to a House subcommittee contradicting the 1994 congressional testimony of Philip Morris USA's CEO, William Campbell. In their sworn statements, the former employees alleged that the company manipulated nicotine levels. One of the former Philip Morris employees, William A. Farone, said, "It is well recognized within the cigarette industry that there is one principal reason why people smoke—to experience the effects of nicotine." Ian L. Uydess, one of the scientists formerly employed by Philip Morris, said, "Nicotine levels were routinely targeted and adjusted by Philip Morris."

FDA commissioner David Kessler, apparently emboldened by the revelations, reopened the FDA's docket for public comment on its proposed tobacco regulations. Kessler issued a statement saying, "This is information we believe the public should know. These documents shed light on the role of nicotine in the design and manufacture of cigarettes." The affidavits served as new ammunition for states with lawsuits against the tobacco industry.[6]

Philip Morris, furious that Mr. Uydess's affidavit was leaked to the *Wall Street Journal*, responded by saying, "Obviously, this is a well-orchestrated public relations gambit involving the FDA and plaintiff's attorneys. We are very concerned that a federal agency would leak a document to an influential Wall Street newspaper as part of an effort to adversely affect public opinion and cloud rather than clarify the facts as a means of pursuing its agenda of prohibition."[7] As a sign that it was willing to cooperate to keep cigarettes out of the hands of kids, Philip Morris offered to support legislation to ban cigarette vending machines and prevent other cigarette sales to minors.

After three years of haggling over whether it had the authority to regulate tobacco, the Food and Drug Administration was forced to take its case to court. Tobacco industry lawyers in Greensboro, North Carolina, challenged proposed FDA regulations that were scheduled to go into effect on February 28, 1997.

The tobacco companies were seeking a summary judgment that the FDA had no authority to regulate tobacco and that regulating advertising violated the First Amendment. The FDA's regulations included vending machine restrictions and a national ban on tobacco sales to children under eighteen, self-service displays, and promotional cigarette giveaways. In addition, they mandated photo ID checks for cigarette purchasers under age twenty-seven. The FDA also wanted to prohibit tobacco billboards within a thousand feet of schools and playgrounds, restrict advertising in magazines that might be read by minors, and ban logo-bearing caps and tote bags.

U.S. district judge William L. Osteen finally issued his ruling in April 1997, giving each side something to be pleased and disturbed about. He held that the Food and Drug Administration did have the authority to regulate tobacco products. But it could not impose severe restrictions on advertising and promotion by the tobacco companies—not because of the First Amendment but because the FDA did not have such statutory authority. FDA commissioner David Kessler called the decision "stunning," "amazing," and "a landmark." "It's a victory for the nation, for the public health," he said. A gleeful, but not completely satisfied, President Clinton described the ruling as "on balance, a great victory." He announced that the Justice Department would appeal the prohibition on strict regulation of tobacco advertising and promotion. An equally pleased Vice President Gore said the decision "validates President Clinton's efforts to protect children from this deadly and highly addictive product."[8]

Second-Hand Smoke Crusade

The anti-tobacco crusade extended to "second-hand" smoke, with the Environmental Protection Agency classifying it as a health hazard. One company that refused to toe the EPA line was targeted for punitive action.

In February 1996 a federal grand jury began investigating Healthy Buildings International, a building inspection company that monitored indoor air quality for public and private buildings. The company's employees had testified in more than a hundred congressional and legislative hearings that second-hand smoke did not pose a health threat in buildings that were properly ventilated. The Justice Department was investigating whether the company had been enticed into giving false testimony by the millions of dollars in fees it received from the tobacco industry. One allegation was that in a 1989 study, the company manipulated data to understate the contrast between smoking and nonsmoking areas in buildings.[9]

Before the year was over, federal prosecutors dropped their investigation, after having reviewed more than 50,000 of the company's documents. Mary C. Spearing, head of the fraud section for the Justice Department, sent a letter to the company's attorneys saying, "Based on the evidence presently available to us and standards of proof applicable in a criminal case, we have closed the file without prosecution."[10]

"State" Action

In mid-1996 the states pursuing the tobacco companies gained a major legal victory. The Minnesota Supreme Court ruled that Blue Cross and Blue Shield of Minnesota had a sufficient interest to sue the tobacco industry for tobacco-related health-care costs. Minnesota was the only state working with insurance companies against big tobacco. "We couldn't be happier," said Minnesota attorney general Hubert H. Humphrey III.

Though the Minnesota decision was not binding in other states, it did offer a precedent for state attorneys general to point to—and there were plenty of other states interested in the spoils of suing the tobacco industry. Ten other states had similar claims. Actions were pending in Mississippi, Florida, and other states, and some states had filed class action suits against the tobacco companies.[11]

State and federal authorities began to coordinate their investigative efforts. Minnesota state officials shared with the Justice Department tens of thousands of documents from their files against the tobacco companies. The Justice Department assigned a task force of FBI agents to search the documents for evidence that tobacco executives had lied to Congress and other agencies. The Food and Drug Administration was also working with the Justice Department developing evidence pertinent to its criminal investigation.[12]

Action on the Criminal Front

For all its investigating, the Justice Department didn't file a criminal case until January 1998. That is when it accused DNA

Plant Technology Corporation of Oakland, a California biotechnology firm, of conspiring with a major tobacco company (Brown and Williamson Tobacco Corporation) to develop a high-nicotine tobacco plant. The charge itself was minor, but it was meant "to send a signal to the industry that the [larger] criminal inquiry is serious and that it is moving," in the words of a Justice Department official.[13] The Justice Department reached a plea agreement with DNA and succeeded in pressuring it into cooperating with the Justice Department's ever growing investigation against the tobacco industry.

A Proposed Comprehensive Settlement

In June 1998 the tobacco companies reached a tentative settlement with the state and private attorneys pursuing action against them. The settlement provided that in exchange for immunity from further class action and punitive damages claims, as well as yearly caps on actual damages claims, the tobacco companies would launch public health initiatives and pay $368.5 billion in damages over a period of twenty-five years. Unfortunately for the attorneys, the settlement required congressional approval and, after heated debate, didn't get it.

The Onset of White House Frustration (and a Plan)

President Clinton now looked to achieve through litigation what Congress had denied him and the other anti-tobacco crusaders. His idea was for the federal government to file a civil action against the tobacco companies seeking reimbursement for Medicare expenditures made by the government on behalf of people who had tobacco-related injuries. The trouble was that Justice Department attorneys had already rejected a civil action against the tobacco companies because the government lacked legal standing to sue them. On April 29, 1997, Justice Department spokesman Joe Krovisky said, "Medicare and Medicaid statutes do not provide explicit authority for the federal government to pursue suit" against the tobacco companies for the costs of tobacco-related disease. Krovisky, as it turned out, was not speaking just for himself. The next day, his boss, Attorney General Janet Reno, testifying before the Senate Judiciary Committee, admitted that the federal government was without authority to bring such a suit. "What we have determined was that it was the state cause of action, and that we needed to work with the states, that the federal government does not have an independent cause of action [to recover health care expenditures]."

Clinton's first hurdle would be to convince attorneys in the Justice Department to change their firm position that there was no statutory authority to support a civil action. One administration official said, "They are looking for a way to do it. But they've got some nervous Nellies in the Justice Department that don't think the Medical Recovery Act permits this kind of lawsuit."[14] Writing for *Roll Call* magazine, Congressman Walter Jones saw it differently: "Ever since the Medicare and Medicaid programs were founded, it has been the position of every Justice Department— Democratic and Republican alike—that the federal government does not have the authority to sue the tobacco industry to recover costs spent on patients who happen to smoke."[15] Jones went on to point out that such a lawsuit would "effectively skirt the role of Congress to create effective tobacco policy." Jones also warned that this kind of unauthorized lawsuit would set a precedent for the government to target for legal punishment wine, beer, and spirits producers; manufacturers of high-fat foods; and other businesses that could arguably be seen as contributing to bad diet or other health problems.

Obstacles to a Government Lawsuit

The proposed civil suit had another problem. Because the government had collected excise taxes on tobacco, it had indirectly supported smoking—or at least upheld it as a perfectly legitimate and legal activity. In fact, President Clinton's ever increasing cigarette taxes ensured that the government received more of the profits from cigarette sales than did the tobacco companies. There were other complications. Until 1974 the military distributed cigarettes to servicemen with their C rations. It also provided major discounts on cigarettes at its post exchange grocery stores and mandated smoking breaks. In addition, it had removed health warnings required for the retail market on tobacco products distributed within the military system.[16] (The surgeon general had warned in 1964 that tobacco is dangerous.) Moreover, the government had consistently exerted pressure on veterans to refrain from filing claims for smoking-related illnesses because they were personally responsible for any smoking-related problems they experienced for having chosen to smoke.

The government had engaged in studies as far back as 1929 concerning the dangers of tobacco and had long subsidized tobacco farmers. In fact, in October 1999, Congress passed an $8.7 billion farmer assistance package that included $328 million in subsidies for tobacco farmers for losses due to declining cigarette sales.[17]

The government had been so aware of smoking risks that in 1965 Surgeon General Luther Terry testified to a Senate subcommittee that the government's "whole attitude is toward giving the general public the most information that we can so that each individual can make his own decision about smoking.... Our purpose... is not to hurt an industry or to forbid anyone to smoke. But it is our responsibility to point out that cigarette smoking is a great national health hazard, and to give you—the citizen—the best available scientific information with which to make up his own mind about smoking."[18]

The Office of the Surgeon General had filed reports on the dangers of smoking for decades. "The federal government," said tobacco industry spokesman Scott Williams, "cannot claim ignorance to the health risks associated with tobacco use. This is political. This is about money."[19] Finally, to prevail in a civil suit the government would have to overcome what some journalists call the "ghoul defense," referring to a well-known study by a Harvard economist showing that smoking actually saves the government money. While smokers fall prey to more diseases in their fifties and sixties—and therefore avail themselves of benefits under Medicare, Medicaid, and veterans programs—on average they also die at an earlier age, which results in huge savings in social security.[20] The study was conducted by Harvard professor W. Kip Viscusi, who concluded that smokers receive less social security, Medicare, and other federal government benefits because they have an 18 to 36 percent chance of dying earlier than nonsmokers. A June 1999 Congressional Research Service report confirmed this finding. It concluded that since smokers die prematurely they save the federal government $29 billion each year in health care costs.[21] The Research Service report stated, "All in all, smoking has apparently brought financial gain to both the federal and state governments, especially when tobacco taxes are taken into account. In general, smokers do not appear to currently impose net financial costs on the rest of society."

Clinton Increases Pressure on Justice Department

In his attempt to federalize the assault on tobacco, Clinton found an ally in Mississippi attorney general Michael Moore and plaintiffs' attorney Richard Scruggs who offered to organize a dream team of attorneys for the federal government against the tobacco companies.[22] Clinton needed all the allies he could get because it was increasingly obvious that his proposed legal war against the tobacco industry was without legal foundation. In August 1998 the Fourth U.S. Circuit Court of Appeals declared that the Food and Drug Administration had no authority to regulate tobacco as an addictive drug. The court ruled that Congress never intended to grant the Food and Drug Administration the authority to regulate cigarettes. The FDA, said the court, had exceeded its authority in 1996 when it issued broad regulations restricting the sale of tobacco to minors and limiting advertising and marketing by tobacco companies. White House press secretary Mike McCurry, speaking on behalf of a defiant President Clinton, said that Clinton remained "fully committed to the FDA's regulatory role and its role in protecting our children. Reaffirming the Food and Drug Administration's authority over tobacco products is necessary to help stop young people from smoking."[23] President Clinton heavily pressured the Justice Department to reconsider an action against the tobacco companies. "If the White House hadn't asked, [the Justice Department] would never have looked at [a lawsuit] again," admitted Clinton aide Rahm Emanuel. Democratic senator Richard Durbin confessed that Clinton was attempting an end run around Congress. The White House, said Durbin, had "seen that the tobacco industry holds such sway over the Republican Congress, they don't feel there is the likelihood of any legislation being passed. So they turned to the courts."[24]

The administration even recruited private attorneys to convince the Justice Department that it could in fact sue the tobacco companies. Justice Department attorneys worked around the clock in search of a legal theory to support its lawsuit. The private lawyers lobbied the government to use the 1962 Federal Medical Care Recovery Act. That law provides that the government can sue to recover medical costs expended on military personnel and other government employees injured because of third party negligence.

Democratic senator Bob Graham of Florida tried to help by proposing legislation that would deny an obvious truth. The tobacco companies had argued that smokers pursued their habit at their own risk because the risks were openly acknowledged on every packet of cigarettes. Graham's legislation would have explicitly forbidden the tobacco companies from asserting that defense. This was Clintonian justice at work: not only denying the truth but forbidding your opponent from speaking the truth.[25]

It was later revealed that one reason Janet Reno and her Justice Department declined to initiate legal action in 1997 (when they properly and honestly determined there was no legal basis upon which to sue) was strong opposition among top Justice officials. A key player in the Justice Department at that time was Frank Hunger, who headed the department's civil division. Hunger had been an enthusiastic supporter of the Justice Department's efforts to empower the Food and Drug Administration to regulate tobacco. But he was strongly opposed to the department bringing a civil lawsuit against the tobacco companies, believing that the government had neither statutory nor common law authority to do so.[26] Hunger could hardly be accused of a pro-tobacco bias. He is Al Gore's brother-in-law. His late wife was Gore's sister, who died from smoking-related lung cancer in 1984. Since that time he has been anti-tobacco and even encouraged Gore to speak about his sister's death in his Democratic National Convention speech in 1996. When Hunger left the department to go into private practice in January 1999 (and then to assist Al Gore's presidential campaign that summer), the coast was clear for Justice to proceed.[27]

The State of the Union Address (Clinton Declares War)

An impatient President Clinton, in his 1999 State of the Union address, said that the federal government would sue tobacco companies to recover the costs of treating Medicare patients with smoking-related ailments. "Tonight, I announce that the Justice Department is preparing a litigation plan to take the tobacco companies to court. Smoking has cost taxpayers hundreds of billions of dollars," Clinton said. Pretending that his motive was to reimburse taxpayers, he added, "Americans should not be held responsible for bearing these costs." And again, "Taxpayers should not pay for the cost of lung cancer, emphysema and other smoking-related illnesses—the tobacco industry should."

Some dismissed Clinton's threat as political pandering to his favorite constituency: trial lawyers. Mary Aronson, a Washington attorney and policy and litigation analyst, said, "Clearly this was motivated by those with the most to gain from a lawsuit—trial lawyers—who have been pressuring the White House."[28] Placating trial lawyers was probably a factor, but Clinton was also engaging in war with the tobacco industry for the sake of punishing it. And he had another motivation, which was to pour the earnings of private industry into government coffers. He separately called on Congress to expand the Food and Drug Administration's authority to regulate tobacco and proposed a 55-cent-a-pack tax on cigarettes.

No one knew yet the exact size of the federal lawsuit that Clinton was contemplating, but most believed it would dwarf the

$246 billion settlement the tobacco companies ultimately agreed to pay the states in 1998. The reason was that the federal suit could extend beyond Medicare to the Federal Employee Health Benefits Program, the Defense Department health program, veterans benefits, Indian health services, and possibly other programs.[29] The Justice Department assured the states that a federal civil suit would not impinge on the states' settlement and would leave that money to the states.[30]

The tobacco companies responded quickly to Clinton's declaration of war, issuing a press release stating, "In April 1997, the Justice Department said Medicare and Medicaid statutes do not provide explicit authority for the federal government to sue tobacco companies. The relevant laws have not changed, and not until last night, during a political speech, did anyone in the Administration publicly suggest such authority exists. Now, the President has ordered the Justice Department to reverse course and concoct a legal basis for this case. It may be good politics to continue such a witch-hunt against a legal industry. But it remains bad law. The industry will vigorously defend itself against this entirely political lawsuit."[31] Another tobacco industry spokesman said, "We have reached the point where there is this kind of state-sponsored terrorism against an industry selling a legal product, and it must stop. The bottom line is that the administration wants its money first. It's not about public health anymore."[32]

Attorney General Janet Reno obediently assured President Clinton and the public that the Justice Department was preparing a case against the tobacco companies. "We're putting together the task force, and they will make the recommendation as to when and where to file the lawsuit," Reno said at a press conference. Reno also shrugged off the suggestion that the federal government had no authority to sue. "I have made the decision, after going through the legal issues that are involved, that we can file a lawsuit," said Reno.[33] Reno did not explain why her opinion had changed, nor did she mention that it differed from that of many of her colleagues. According to the *Wall Street Journal*, senior Justice Department officials remained uncertain they had authority to bring such an action without congressional approval.[34]

Nevertheless, Janet Reno pressed forward, hiring Michael Ciresi, a Minnesota attorney who had played a major role in extracting a $6.5 billion settlement from the tobacco industry, to advise her tobacco litigation task force.[35] David W. Ogden, head of the task force, said Ciresi and his firm were chosen because "they have devoted thousands of hours to uncovering and learning the facts relating to tobacco litigation. Their extraordinary experience in this area will be very valuable to the department's tobacco litigation team." Reno's critics charged that she had turned the Justice Department over to trial lawyers.

To fund its case, the Justice Department asked Congress to allocate it an additional $20 million over the fiscal year beginning October 1, 1999. The money would cover the expenses for the task force and expert witnesses. Senate Republicans initially blocked the funding request. They also inserted a provision in an appropriations bill that would restrict the Justice Department from spending any of the money in its budget to fund a tobacco lawsuit. (Less than a month later, the Senate reversed itself and removed the restriction, but held fast to its decision denying the additional $20 million.) President Clinton immediately turned the Senate's funding refusal into political ammunition. "Given the power of big tobacco in this Congress," he said, he knew the funding "would be hard to get."

To hedge her bets, Reno lobbied Congress for "clarifying" legislation to ensure that the federal government could bring the suit. But the legislation was designed to do more than clarify; it would strengthen the government's case by removing standard defenses that are available to other defendants in civil cases. The legislation would have forbidden tobacco companies to argue that smokers were contributorily negligent or willingly assumed the known risks of their habit. Just as important, the legislation empowered the government to sue directly rather than on behalf of injured smokers, even though the government—because it cannot smoke—would normally not be allowed to file such a suit. Legal experts were very concerned that this type of legislation would overturn two hundred years of traditional tort law practice. By stripping the tobacco companies of standard legal defenses, the industry would be literally "defenseless" and forced to settle.[36]

The precedent set by this legislation exposed many other industries to liability including auto manufacturers, fast food restaurants, and any other industry that could pose a potential health risk to consumers, and whose costs would partially be borne by Medicare.[37] "I've asked Reno under what legal authority [they are] doing this," said Senator Orrin Hatch. "It could be any industry this administration doesn't like. It's a dangerous thing in my eyes." The United States Chamber of Commerce voiced its concern too. "If the Department of Justice sues tobacco, then there's no business that's really safe from revenue-raising lawsuits," said chamber official Jim Wootton. The chamber was concerned that a government suit against the tobacco industry was a politically motivated ploy to use litigation to acquire money to fund government programs.

Clinton Pulls the Trigger

After posturing for the better part of 1999, Clinton announced on September 22, 1999, that he was going to make good on his threat to unleash the Justice Department against the tobacco industry. "Over the years, smoking-related illnesses have cost taxpayers billions of dollars through Medicare, veterans' health, and other federal programs. Today, the Justice Department declared that the United States is in fact filing suit against the major tobacco companies to recover the costs borne by taxpayers. I believe it's the right thing to do.... It is time for America's taxpayers to have their day in court," said Clinton.

The day of Clinton's press conference the Justice Department filed an action against eight major tobacco companies, alleging that they had "waged an intentional and coordinated campaign of deceit" for the past forty-five years. Janet Reno said that in the interest of making "enormous profits," the companies had conspired to defraud and mislead the American public and to conceal information about the dangers of smoking. She pledged that the Justice Department would "work tirelessly to see that justice is done."

Tobacco executives denounced the suit as politically motivated and said they would seek to have it dismissed. "We will not succumb to politically correct extortion," said Greg Little, Philip Morris's associate general counsel. "We're right on the law. We're right on the facts. We will prevail in the lawsuit," he said. Little added, "It is absurd for the federal government to stand up today and announce that somehow it was unaware of the health risk of smoking and has no responsibility for the tobacco policy of the last 50 years." The Chamber of Commerce also weighed in again. "No business can feel secure in the United States when the enormous power of the Justice Department can be unleashed against them for the purpose of raising revenue and scoring political points. This is nothing more than taxation through litigation," said Bruce Josten, executive vice president.[38]

Georgetown law professor Jonathan Turley was skeptical about the suit. He said the government was trying a hodgepodge of legal theories because of its uncertainty about the merits of its case. "Remember," said Turley, "it wasn't that long ago when Janet Reno told the Senate, 'We don't have a good-faith basis to sue.'... But after she made that statement, the president went to the State of the Union and said, 'We are going to sue. We are going to ask for billions in damages.' And so you have this sort of reverse engineering at Justice. They're trying to find a theory to meet the verdict, essentially, that the president announced." Turley went on to say that the government had no more than a long shot with many of these theories and that some of the statutory claims were beyond the scope of the statutes. "What the Clinton administration is trying to do," said Turley, "is essentially convert statutes which were designed for a different purpose."[39]

Within a day or so of announcing its civil suit, the Justice Department formally closed its criminal investigation without bringing charges against the tobacco executives for allegedly lying to Congress and regulatory agencies about the addictiveness of nicotine. But all was not lost. The Justice Department would still be able to use in the civil suit many of the documents it acquired from the industry in the course of its criminal investigation.

Dubious Legal Claims

In its lawsuit the government alleged that the tobacco companies made false statements about whether smoking is harmful, made false promises about conducting research to determine the long-term effects of smoking, and denied the existence of clinical evidence that nicotine was addictive. It also charged that the companies failed to develop less harmful and addictive products and that the industry targeted minors in marketing strategies and ad campaigns.[40] The government was seeking to recoup more than $20 billion a year over the course of five decades—a trillion-dollar penalty against the tobacco companies.

The Justice Department sought these damages under the veils of the Medical Care Recovery Act (MCRA), the Medicare Secondary Payer (MSP) provisions of the Medicare Act, and the Racketeer Influenced and Corrupt Organizations Act, known as RICO.

But the Medical Care Recovery Act was passed in 1962, three years before Medicare was even created—so the statute couldn't possibly have contemplated authorizing the recovery of Medicare expenditures. When Congress amended the act in 1996, there was no reference to Medicare in the act or its legislative history. Legal experts agree that this act was never intended to be a "Medicare Recovery Act" that would allow the government to seek reimbursement for Medicare expenditures. Prior to the tobacco suit the Justice Department had never brought a claim under the act seeking reimbursements for the Medicare program. Indeed, there have been no cases in which a court permitted recovery of Medicare expenses under the act.[41] The Medicare Secondary Payer Act was also a dubious basis for the government to sue the tobacco companies because it targeted the *insurers* of third parties who injured Medicare recipients. It made these insurers liable for Medicare costs, but it did not allow recovery directly from the third parties that caused the injury. When Congress amended the 1980 act in 1984, it again failed to permit recovery against third parties. [42]

As for the RICO claim, it was based on the allegation that tobacco executives met at the Plaza Hotel in New York City in 1953 and conspired to formulate a long-term public relations campaign to fraudulently conceal the harmful and addictive nature of tobacco products. The executives also allegedly planned to market their products to teenagers.

The tobacco companies responded to the lawsuit by filing a motion to dismiss the case, saying the government had no right to recover under any of the three federal statutes. "The Government," said the tobacco lawyers responding to the Medicare claims, "is asserting causes of action for Medicare recovery that have never been recognized by any court before, that it has never asserted before, that it has publicly stated it does not have, and that it has to this date never asserted against anyone other than this one group of defendants which it has chosen to target in this selectively filed lawsuit."

With regard to the RICO claim, the tobacco attorneys contended that the $246 billion settlement the companies had already reached with the states included an agreement by the companies to "radically transform the way tobacco products are marketed in this country." As such, they argued, the RICO claim was groundless, because the government could not rely on past violations alone but would have to establish that there was a likelihood of future violations.

Round One in the Court Battle

The opposing sides met in court in late May 2000 to argue the tobacco companies' motion to dismiss the lawsuit. An exasperated lawyer representing the defendants told the court, "This just absolutely, independently cannot fly." The government's claims "are entirely lacking in any foundation in law," said attorney Herbert Wachtell. The government practically conceded the weakness of its case when Justice attorney Frank Marine implored the court not to dismiss the suit. "We have an overwhelming case to go to the next step. It's not whether we have proof at this point, it's whether we are entitled to put the proof before your honor at trial," he said. In an interesting exchange during the hearing on the motion, Judge Gladys Kessler asked Justice attorney Mark Stern about the department's previous position—that it did not have the authority to sue under the two medical recovery statutes. Stern insisted that the government had never taken an official position based on a full analysis.[43]

The Justice Department did not deny that it was trying to use these statutes in ways they had never been used before. The unprecedented use of the statutes was justified, they argued, because of the unprecedented deceit perpetrated by the tobacco industry. "What makes this suit unique is the conduct of these corporations, which for decades have deliberately and successfully addicted millions of citizens to a product that [the] defendants have long known causes suffering and death," said the Justice Department in its court pleadings. In other words, according to the Justice Department, it was okay to ignore the clear meaning of the statute because the tobacco companies' conduct was so egregious.

On September 28, 2000, Judge Kessler dismissed outright the government's two medical reimbursement claims but overruled the motion to dismiss the racketeering (RICO) claim. In her ruling, Judge Kessler said that it is inconceivable "that after more than 30 years the government could now hold the tobacco industry responsible for an estimated $20 billion a year for smoking-related costs." But she said it would be premature to dismiss the RICO claim before hearing the government's evidence on the merits. "Based on the sweeping nature of the government's allegations and the fact the parties have barely begun discovery to test the validity of these allegations, it would be premature for the court to rule

[now]," wrote Kessler. "At a very minimum the government has stated a claim for injunctive relief; whether the government can prove it remains to be seen." Judge Kessler acknowledged that the remaining claims were potentially substantial. "In sum," she said, "while the government's theories of liability have been limited, the extent of the defendants' potential liability remains, in the estimation of both parties, in the billions of dollars."

Despite having survived the tobacco companies' motion to dismiss the RICO claim the government still faces substantial obstacles in making a case under this statute.

Justice vs. Congress in the Battle for Funding

When Congress denied the Justice Department the $20 million it had requested to fund the tobacco suit, Janet Reno did an end run. Without telling Congress of her plan, she approached other federal agencies to help subsidize the administration's litigation crusade. Congress discovered it when staff members of the House Appropriations Subcommittee were reviewing Clinton's 2001 budget. That prompted them to ask questions. Reno was forced to admit to a congressional subcommittee that she had secured $8 million from the departments of Defense, Veterans Affairs, and Health and Human Services. Reno justified this bizarre move by asserting that those agencies incurred costs from treating smokers. She cited an obscure 1995 statute that supposedly permitted the Justice Department to accept money from other agencies to underwrite litigation that involved "unusually high costs."[44] Congressman Harold Rogers, chairman of the Commerce, Justice, State and Judiciary Appropriations Subcommittee (responsible for overseeing Justice Department funding) was outraged at Reno's effort to bypass Congress. "I'm ticked off at them for circumventing the clear legislative intent," he said. Rogers said he was looking for ways to block other departments from funding the suit. He also said that some congressmen were so upset that they were considering whether to repeal the 1995 law. Referring to the potential loophole in the law, Senator Mitch McConnell said, "It will not be tolerated. It will be fixed."[45]

When Congress announced it was going to vote to prevent the Department of Veterans Affairs from granting Justice $4 million, Janet Reno said she would have no choice but to drop the lawsuit if the funding were denied. "Some members of Congress are now trying to shut America's taxpayers out of the courtroom," she said. "Without these critical funds, we will have no choice but to seek to dismiss the litigation." President Clinton, in a written statement, pressured Congress not to deny the funds. If Congress prevents this funding, it "will be capitulating to the tobacco industry once again at the expense of taxpayers and their children," he said. On June 19, 2000, the House voted to bar the funding in a 207-197 vote. The very next day, however, Congress inexplicably reversed itself—undoubtedly under White House pressure—and voted to allow the interagency funding. A jubilant President Clinton crowed, "This bipartisan victory should be a model for Congress. The legal responsibility of the tobacco companies should be decided in the courts by the judicial process."[46] That same week congressional Republicans made one more effort to deny the funding, but it failed by a 215-183 vote.

The Clinton-Reno War on Business

Janet Reno's actions in an entirely different arena provided an insight into the real agenda of the Clinton administration with regard to tobacco—and it certainly wasn't to protect children. In

March 2000, Reno again invoked the two arcane federal statutes (the Medical Recovery Act and the Medicare Secondary Payer statute) in a shameless effort to enrich the federal government. This time she was targeting the manufacturers of breast implants. She announced that the Justice Department would lay claim to part of the $3.2 billion settlement monies that the manufacturers had agreed to pay to women in their class action suit that began in the early 1990s. Her goal was to siphon off a huge portion of the funds designated for the allegedly injured women and disburse it to government agencies to recoup the government's health care costs (Medicare and otherwise) incurred on behalf of these women. Irrespective of the merits of the underlying lawsuit, Reno's manifest objective was not to help injured people but in fact to further injure them by depriving them of a portion of their settlement claim—all for the sake of the insatiable, money-absorbing federal government.[47] This collateral action brought into stunning focus the character of the Clinton-Reno Justice Department—a character of governmental greed. In its avarice it is an equal opportunity exploiter all its subjects, whether big business or little citizens.

Throughout its crusade against Big Tobacco the Clinton-Reno Justice Department showed that its primary allegiance was not to justice and the rule of law but to the political ends of the Clinton administration.

Chapter Three

A Genuine Conspiracy

On President Clinton's one hundredth day in office a messenger appeared at the White House travel office and delivered a couple of long-stemmed red roses to the staff along with a card from Mr. and Mrs. Clinton thanking them for their hard work. Within a few minutes the messenger returned and reclaimed the flowers, saying, "You were not supposed to get these." No truer words were ever spoken.

The Clintons could ill afford to be doling out praise for the travel office employees considering their plan to fire and replace them with their Arkansas cronies. Even before Bill was inaugurated, the Clintons were anxious to get "[their] people in." An article appearing in an obscure Arkansas business publication shortly after the election unwittingly revealed the Clintons' plan. The story quoted an official of World Wide Travel, Inc., a Little Rock travel agency, as saying that the firm expected to get the White House travel business based on its ties to Clinton confidant David Watkins.[1] In a separate incident, Clinton campaign aide Jeff Eller told reporters as early as December 1992 that there were problems in the travel office and he wouldn't be surprised if some people got fired.[2]

The travel office functioned as an in-house travel agency that arranged charter flights and other travel amenities for the White House press corps. Its seven employees worked for the government but handled no government funds, as the media paid their own travel expenses. Though referred to as career employees, the travel office staff actually served at the will of the president. Billy R. Dale was in charge of the operation, having worked there for more than thirty years.

David Watkins, a Clinton campaign official, and Betta Carney, World Wide's primary shareholder, recruited Clinton's third cousin, Catherine Cornelius, to formulate a plan for an Arkansas coup of the travel office.[3] Cornelius, who made travel arrangements for the press traveling with the Clinton campaign, mostly used World Wide as the campaign's travel agency. In a series of memos to the White House (sent to the attention of David Watkins), Cornelius proposed that she and another Clinton campaign worker, Clarissa Cerda, take over the travel office with the professional assistance of World Wide. Cornelius projected that they could reduce costs by $210,000 annually. Watkins readily approved the plan and immediately appointed Cornelius and Cerda as White House office assistants, with the objective of transferring them to the travel office as soon as it could be arranged.[4] Though Watkins masterminded the Cornelius scheme from the get-go (presumably with the blessing of the Clintons), White House aide Patsy Thomasson allegedly told Cornelius to lie if she were ever asked whether Watkins had read her memos before Clinton took office.[5]

Watkins placed Cornelius in the travel office early in Clinton's first term to spy on the employees. She was instructed to keep "her eyes and ears open" in order to build a case against them. She began eavesdropping on employees' conversations, secretly copying records and making reports. She continued to do so until she was exposed when a check she was copying got caught in the copier. From that point forward the travel office employees were on to her and secreted files from her.

While Watkins and Cornelius were preparing to implement their little conspiracy to oust the employees, others were also goading them to take action. Hollywood television producer Harry Thomason, one of the Clintons' closest friends and biggest contributors from Arkansas, had an interest in Thomason, Richland & Martens Inc. (TRM), an aircraft charter company. He and co-owner Darnell Martens were anxious for TRM to acquire some of the White House travel business. At Thomason's suggestion, Martens called travel office director Billy Dale and tried to talk him into using TRM's brokerage services. Dale politely declined, saying he had no need for "a middleman," since that is basically the function served by the travel office itself. Martens and Thomason did not take this rejection kindly. This was Bill Clinton's White House, after all.

At Thomason's urging, Martens faxed a memo to the White House on May 10, 1993, stating that because of its volume TRM could provide travel consulting services to the White House at a reduced cost. He argued that the travel business should be put out for competitive bids. He also complained that Airline of the Americas, the charter company used almost exclusively by Mr. Dale, was "decidedly anti-Clinton" and "Republican-operated." Around this same time Thomason and Martens both acquired

White House passes, giving them unrestricted access to the White House. Thomason also acquired an office at the White House. Armed with his own office and White House pass, Thomason virtually had the run of the place. Indeed, Thomason testified before the House Government Reform Committee that "for some reason, all the employees of the White House thought if they needed to unload things or tell things, that they could see me."[6] Thomason complained to Hillary about his difficulty in obtaining some of the travel office business for his private company. He allegedly passed on rumors to the Clintons that travel office employees were taking kickbacks.[7]

Just three days after Martens faxed the memo to the White House, White House deputy counsel Vincent Foster instructed assistant counsel William Kennedy, a former partner of Hillary at the Rose law firm in Little Rock, to call the FBI to express concerns about the travel office. When the FBI agents came to the White House, Cornelius shared with them the fruits of her travel office spying operation. In an effort to convince them to begin a criminal investigation, she told them of suspected kickbacks, petty cash discrepancies, and employee lifestyles too lavish for government salaries. She concealed from the agents her conflict of interest in wanting to take over the travel office for herself.

During this same period other White House aides were also trying to build a case against the travel office employees. An FBI agent on White House duty at that time later told Senate Judiciary Committee staff members that three White House political appointees—William Kennedy, Jeff Eller, and Patsy Thomasson—pumped him for information on travel office employees. The agent, Dennis Sculimbrene, reported that he had complained to his bureau supervisor that the aides were simply looking "for a reason or an excuse to fire [these] people" and that the FBI was being used. He said that he tried to set the aides straight concerning their erroneous allegations about travel office employees, such as that they were all Republicans and liked George Bush.[8]

In the meantime another senior White House aide, Jeff Eller, a personal friend of Cornelius, strenuously argued that the employees should be fired. Only Vince Foster counseled restraint. He advised that before firing them, the White House—presumably to cover its tracks—should have the travel office books professionally audited. As a result of Foster's advice, officials hastily arranged for the accounting firm of Peat Marwick to conduct an audit. The auditors came on Friday and frantically completed their work by the following Monday.

The Wednesday Morning Massacre

On the morning of May 19 the White House director of administration, David Watkins, abruptly fired all seven of the travel office employees, telling them the White House was trying to reorganize and pare down the travel office. He told them they had to pack their things and be out by noon. Watkins did not tell them they were under suspicion for misconduct or that the FBI had been charged with investigating them. That's why they were astonished when they heard White House press secretary Dee Dee Myers tell the press that an outside review by Peat Marwick had turned up evidence of "gross mismanagement" and "very shoddy accounting practices." One of the firm's partners, said Myers, found evidence of possible illegalities and a lack of documentation for the petty cash. Myers reported that the FBI had been called in to examine the books and operations of the office. She said the White House was holding all seven employees accountable for the "wrongdoing," which "had been going on for years." Myers said that the White House could get cheaper and better service elsewhere (obviously discounting the myriad contacts the fired employees enjoyed all over the world from their years of experience). The official White House line was that the travel office was being reorganized as part of Vice President Gore's initiative to reinvent government.

Travel office employee Barney Brasseaux said that he was shocked by Myers's suggestion of wrongdoing. Another, Ralph T. Maughan, accused the Clintons of angling to secure the position for the president's relative. "In a nutshell, they wanted Ms. Cornelius in there. We got stabbed. There's no way they can bring criminal charges against anybody." Employee Robert Van Eimeren said he was puzzled by the firings and the allegations of wrongdoing. "I handled staff travel for employees. I know nothing about the books. I'm upset by it. I feel wronged. It's been alleged I've done something wrong; I have not."[9] When asked about this, Dee Dee Myers responded superciliously that the employees were not given an opportunity to defend themselves "because dismissing them was the best course of action given the evidence of mismanagement."

At the time of the firings, Thomason's partner, Darnell Martens, arranged for his and the Clintons' mutual friend from Little Rock, Penny Sample, to come to Washington to work in the travel office and temporarily book flights along with Catherine Cornelius and World Wide.[10] Sample was president of Air Advantage, a firm that acted as a commissioned broker between airlines and business customers. During the Clinton campaign, TRM subcontracted work to Air Advantage, which had access to the larger aircraft needed by the campaign. In the first week of the new operation Sample earned a $1,400 commission while supposedly working in the travel office on a volunteer basis.[11] When officials discovered this fee payment, Sample sheepishly returned it. George Stephanopoulos said, "It was a mistake. She did not realize the funds were going to her firm." Sample left the White House to return to her business a few days later. World Wide also bowed out, and was replaced by American Express Travel "on a temporary basis."

Let's Get Our Story Straight

The Wednesday morning massacre didn't go as smoothly as the Clintons had planned. Within less than a week even their media supporters, such as the *Washington Post*, were suggesting foul play. The *Post* correctly noted that the financial audit did not precede the allegations of impropriety or the administration's contacting of the FBI. Rather, the audit was performed "to justify its earlier decision to replace the seven career workers with political appointees."[12] The actual sequence of events was that the White House first decided to terminate the employees, then it installed its would-be replacement (Cornelius) in the office to fish for evidence. Next, it called in the FBI and misled its agents into believing that criminal charges should be filed against the travel office employees, then scurried to arrange for an audit to cover its tracks.

If this weren't bad enough, the White House also tried to manipulate the FBI into massaging its report to conform with the administration's version of events. Presidential aides summoned agent John E. Collingwood to the White House to pressure him into characterizing the FBI's probe as a "criminal investigation." Clinton misled the press about this. When asked why he called the FBI in as the employees were being fired, he said that it was "not to accuse any of these people of doing anything criminal" but to look at an auditor's report. The exact opposite was true. When FBI agents came to the White House, officials did not discuss the auditor's report with them but focused on covering Clinton's tracks.

Janet Reno was infuriated that the White House contacted the FBI directly, in contravention of a recently implemented policy. The rule was that any requests for information or assistance from any branch of the Justice Department, including the FBI, be cleared through the Attorney General's office. When the press asked Clinton about this, he tried to pass it off country-boy style. He said, "I had nothing to do with any decision except to save the taxpayers and the press money. That's all I know." Clinton added, "The FBI sounds like a huge deal to you, but when you're in Washington, you're the president, you can't call the local police or local prosecutor, that's who you call."[13]

Enter the IRS

Just two days after the travel office firings three IRS agents appeared unannounced at the offices of UltrAir (formerly Airline of the Americas), in Smyrna, Tennessee, and served it with a subpoena for its corporate records. UltrAir was the Houston-based airline company that handled most of the White House press corps charter business the previous year. The revenue agents said they were conducting an audit based on newspaper reports about the company's connection to the White House travel office. This was highly unusual for the IRS, which usually doesn't conduct audits before a tax return has been filed. UltrAir had just been formed in 1992 and had not even filed its first tax return because it had obtained an extension.

The White House denied initiating the audit. FBI agents later testified, however, that when associate White House counsel

William Kennedy called the FBI to prod it into investigating the travel office, he threatened to turn to the IRS for action unless the bureau acted immediately. This revelation illustrated how desperate the White House was to garner evidence of criminal wrongdoing against the employees. Kennedy later served as one of the fall guys for the administration. The White House forced him to resign in November 1994 for his role in the travel office affair and for failing to disclose that he hadn't paid taxes on his children's nanny.

Oops

President Clinton had a rough week following the firings. In addition to taking heat over the travel office he also came under fire for treating himself to a $200 haircut on Air Force One. Coiffeur to the stars, Christophe of Beverly Hills, clipped him while the jet's engines were running and other planes were circling above the L.A. airport waiting to land. Clinton did little to promote his image as a man of the people by firing seven low-level employees and tying up an airport for several hours of extravagant pampering. After a week of nonstop criticism, the White House rescinded the firings of five of the seven travel office employees and placed them on administrative leave with pay—apparently as part of Clinton's promise of a more efficient operation. These five were exonerated because—just as they had claimed—they did not have access to the travel office's cash or bank account. Their reinstatement did not change the fact that the White House had publicly smeared them without any evidence of wrongdoing. When the firings had occurred, White House officials had insisted that the evidence of impropriety and mismanagement was so great that the entire staff had to be dismissed immediately. Dee Dee Myers had said, "We absolutely stand by our decision" to fire the seven employees. Adding insult to injury, George Stephanopoulos denied that the five had ever been fired, saying they had merely been put on administrative leave.

Meanwhile, the Justice Department was still investigating them, notwithstanding their reinstatement. During that period Congress allocated $150,000 to their legal defense costs. The White House eventually placed them in new government jobs, but the government spent $103,300 paying them while they were out of work. In other words, these firings cost taxpayers more than $250,000 in salaries and legal fees, more than Catherine Cornelius wrongly estimated she could save by reorganizing the travel office. Three years later the House passed legislation to reimburse the employees an additional $500,000 in legal fees, most of which were incurred by Billy Dale.[14] President Clinton promised to support the legislation in the Senate and to sign it if it passed. After repeated assurances over a period of three months that he would sign the bill he angrily reneged during a White House press conference. He was upset because various congressional investigations had subjected his staff to "abject harassment." "What did I say? What word did I give, sir? I never gave my word on that," he said. "I don't believe that we should give special preference to one group of people over others. Do you? Do you?"[15] Thereafter, Clinton tried unsuccessfully to block the bill in the Senate, where it passed 52 to 46. Senator Orrin Hatch decried Clinton's hypocrisy in opposing the reimbursement of travel office employees' legal fees while pushing a similar request for reimbursement for his own advisors.[16]

The new and improved travel office didn't produce the efficiency the White House had promised. A few months after the firings the travel office got in a major dispute with the four major television networks about the exorbitant airfare their reporters were charged for a trip to Asia with the president. "We felt they were out of whack in terms of cost," said Bill Headline, the CNN Washington bureau chief who helped organize the trip and was billed $87,000 for airfare. "We said we're not going to pay these [bills] until we have some answers." Another executive said his network was billed for portions of a trip on which his correspondents didn't travel. "We've never had this problem before," said the unnamed executive.[17]

Press Secretary Dee Dee Myers tried to pawn off this overbilling on Billy Dale and crew. She said that the old travel office "subsidized [foreign travel] with money averaged in from other domestic trips.... They were not billed on a per-trip basis, which is something we plan to change." Bill Headline contradicted her, saying, "I don't think we ever had the feeling we were being overcharged." This was not the first time Myers had attempted to discredit the former crew. In an earlier press conference she had attempted to deflect criticism for the firings by saying that the travel employees were working only four days a week. Many members of the press corps disputed Myers's characterization. One of those, Ann Devroy, staff writer for the *Washington Post*, said that to the contrary she had known the travel employees to work twenty hours a day, seven days a week. The White House's description of the agents as being guilty of financial misconduct, she said, "in no way matched my reality. I know them as decent, helpful, honest men, and the White House was virtually calling them criminals. I asked questions."[18]

White House pledges of efficiency never came to pass. Almost two years after the firings the travel office had one more employee than it did under the dog days of Dale: four from American Express and four from the White House staff.

FOBs and Their Privileges

The travel office scandal provided the public a glimpse of the Arkansas-style Clinton White House in operation. Friends of Bill [FOBs] were given unprecedented access and were treated as dignitaries. Clinton had allowed his buddies not only to influence his decisions but also to involve themselves directly in the decision-making process concerning matters in which they had a plain conflict of interest. Harry Thomason attended many meetings and was even allowed to question White House employees and others as the travel office events unfolded.[19] With Clinton's blessing, Thomason ventured into other policy areas as well. He and his actress friend Markie Post spent two days in April 1993 "meeting intensively with senior White House staffers" involving Hillary's scheme to nationalize health care.[20] Some argued that with such access to official White House meetings, these FOBs loose in the halls of the White House had become de facto government employees subject to ethics laws and regulations. White House official Beth Nolan, after claiming to have looked into it, summarily concluded that Thomason was not covered by the law (no controlling legal authority). The General Accounting Office (GAO) later determined that the White House should not have allowed private individuals with personal interests at stake to influence its management decisions. White House chief of staff Thomas F. "Mack" McLarty also admitted that the White House had granted access too freely to nongovernmental people and promised to make a review of pass holders.

During the week following the firings, Harry Thomason and Linda Bloodworth-Thomason denied that Harry was trying to use his relationship with Clinton to procure business for himself or his partner. Bloodworth-Thomason said her husband was too wealthy to have a motive. With his six-figure weekly salary, she said, it would be "sort of the equivalent of taking over a lemonade stand."

Despite these denials, reports later emerged showing that Thomason's efforts to procure cushy government contracts for TRM (more lemonade) were not limited just to the charter business. TRM also engaged in the business of evaluating aircraft to find ways to cut costs. Thomason met with President Clinton very early in his first term and tried to sell him on a proposal for a $500,000 consulting contract for TRM to evaluate government aircraft for cost savings. As a result of the meeting, Clinton forwarded Thomason's proposal to senior White House officials recommending action, along with a handwritten note saying, "These guys are sharp. Should discuss with Panetta and Lader." Leon Panetta was in charge of the Office of Management and Budget at the time, and Philip Lader was deputy White House chief of staff. The deal never came to fruition, being abandoned when the travel office scandal erupted.[21]

The Trial

After making Billy Dale wait in suspense for almost two and a half years, the government finally brought him to trial on October 26, 1995, on embezzlement charges. The principal allegation against Dale was that he converted $14,000 from a petty cash fund and more than $54,000 of press corps funds (the travel office did not handle government funds) into his personal checking account between 1988 and 1991. After all the effort the administration expended in creating the false impression that the Peat Marwick audit uncovered wrongdoing, the government didn't charge Dale with any misconduct for the period the audit covered, January 1992 through May 1993. Perhaps Clinton was trying to tie Dale's wrongdoing to previous administrations, just as he had done with many other scandals. During congressional hearings on Travelgate, Democrats claimed that irregularities in travel office accounts occurred during previous Republican administrations.[22]

Dale kept his petty cash records in a black notebook and an envelope. These records, which Dale's lawyer, Steven C. Tabackman, claimed would exonerate him, disappeared. Catherine Cornelius had admitted taking some travel office records home with her, and Dale's records may have been among them. The defense also elicited testimony from a witness who said he saw White House aide Patsy Thomasson in the travel office early one morning after the locks had been changed.[23] Another defense witness, twenty-three-year FBI veteran Dennis Sculimbrene, testified that he saw several people he did not recognize with visitor's passes inside the travel office on the day of the firings and was worried that the office's records had not been properly secured. "I was amazed that the office was open and there was access to it. I felt that the records probably should have been secured."[24] Sculimbrene said his superior was so concerned when he learned of this security breach that he wrote a letter to White House official John Podesta.[25] When Justice Department attorneys attempted to impeach their own man (the FBI agent) by asking him why he didn't report his concerns to the Secret Service, Sculimbrene fired back, "I would've been doing that every day I was there if I had." Such was the atmosphere at the Clinton White House. Finally, another travel office employee testified that when he returned to the office to pick up some personal items more than a week after the firings Catherine Cornelius "bolted from the room."

The government argued that Dale pocketed the funds to build a second home on a Virginia lake. Tabackman denied the charge, saying the couple lived within their means and spent their thirty-seven years of marriage accumulating savings and then took out a loan for the balance to build the summer home.[26] Tabackman admitted that Dale made a "disastrous mistake" in commingling travel office funds with his personal funds but explained that he had a legitimate need for a healthy petty cash fund. It was used to provide "tips" demanded by foreign airport and hotel employees that were necessary to quickly move groups of reporters through foreign countries. He acquired the petty cash funds through refunds from various hotels and companies that were paid for more services than they provided. Dale began depositing the refund checks into his personal account and used the money to cover those "tips" and other off-the-books payments. With the press complaining about high costs and the administration not offering any suggestions, "[he] was at [his] wit's end" and had to come up with a solution on his own. His strategy of using refunds to pay some of the expenses led the media to believe that certain trips were not as expensive as they actually were.[27]

The Justice Department prosecution was as petty as it was absurd. Prosecutors had no direct evidence that Dale had embezzled any funds so the case centered on a meticulous, tedious review of Dale and his wife's bank records. At one point Mrs. Dale was questioned extensively about a $9 deposit she made to her checking account. "How often do you go to the beauty parlor?" U.S. attorney Goldberg asked Blanche Dale. "Doesn't the garage have an automatic door opener, Mrs. Dale?"[28]

One indication that this prosecution was a government-initiated witch-hunt was that the people who were allegedly victimized by the embezzlement didn't believe Dale had stolen their money. There were no victims here. This was not the government's money at all, but the press corps'. The press corps never complained about any anomalies in the fund. They uniformly trusted Dale, having enjoyed a long, satisfactory relationship with him. Some of them testified on his behalf at the trial saying they trusted him when he ran the travel office and still trusted him "today." Wendy Walker Whitworth, a vice president for CNN and senior executive producer of *Larry King Live* who was formerly assigned to the White House, said, "It doesn't surprise me. Billy is not an e-mail kind of guy. He doesn't have a lot to do with computers. If he was doing this, he was doing it to run the kind of operation he had to run [as] efficiently [as he could]." Robert Hartman, a CBS producer, said, "I found him to be a stand-up, straight-up guy."[29] ABC's Sam Donaldson testified that Dale was always there for the news media in "big ways and in small ways.... He never let me down."[30]

A specialist on fraud, who had often worked as a government expert, testified for the defense. He said that Dale did not need the travel office money he was accused of embezzling because he had more than enough money to cover his family's needs during the time in question. The Dales, he said, had "a very modest standard of living. The Dales were not spending money at Tiffany's or Nordstrom's.... They were spending money at Kmart, Sears... and Bradlees.... They were not in financial difficulty. They were easily able to meet all of their commitments."[31]

The government's theory was so obliterated by the close of the trial that prosecutors were reduced to arguing that "you don't have to be hungry to steal.... Rich people embezzle money. People with savings embezzle money." Having spent much of their case trying to prove that Dale needed the money to supplement his income and lifestyle, U.S. attorneys carped, "This case isn't about whether he needed the money. He took the money because he wanted the money."

When Dale's attorney, Mr. Tabackman, was delivering his summation and recounting the abundant character-witness testimony from coworkers and journalists, Dale was visibly moved, choking back tears.[32]

On November 16, 1995, the federal jury of six men and six women acquitted Dale after deliberating only two hours and twelve minutes. It's noteworthy that the jury acquitted Dale even without being allowed to hear certain extremely damning evidence against the government. The jury was precluded from learning that the very people who had access to the travel office at the time of the firings and therefore to Dale's missing records were the same people who had an interest in taking over the travel office operation. Upon hearing of the verdict, Dale held back the tears no more. Displaying the class and character that gave rise to the testimony in his favor at the trial, Dale resisted lashing out at the Clinton administration. "It's been thirty long months. I've been angry for two and a half years, but I've had to keep my mouth shut."

When President Clinton heard about the verdict he said, "I'm very sorry about what Mr. Dale had to go through and I wish him well. I hope that he can get on with his life and put this behind him."[33] Kind of reminiscent of "better put some ice on that." The ordinarily liberal *Washington Post* upbraided Clinton for that non-apology. It editorialized that Clinton misspoke when he expressed sorrow about what Billy Dale "had to go through." It would have been more accurate to say, "he was sorry for what Mr. Dale was 'put through' by the White House."[34]

Steve Tabackman called the verdict "a vindication not just of Billy Dale and the life he led but of all of the [people] who worked in the travel office who suffered the consequences of the misguided and outrageous decision by the White House."[35] A few days after the verdict Billy Dale broke his silence during an interview with reporters. He and his wife said that their experience shattered their trust in government. "I feel like the victims of Ruby Ridge and Waco. The only difference is they didn't use guns on us," said Billy Dale. Mrs. Dale added, "Nobody will ever know the number of times we, as a family, sat and cried together.... But we've lost a lot of faith and trust in the system." She said that she and her husband had always taught their children to respect the presidency. But their belief in the White House was shattered "after seeing what the office of the president can do to people... and have them go through the agony that we went through... and having our life history up there for anybody to pick apart and to twist and to turn into anything that suited their purpose."[36]

Billy Dale also related how he was told early on that the travel office scheme was being orchestrated directly from the office of the president. He said that a lady who used to work in administration at the White House told him, "There is one person and one person only responsible, and that person occupies the Oval Office."[37] Perhaps Dale wasn't yet aware of the significant role Hillary Clinton played in cashiering him and his colleagues. But others were.

Hell to Pay

In January 1996 a shocking memo surfaced. It had been almost three years since the firings and more than a year after congressional investigators and the Independent Counsel's office had served subpoenas on the White House for travel office documents. The White House belatedly released a nine-page memo written by former aide David Watkins to his then superior, Chief of Staff Mack McLarty, contradicting the first lady's contention that she had played no role in the decision to fire the employees. Watkins said in the memo that he fired the travel office employees at Hillary Clinton's "insistence," saying he knew there would be "hell to pay" if he "failed to take swift and decisive action in conformity with the First Lady's wishes."[38]

When Kenneth Starr learned of the memo, he wrote the White House counsel to express "distress" that the White House had withheld this vital information. "The White House had an obligation to turn this memorandum over to the Office of Independent Counsel as soon as it was discovered." Congressman William Clinger, chairman of the House Government Reform Committee, said the memo was evidence of a White House "cover-up" that, together with the travel office firings, was "orchestrated at the highest levels of the White House."[39]

The Watkins memo was inconsistent with Hillary's (and Watkins's) earlier statement to GAO investigators that she had no knowledge of who ordered the firings and played no role in the incident. The memo also included a chilling revelation about Watkins's previous efforts to cover up for the Clintons. He said that coming clean involved "a soul-cleansing. It is my first attempt to be sure the record is straight, something I have not done in previous conversations with investigators—where I have been as protective and vague as possible."[40] In the released memo, Watkins was anything but vague. He told McLarty, "At that meeting you explained to me that this was on the First Lady's radar screen. The message you conveyed to me was clear: immediate action must be taken. I explained to you that I had decided to terminate the travel office employees, and you expressed relief that we were finally going to take action (to resolve the situation in conformity with the First Lady's wishes)." He added, "the pressure for action from the First Lady and you became irresistible. This demand for immediate action forced me to accept hastily formulated plans for hasty, inadvisable action.... If I thought I could have resisted those pressures, undertaken more considered action, and remained in the White House, I certainly would have done so." Watkins had also written that Hillary said, "We need these people out. We need our people in. We need the slots."

In testimony before a House committee Watkins stood by his story that he felt intense pressure from the Clintons to fire the travel office employees. He said he probably would have been removed from the White House had he refused to act. Hillary was responsible for generating the pressure, but it came to Watkins through two intermediaries, late deputy White House counsel Vince Foster and Hollywood producer Harry Thomason. Watkins said that four days before the auditors were hired to examine the travel office records Hillary was "ready to fire them all that day."[41] Mack McLarty, in deposition testimony for the House Reform Committee, corroborated Watkins's version of events. He said that although first lady Hillary Clinton never explicitly told him to fire the travel office staff, she expressed concerns to him about them and he felt "pressure to act" on the removal of the seven employees.[42]

Not long after the Watkins memo came to light another bombshell exploded. Hillary Clinton's Rose Law Firm billing records that had been evading investigator's subpoenas for years were miraculously discovered in the White House residence. Hillary had denied doing appreciable legal work for the failed Madison Guaranty Savings and Loan (of Whitewater fame), which cost federal taxpayers $60 million. Congressman Jim Leach, chairman of the House Banking Committee, said that to the contrary the billing records proved that Mrs. Clinton performed extensive and detailed legal work on Madison, including its dubious purchase of Castle Grande.[43]

Prominent *New York Times* columnist Bill Safire wrote his now famous column on January 9, 1996, wherein he denounced Hillary Clinton as a "congenital liar." The billing records, said Safire, "show Hillary Clinton was lying when she denied actively representing a criminal enterprise known as the Madison S&L." The column prompted the also now famous response of Bill Clinton that if he weren't president he would have been tempted to punch Safire in the nose. "I've said it before, I'll say it again, if everybody in this country had the character that my wife has, [it would] be a better place to live."

Hillary's feminist comrades, appalled that she was under attack, rushed to her defense. Betty Friedan said, "This whole thing is so diversionary. I have no idea what went on way back in the past, God knows, but I don't think it's at all relevant to the state of our nation today. I'm ashamed of the media. Don't try to make Hillary a red herring." In other words, feminist causes are way too important to be deterred by the scandals of their advocates, so the media should suppress any such stories. Judith Lichtman, president of the Women's Legal Defense Fund, expressed similar sentiments. "The more I talk to you about this, the more I realize how angry I am that this takes up so many inches in newspapers and minutes on TV instead of the real debate we should be having about the heart and soul of this country."

For all their protesting, Hillary's apologists did not address the heart of many of the first couple's problems. From the travel office scandal, to the billing records, to the disastrously failed effort to force socialized medicine on the nation, Hillary Clinton displayed incompetence, political paranoia, an allergy to telling the truth, and an unrivaled arrogance and abuse of power. Assessing Hillary's recurring difficulties, the *Washington Post* opined that "the history of the first three years shows that many of the most spectacular misjudgments of the administration bear her imprimatur. Mistrust of people outside her circle of loyalists was a common theme."[44] For example, she was behind the reversal of a long-standing White House practice of allowing reporters to walk unescorted to the press secretary's office. According to one former official, "She said the press were scum. That they would be standing around trying to read papers upside down on people's desks and doing gotcha interviews and just trying to make us all look bad."[45] An even more revealing incident occurred earlier in Clinton's term after Hillary read an item in *Newsweek* reporting that she'd thrown a lamp at the president during a marital spat. Her fury was directed not at the magazine but at the Secret Service, which she suspected of planting the story. According to a Democratic official, "she freaked. She could not abide the idea of having spies in her own home.... She really does have a feeling that if you are not with us, then you are against us."[46] Indeed.

We're Mad As Hell and We're Not Going to Take It Anymore

A few months after the trial Billy Dale wrote an article with his attorney, Steven Tabackman, for the *Washington Post*. He said he assumed that after the jury acquitted him so quickly he would be able to return to his normal quiet lifestyle, but the release of the David Watkins's memorandum subjected him to renewed attacks "at least as vicious as the ones for which I was tried and acquitted." He said he had kept quiet for the two-and-a-half-year period between the firings and the trial but was not going to anymore. "This time, however, there is no trial pending. This time I will not sit silently and take it."

Dale accused the Clintons of reverting to full attack mode against him to obscure the hideousness of their own actions. They unleashed their attorneys to further smear him by falsely suggesting that he had tried to enter a guilty plea to the embezzlement charges. (In a confidential letter to the Justice Department before the trial he had admitted to commingling funds but denied that he ever spent the money on himself—an essential element of an embezzlement charge.) Dale was just as outraged about the origin of this story as the lies it contained. The only way the press could have learned of the letter was through a Justice Department leak. As Dale noted, "the Justice Department's own rules prohibit the release of this kind of confidential communication." [47]

Dale also said that Hillary was appearing on various TV shows denying that she had anything to do with the firings. Dale said that it didn't matter to him who fired him. "What does matter is that the public understands that the firings had nothing to do with 'financial mismanagement.'" That allegation, he said, was just a convenient excuse to carry out a decision that had been in the works a long time. Indeed, Hillary indicated that by May 12, 1993, she wanted the travel office employees replaced, but it wasn't until May 13 that the decision was made to retain Peat Marwick to conduct the audit. "So I am forced to wonder," said Dale, "what is the financial mismanagement that she was concerned with before Peat Marwick even began its work?"

Dale related the previously unknown story that his office began to get calls "around inauguration day" from people looking for the "new director," Catherine Cornelius—strong proof that the plan to fire him preceded Clinton's assumption of the presidency. Moreover, World Wide's people, said Dale, were already occupying desks in the travel office by the time Dale and his staff returned from the fifteen-minute meeting in which they were fired. Dale said he later learned how World Wide had ingratiated itself to the Clintons. During the campaign, through their "creative billing procedures" of the traveling media, they ensured that the campaign would have the cash flow to spend on crucial primaries.

The travel employees continued their PR counterattack against the Clinton smear machine when they testified at the House Reform Committee hearings. Their voices were shaking with emotion as they accused the Clinton administration of abusing its power when it fired them three years before. All of them said their lives had been turned upside down by the affair. Three of the employees' fathers had died before their names were cleared. When certain Democrats downplayed their distress by saying they were not the only federal workers to have lost their jobs, travel office employee John McSweeney retorted, "Can you point to one of them who turned on the television and heard himself being accused of being a thief?"[48]

Cover-up and Dead Ends

In the aftermath of the travel office scandal and the ensuing congressional investigations, the White House went into its familiar stonewall mode. As usual, the White House hid behind a bogus executive privilege claim to block investigators from viewing key travel office documents. In addition, Bill and Hillary Clinton denied any wrongdoing in connection with the firings, and their trusted aides circled the wagons in their defense, as had been their custom for Clinton's entire two terms. As part of Clinton's damage control efforts, his aides were extraordinarily uncooperative when testifying before the committee. For example, former aide William Kennedy, who implemented the firings under pressure from Hillary Clinton, denied that he told the FBI that concern about the travel office was coming from "the highest levels" of the White House. Yet four separate FBI agents directly contradicted him. Similarly, the committee cited former White House counsel Bernard Nussbaum for "incomplete testimony" involving relevant documents about the travel office dispute. Many other aides contradicted each other as well. Committee chairman William Clinger submitted a fifty-three-page summary to the independent counsel detailing "the most egregious examples" of conflicting testimony and asked him to examine the materials for possible federal perjury and obstruction of justice violations.[49]

On another front, Independent Counsel Kenneth Starr, whose investigative scope had been expanded to include the travel office affair, was trying to get to the bottom of Hillary's involvement in the firings. Deputy White House counsel Vincent Foster was reputedly among those who had tried to trump up charges against the travel office employees to make way for Clinton's Arkansas friends to assume the operation. Foster, apparently fearing he would be implicated in a criminal investigation, went to see attorney James Hamilton for advice on how to handle his coming troubles. Just nine days later, on July 20, 1993, Foster's dead body was discovered at Fort Marcy Park in Washington, D.C.

The independent counsel was aware that when Foster met with his attorney he was concerned not only about his own criminal liability but also about problems facing his close friend and confidante Hillary Clinton. Starr learned that James Hamilton had taken three pages of handwritten notes during his meeting with Foster. At

Starr's request the federal grand jury issued subpoenas to Hamilton for his notes. He was determined to find out whether Foster had revealed anything to Hamilton that could be useful to his criminal investigation. Hamilton refused to honor the subpoena on the basis of his attorney-client privilege with Foster. The federal district court sided with Hamilton and said the notes were protected by the privilege. Though the court of appeals reversed the district court's decision, the Supreme Court ultimately ruled in a 6-3 decision that the notes were protected by the attorney-client privilege even after the death of the client (Vince Foster). The ruling, one of Ken Starr's few appellate defeats, foreclosed another potential avenue for ascertaining the extent of Hillary Clinton's role in the firings.

Ken Starr's successor, Robert W. Ray, formally concluded his investigation into Travelgate in June 2000. He announced that there was "substantial evidence" that first lady Hillary Rodham Clinton had a role in the 1993 travel office firings but insufficient evidence to prove to a jury beyond a reasonable doubt that her statements to the contrary were knowingly false. In his report, which the three-judge panel released to the public on October 18, Ray made clear his belief that Hillary lied in sworn statements to independent counsel investigators, to Congress, and to the General Accounting Office, when she denied she had any role in the firings.

The travel office scandal thus ended like so many of the other Clinton scandals: justice perverted and justice denied. Once again, with the concerted assistance of the politicized Justice Department, the Clintons escaped accountability. Everyone knew, based on the Watkins "hell to pay" memo and the testimony of other witnesses, that Hillary Clinton was one of the prime movers in the travel office firings and that she lied about it to investigators. Her statement in written answers to Congress in 1996 that she "had no decision-making role with regard to the removal" was obviously false. But Ray was aware that he would have a very difficult time convicting Hillary Clinton before a Washington, D.C., jury and he surely understood the public's distaste for criminal pursuit of the first lady.

Travelgate represents as clearly as any other scandal the Clintons' wholesale appropriation of the Justice Department for political ends. The Reno Justice Department again reserved its prosecutorial fervor for enemies of Bill and Hillary Clinton rather than enemies of justice. The political prosecution of Billy Dale will serve as a chilling illustration of what can happen when the nation's chief executive officer and his primary law enforcement agency decide to turn the law upside down and abet the cause of politics rather than justice. Only political motivations can explain the Justice Department's monomaniacal determination to proceed criminally against a fifty-seven-year-old government employee whom everyone trusted and who was handling private, rather than public, funds. Even the most ingenious system of constitutional checks and balances in the history of the world cannot always prevent the misdeeds of dishonorable officials nor ensure their accountability.

Chapter Four

Investigating the Investigator

W hen the Lewinsky scandal erupted on January 21, 1998, President Clinton's political strategist Dick Morris and friend Harry Thomason rushed to his aid. Thomason flew to Washington immediately and remained at the White House for thirty-four days by Clinton's side. Morris was in touch by phone. Both confidants advised him to tell the truth. Otherwise, the scandal would become a public relations disaster.[1]

Morris actually composed a speech for Clinton to deliver to the American people. In it Morris had Clinton conceding his "personal flaw" (marital infidelity) and the "great pain" he had caused Hillary because of it. He had Clinton directly admitting his affair with Lewinsky and clearly apologizing for it. The proposed speech closed with Clinton offering to resign. "If the American people want me to step down as President, I will do so. With a heavy heart, but I will do so.... My future is in your hands, my fellow Americans."[2]

With Clinton's blessing, Morris secretly enlisted a research firm in Melbourne, Florida, to conduct a poll to gauge the public's likely reaction to the speech. Morris personally absorbed the $2,000 cost of the poll, just to ensure that Clinton could not be tied to it. The poll results surprised Morris. The respondents favored resignation, 47 to 43 percent. Morris, conveying the bad news to Clinton, said, "They're just not ready for it." Clinton's reply would form the blueprint for the White House strategy over the next year: "Well, we just have to win then."[3]

Clinton's Counteroffensive

Knowing that the truth was not on their side, Clinton and his trusted aides and loyalists decided to launch a blistering and sustained counterattack against Kenneth Starr and his deputies. Its purpose was to shift the public's disfavor from Clinton to Starr and to divert Starr's energies from prosecuting Clinton to defending himself. The counteroffensive was unprecedented in its scope and intensity. Clinton's lawyers and henchmen accused Starr and his assistants of violating Justice Department guidelines, conflicts of interest, illegal leaks of secret grand jury information, colluding with Paula Jones's attorneys to entrap the president, and more.

Several female witnesses simultaneously accused Starr of suborning their perjury in order to incriminate Clinton. James Carville formed the Education and Information Project for the express purpose of targeting Starr and congressional Republicans "to expose their hypocrisy." Larry Flynt, owner of *Hustler* magazine, conducted his own campaign to smear the president's accusers, also on grounds of hypocrisy. The president's lawyers hired private investigators to gather "information" about Clinton's political accusers. The Democratic National Committee attempted to discredit Starr's deputies with rumors about alleged improprieties they had committed while working in the Justice Department.

Worst of all, the Department of Justice tacitly participated in this well-coordinated campaign of character assassination. Almost every step of the way, Reno and her troops used their awesome power to undermine the Office of the Independent Counsel and others who were attempting to bring Clinton to justice. The message: Don't mess with Bill.

Six months before the Lewinsky news broke, the White House hadn't yet developed a comprehensive strategy to combat the Office of the Independent Counsel, but it was beginning to ratchet up its attacks against Starr, and it was getting assistance from its congressional allies. In June 1997, Clinton lawyer David Kendall accused Starr of an unethical "leak-and-smear" campaign against the president. Another attorney for the president, Bob Bennett, threatened to investigate the past sex life of Clinton accuser Paula Jones. He vowed to wage "nuclear war" to defend Clinton.

Meanwhile, Senate Democrats were lashing out at Republicans for conducting a partisan investigation in their campaign finance probe against the administration. Yet White House officials denied that there was any coordinated strategy to take the offensive against Clinton's accusers. In a commencement address Clinton himself warned the graduates to avoid being tempted by thoughts of retribution. "No one ever really gets even in life."[4] This is one case where Clinton, probably, wasn't lying. His primary motive, probably, was not to get even but to ward off his attackers. Revenge could wait until later.

Indeed, White House press secretary Michael McCurry admitted that the White House was behind Kendall's allegation that Starr was leaking material. "This is not a strategy; it's an anxious desire to see this matter come to some kind of completion," said McCurry. Another Clinton ally said Kendall's accusations weren't meant to create legal problems for Starr. The purpose was "to stop the smears."[5]

A Declaration of War and Rallying the Troops

Following the Lewinsky revelation, evidence of a White House conspiracy to smear Starr began to emerge. Appearing on NBC's *Meet the Press* shortly after Clinton's finger-wagging denial of sexual relations with Monica Lewinsky, James Carville issued some bold statements. He said repeatedly that the independent counsel was engaged in a systematic leak of grand jury information in "a concerted effort to get the president." "I think the real focus here is on the methods of the independent counsel, on the motives of the independent counsel and what's going on here, and I think that's what people want to hear about. And I think that they're going to hear a lot about it in the coming weeks and months."

Carville then took it upon himself to declare war against Kenneth Starr on behalf of the president. "And there absolutely is not going to be any resignations or any such things as that. But I tell you what there is going to be. There's going to be a war.... [T]he friends of the president are disgusted by these [kinds] of tactics. And we're going to fight, and we're going to fight very hard, to defend this president." Carville revealed that Hillary Clinton was "very much appalled by all this, is very much in a fighting mood and is rallying the troops." Carville telegraphed another impending Clinton strategy. "I think there's going to be an investigation when it's over and I think it's going to be an investigation of the leak of material out of the independent counsel's office. I really believe that."[6]

Within a week of Carville's TV appearance reports surfaced shedding light on who was behind this well-organized plan to discredit the prosecutors. With the outbreak of the Lewinsky scandal the White House was no place for the faint-hearted. "It would be fair to say it was a disaster area," said an administration official. Some low-level staffers were initially discouraged to the point of privately discussing Clinton's resignation. Then Hillary Clinton stepped in and took charge of damage control for the president. She assembled a nucleus of fellow guerrilla warriors whose mission was to cripple the president's enemies and reinvigorate his waning popularity.

Hillary's Lewinsky troops comprised two categories, legal and political. Every member of each group was unquestioningly loyal. The legal team included David Kendall, Charles Ruff, Mickey Kantor, Harold Ickes, Lanny Breuer, Bruce Lindsey, and Cheryl Mills. Bob Bennett was peripherally involved, but Hillary saw to it that his services were relegated to the Paula Jones suit. Paul Begala, Rahm Emanuel, John Podesta, Doug Sosnik, and Ann Lewis formed the political group.

Hillary's strategy consisted of:
- stonewalling the media about factual details;
- orchestrating attacks on Ken Starr, depicting him as a partisan participant of a right-wing conspiracy;
- simultaneously assaulting Starr in the courts;
- presenting an image of the president as being too engaged in important affairs of state to be troubled by these allegations;
- preparing a counterattack on the media as biased and irresponsible;
- escalating Clinton's level of domestic travel to simulate a "campaign mode," the environment in which he is most comfortable;
- abstaining from attacks on Lewinsky while encouraging others, including the press, to do it behind the scenes.[7]

When her plan was in its earliest phase of implementation, Hillary achieved results that surely exceeded her most optimistic expectations.[8] As far-fetched as it sounds, in terms of popular opinion she almost turned the Lewinsky nightmare into a positive, with the president's popularity levels reaching new highs. According to a *Washington Post* poll in early February 1998, 67 percent of the American people approved of his job performance and a stunning 57 percent said they were satisfied he had sufficient honesty and integrity to serve as president. Fifty-nine percent believed that Clinton's political enemies were "conspiring" to bring him down.[9] So far, mission accomplished.

"Intolerable, Unlawful Leaks"

As Hillary's strategy was unfolding, the two White House groups were in constant conflict. The political group was pressing for unmitigated attacks against the independent counsel, while the lawyers were urging caution.[10] This tension was resolved, however, when the president's lawyer stood before cameras in the first week of February and again publicly accused Starr's office of leaking secret grand jury information. Attorney David Kendall, in a public statement, accused Kenneth Starr of being "obviously out of control when it comes to leaking." Kendall sent a letter to Starr saying, "The leaking by your office has reached an intolerable point." He accused Starr of an "appalling disregard" for the Federal Rules of Criminal Procedure, specifically Rule 6(e), prohibiting the disclosure of grand jury testimony and evidence. Kendall described the leaks as being part of a pattern of "selectively releasing both information and falsehoods in an attempt to pressure, manipulate and intimidate witnesses and possible witnesses." Kendall threatened to seek a court order holding Starr in contempt of court.

Starr was taken aback by all of this. At the time he was appointed independent counsel he enjoyed a distinguished record and was not considered to be excessively partisan. In fact, when the Senate Ethics Committee needed an unbiased mediator to assist it in making certain factual determinations in Senator Bob Packwood's sexual harassment case, it chose Starr. Notably, no one ever accused him of leaks when serving in that role.[11]

In a letter, Starr crisply responded that Kendall's allegations were "reckless" and had "no factual basis." "Your role as private defense counsel and your loyalty to your client does not qualify you to lecture me on professional conduct and my legal responsibilities," wrote Starr. Nevertheless, Starr reported that he had begun an investigation to determine if anyone in his office was responsible for the leaks, which he conceded would be "a firing offense" and criminal. In a more pointed jab, Starr noted that the president's lawyers, not the Office of the Independent Counsel, had a motive for leaking information.[12]

Right on cue, Congressman John Conyers, senior Democrat on the House Judiciary Committee, asked Attorney General Reno to investigate whether Starr should be removed or disciplined for "repeated instances of alleged misconduct and abuses of power." A Justice Department spokesman said the department would review the congressman's request.[13] And Kendall, true to his promise, filed a sealed motion in federal court in Washington within days of his letter, seeking to have Starr held in contempt and his office investigated.

Some Republican officials, such as Missouri senator John Ashcroft, came to Starr's defense. "This is a diversion," said Ashcroft. "The real need in this country is for the president to tell us what happened [and for] the president to be accountable to the

American people.... If there's nothing behind this stonewall, it's time for the president to tear down the stonewall and to tell the American people the truth."[14] But overall, Republican efforts were lame compared to the relentless barrage from Clinton's minutemen.

Every weekend and on most weeknights they packed the television talk shows armed with talking points, blasting Starr, and decrying his "transgressions." White House aide Paul Begala appeared on *Meet the Press* and accused Starr of criminal leaks, "a much more serious crime, frankly, than signing a false affidavit by a 24-year-old kid in a civil lawsuit." On CNN's *Late Edition*, White House adviser Rahm Emanuel charged that the Office of the Independent Counsel had spent more time and money investigating Clinton than federal investigators trying to determine the cause of the crash of TWA Flight 800. "And I'll tell you the difference is one is done professionally, the other is done with real questions being raised by serious, serious former prosecutors and legal scholars, wondering what is going on," said Emanuel.[15]

A Two-Pronged Approach

As the weeks passed, Clinton's lawyers added sophistication to their plan. While some White House attorneys were busy gathering information that could be used behind the scenes in their legal battles, Kendall and various Clinton aides bludgeoned Starr publicly. They employed this two-pronged approach because they understood that the legal battle would be greatly affected by the public relations battle.

Behind the Scenes: Conferences and Debriefings

Clinton's lawyers conferred with potential grand jury witnesses to help them find Clinton-friendly lawyers. These lawyers could then share with Clinton's lawyers what their clients had revealed to Starr. Clinton's lawyers also routinely debriefed the grand jury witnesses. This wasn't the first time this embattled White House had employed such tactics. White House counsel Jane Sherburne admitted that she and her colleagues had often debriefed lawyers for witnesses in congressional investigations of other scandals, such as Whitewater, Filegate, and Travelgate. These sessions provided Clinton's lawyers with the same information that Starr had, which means they could have been responsible for all the leaks they were accusing Starr of making. Starr pointed this out to the press, saying that the president's defense lawyers "had most if not all" of the information that was leaked several days before the leaks occurred.[16]

Public Bludgeoning

The president's lawyers hired private investigators to assist in the president's PR defense, or, perhaps more accurately, his offense. Terry Lenzner admitted that his firm, Investigative Group Inc., had been retained by David Kendall's law firm, Williams & Connolly, but would not divulge the scope of his investigation. Lenzner had been working for the Clinton White House at least since 1994 in connection with the Whitewater and Paula Jones cases. Some referred to him as President Clinton's private CIA.[17]

Lenzner's reputation was that of a tough, complex man. A neighbor and friend described him as a man who's "got a dark side that's pretty scary." Another friend said, "He's certainly not characterized by restraint. He's like a guy walking around with gasoline poured over him, just looking for a match." A colleague described him as having a confrontational nature, whose "scorched-earth tactics eventually turn people against him." *New York Times* columnist

William Safire described Lenzner, who had worked for the Senate Watergate Committee, as a "bully" who pursued his work for that committee with a "gleeful savagery."[18] Without admitting direct involvement, Lenzner commented that if his investigators were looking into the backgrounds of Kenneth Starr's staff, "I'd say there was nothing inappropriate about that." Predictably, the White House denied it had hired private investigators to look into the prosecutors' backgrounds but did not dispute that the investigators were being used for other purposes.[19]

It wasn't long before the investigations produced some dirt. Starr learned that certain White House aides, such as Sidney Blumenthal, allegedly had been spreading rumors that two of Starr's deputies, Michael Emmick and Bruce Udolf, had engaged in prosecutorial misconduct in their previous positions at the Justice Department. According to Susan Schmidt and Michael Weisskopf in *Truth at Any Cost*, Clinton's aides "stirred up numerous media investigations of Emmick and Udolf." The White House admitted that Clinton's allies might have provided reporters with "detailed background information."[20]

Specifically, David Kendall's partner Nicole Seligman reportedly provided Blumenthal with a videotape of a Los Angeles television news broadcast containing false allegations of prosecutorial misconduct against Emmick. Blumenthal then allegedly distributed copies to the media and the Democratic National Committee's opposition research coordinator. Clinton allies were also circulating a false story that a California federal judge had questioned Emmick's integrity, when actually the federal judge had been talking about a different federal prosecutor and had, in fact, referred to Emmick as a "man of integrity." The White House employed similar tactics against Udolf.

Starr was incensed that the White House personally attacked his prosecutors, whom he regarded as dedicated public servants. He referred to the charges against his team as "an avalanche of lies."[21] In an effort to combat some of the assaults on his office, Starr subpoenaed Blumenthal to turn over any documents he had about Starr's staff.

Starr's move subjected him to a renewed round of attacks from all quarters. White House spokesman Joe Lockhart accused Starr of "a clear abuse of power."[22] The ubiquitous Clinton attack dog James Carville publicly ridiculed Starr again. "This man is out of control. And he's not going to shut me up—period. He goes down by the Potomac and listens to hymns, as the cleansing water of the Potomac goes by, and we're going to wash all Sodomites and fornicators out of town," mocked Carville.[23]

Other Clinton mouthpieces were in sync with their talking points. Both Paul Begala and Lanny Davis parroted the White House line that Blumenthal was "fined $10,000 for the crime of criticizing Ken Starr," presumably referring to legal fees Blumenthal incurred as a result of being subpoenaed. Congressional Democrats also stepped up to the plate for Clinton and began piling on Starr. Senator Patrick Leahy said that Starr should step down: "Kenneth Starr has gotten totally out of control. He has this fixation of trying to topple the president of the United States. He's doing everything possible to do it."[24]

Many in the media also went ballistic. Clinton couldn't have asked for greater support if these reporters had been on his personal payroll. "This just seems to be totally wacko. Here's a guy whose job it is, in part, to talk to the press. If he is charged in the Lewinsky case, we really are living in a police state," said Nina Totenberg, legal correspondent for National Public Radio, rallying to the defense of subpoenaed Clinton aide Sidney Blumenthal. Alan Murray of the *Wall Street Journal* called Blumenthal's subpoena "a very disturbing development that could have an impact on our ability to gather information for the public."

Doyle McManus of the *Los Angeles Times* went even further: "The independent counsel has already been accused of criminalizing the political process. This looks perilously close to taking that one step further and potentially criminalizing the journalistic process." Jane Kirtley, executive director of the Reporters Committee for Freedom of the Press, implied that Starr's office was guilty of leaks and that Starr was investigating Blumenthal as an act of revenge. "If Ken Starr is serious about finding out where leaks are coming from, he ought to start by investigating his own office. It's disgraceful to do investigations of this nature that appear to be founded on the notion that Blumenthal criticized Ken Starr," she said.[25]

Starr responded strongly to the suggestion that he was acting improperly by subpoenaing Blumenthal. "The First Amendment," said Starr, "is interested in the truth. Misinformation and distorted information have come to us about career public servants.... The grand jury has a legitimate interest in inquiring into whether there is an effort to impede our investigation."[26]

The mainstream media also came to the president's defense on other fronts. One piece in the *Washington Post* was particularly critical of what Clinton accusers were doing to the right of privacy. It related with disapproval that the president was subjected to extensive questioning in the Jones case about "his possible involvement with other women." It lamented Starr's investigation of Clinton's relationship with Monica Lewinsky, and it questioned Starr's conduct in obtaining Linda Tripp's secretly recorded tapes of Lewinsky. "Whatever happened to privacy?" protested the *Post*.

"In one sense, Starr is focusing on serious allegations.... But at the same time his inquiry involves quintessentially private matters—sex, which if it occurred, took place apparently between two consenting adults—that have only been wrenched into public view by the existence of the Jones litigation and the broad discovery that has been permitted in that case."[27]

Other friends of Clinton pitched in on his behalf. The president of the American Bar Association criticized Kenneth Starr for his "prosecutorial zeal." At a Georgetown Law Center symposium on the Independent Counsel Act, without mentioning Starr by name, the ABA president asked a series of rhetorical questions riddled with innuendo. "Does prosecutorial zeal justify sting operations and unauthorized wiretapping in order to leverage the hiding of noncriminal, sexual indiscretion into a criminal obstruction of justice? Are prosecutors entitled to ignore ethical prescriptions on the grounds that their pursuit of truth or common practice justifies departure from professional standards? Is the special counsel a fourth arm of government lacking any meaningful accountability and realistically immune from removal?"[28]

An Escalation in the Counterattack

Regardless of whether a conspiracy can ever be conclusively proven against Starr's enemies, the sheer number of his attackers and the similarity of their unlikely claims constitute convincing circumstantial evidence that the White House and its closest allies were coordinating the assault on Starr. During the Whitewater investigation before the Lewinsky revelations, the president's attacks against Ken Starr were much less frequent. But in the first six weeks following Clinton's denial, no fewer than seven formal complaints were filed (or appealed) against Starr. Two of them were filed in federal court and five with the Justice Department. The majority of them involved allegations of leaks, but there were other charges.

Federal Court Complaints

In addition to Kendall's complaint with the federal court in Washington, D.C., there was also action in another federal circuit. In 1997 attorney Frank Mandanici had filed a bizarre ethics complaint against Starr in federal district court in Little Rock alleging that Starr had conflicts of interest that should preclude him from serving as independent counsel and subject him to disciplinary action. Specifically, he charged that Starr's plan to accept a position at Pepperdine University was improper in that one of the university's major contributors was Clinton nemesis Richard Mellon Scaife. Judge Susan Webber Wright, along with two other judges, dismissed Mandanici's complaint because Mandanici could not show he was personally affected by any of the cases. "In the absence of specific evidence... this court declines the opportunity to provide Mr. Mandanici a forum for pursuing his vendetta," wrote Judge Wright.

Driven by an intensity and persistence seemingly common to Starr's foes, Mandanici appealed to the Eighth Circuit Court of Appeals. Mandanici admitted not having a personal stake in the litigation but claimed that the actual defendants, such as Susan McDougal, were too intimidated to bring a complaint against Starr. Mandanici insisted he was operating on his own and was not a tool of the White House.[29]

Justice Department Complaints

Starr's pursuers also bombarded the Justice Department with complaints. In addition to his court action, Frank Mandanici filed a complaint with the Justice Department concerning Starr's alleged conflicts of interest. Congressional Democrats filed two separate complaints with the Justice Department alleging illegal leaks and demanding an investigation,[30] and Monica Lewinsky's attorney, William Ginsburg, piled on with his own leak allegation.

Kendall Few, a South Carolina attorney who had opposed Starr in litigation involving General Motors, filed a complaint with the Justice Department asking it to investigate Starr for obstruction of justice. The allegation was based on Starr's conduct as a private attorney. Receiving the complaint in March 1998, the Justice Department opened a review to determine whether Starr concealed perjury while defending General Motors in lawsuits over fatal automobile fires. Few's complaint alleged that Starr had withheld from the court evidence that his client had committed perjury.

Some questioned whether it was coincidental that this complaint against Starr involved perjury, the very crime most central to Starr's investigation against President Clinton in the Lewinsky matter.[31] Irrespective of whether the White House was behind the complaint, there is no doubt that it enthusiastically supported it. The *New York Times* reported that just a week after Starr called Sidney Blumenthal before the grand jury, Clinton's aides "circulated a batch of material critical of Mr. Starr's performance as a lawyer for the General Motors Corporation in the early 1990s." According to the *Times*, the material being disseminated was a summary of Kendall Few's complaint against Starr with the Justice Department. General Motors said Starr's representation of the company "was proper in every respect" and that any accusations to the contrary were "unfounded."[32]

As unlikely as it seems, Geraldo Rivera's television show, *Rivera Live*, was responsible for spawning another Justice Department complaint against Starr. Discussions on the show revealed that Starr had engaged in several conversations with Paula Jones's attorney Gilbert Davis in 1994, before Starr had been appointed independent counsel to investigate the president. Davis had consulted with Starr, an expert in constitutional law, concerning the issue of whether a sitting president was immune from civil lawsuits. Starr's view was that the president could be sued, an opinion later validated by a unanimous decision of the United States Supreme Court. This new complaint alleged that Starr deliberately concealed from Janet Reno his previous contacts with Davis when he was seeking her approval to expand the scope of his investigation to include the Lewinsky matter.

In addition to the filings against Starr with the courts and the Justice Department, Democratic congressman Jerrold Nadler, a member of the House Judiciary Committee, threatened a congressional inquiry against Starr. "He wired Linda Tripp before he had jurisdiction, he bullied Monica Lewinsky, he may have set up perjury traps for the president. Starr deserves an investigation of his own, maybe in the context of oversight hearings next year," said Nadler.

Vilifying the Accusers: American Spectator/David Hale/ Richard Mellon Scaife

On August 9, 1998, Deputy Attorney General Eric Holder suggested Starr investigate allegations that conservative philanthropist Richard Mellon Scaife paid David Hale to testify against Bill Clinton in the Whitewater investigation. Hale's testimony had helped convict Clinton's Whitewater business associates. Hale was also prepared to testify that President Clinton engaged in a fraudulent land scheme when he was governor of Arkansas and pressured Hale to make a $300,000 loan to a former business partner of the Clintons.

The allegation, which first appeared in an article on the Web site Salon.com, was that Scaife channeled the money to Hale through the *American Spectator*, a conservative magazine. Scaife reportedly donated more than $2 million to the magazine between 1993 and 1997. Part of the money was used by "the Arkansas Project," a research initiative organized by the *American Spectator* to look into Clinton's past. One of Hale's old friends, Parker Dozhier, a bait shop owner, was working as a research assistant for the Arkansas Project. Caryn Mann, Dozhier's former girlfriend, and her son Josh Rand, claimed that Dozhier paid Hale some $5,000 from his bait shop cash register and allowed Hale free use of his car at the time Hale was cooperating with Starr in his Whitewater investigation. Both Hale and Dozhier denied that any such payments were made. Dozhier said that Caryn Mann was a strong Democrat and a believer in the occult, given to wild fantasies and bent on ruining him.[33]

In his letter to Starr, Holder told him that if he believed he had a conflict of interest precluding his investigation of the matter, he should refer it back to the Justice Department, which would conduct the investigation.[34] Of course, Holder added his observation that Starr probably did have such a disqualifying conflict of interest "because of the importance of Hale to your investigation and because the payments allegedly came from funds provided by Richard Scaife."[35]

Within days of Holder's letter to Starr, Clinton's personal attorney, David Kendall, followed up with his own letter further detailing the alleged links between Richard Mellon Scaife, the *American Spectator*, David Hale, and Ken Starr, and demanded that Starr refer the matter back to the Justice Department for investigation. "You have publicly embraced Hale as a model witness," said Kendall. "A thorough investigation of the Hale allegations could jeopardize the convictions your office has obtained."[36] As it turned out, neither Starr nor the Justice Department handled the investigation. Janet Reno appointed a former Justice official, Michael E. Shaheen Jr., to conduct an independent investigation into the allegations.[37]

Brill's Content *"Leaks"*

The next volley against Starr arose from his interview with the magazine *Brill's Content*. In the interview, Starr candidly revealed his background contacts with various media outlets concerning his investigation. In the article Steven Brill added fuel to the numerous leak allegations against Starr by identifying twenty-four news stories that supposedly came from Starr's office.

The article went so far as to suggest that Starr orchestrated the "leaks" to pressure Monica Lewinsky and her attorney into cooperating with Starr's investigation.[38] The media lent legitimacy to the charges against Starr by persistently referring to Starr's discussions with the press as "leaks." The *New York Times*, for example, titled one of its stories, "Starr Admits to Leaks, Denies Acting Illegally." But Starr denied his communications were leaks at all, stating that they were proper background information having nothing to do with grand jury secrets.[39]

Starr, incensed by the article and believing Brill had sandbagged him, fired off a letter to Brill accusing him of making "reckless and irresponsible" allegations and reiterating his denials of doing anything improper. He said that providing nonconfidential information to the press was necessary to counter the "misinformation that is being spread about our investigation in order to discredit our office and our dedicated career prosecutors."[40]

Starr also issued a one-page public statement denying the charges. "The OIC does not release grand jury material directly or indirectly, on-the-record or off-the-record; the OIC does not violate Department of Justice policy or applicable ethical guidelines; and the OIC does not release [and never has released] information provided by witnesses during witness interviews, except as authorized by law. Mr. Brill's statements to the contrary are false."[41]

Again, the White House called on Janet Reno to open another investigation into Starr's conduct. The White House had everything to gain by these diversions as they significantly delayed and obstructed Starr's investigation against Clinton, while the public was growing increasingly impatient and dissatisfied with Starr.

Federal district judge Norma Holloway Johnson questioned Starr about his alleged leaks, and in a sealed ruling on June 19, 1998, she found that a prima facie case—evidence that at first sight supports an allegation—for contempt of court had been established against him. She ordered him to "show cause" why he shouldn't be held in contempt. She also ruled that President Clinton's lawyers could participate in the investigation against Starr. This was a particularly devastating blow to Starr because it would allow Clinton's lawyers an inside track into his investigation of their client, the president. Ultimately, the court of appeals restricted the participation of Clinton's lawyers in the investigation because it would be "an unnecessary detraction from the main business of the grand jury's investigation" and would allow the possible targets of a grand jury investigation too much information about the case being built against them.[42] When Judge Johnson's sealed ruling was made public, other legal documents came to light revealing the extreme extent to which Clinton's lawyers had tried to impede Starr's investigations. Among their gambits was an unsuccessful effort to subpoena Starr "to appear at their office and testify on July 13, and from day to day thereafter until completed."[43]

After further reviewing the evidence, Judge Johnson, in another sealed ruling on September 25, 1998, found that Starr had committed "serious and repetitive" violations of the Federal Rules of Criminal Procedure. She appointed John W. Kern III, a senior judge on the D.C. Circuit Court of Appeals, as special master to investigate and report back to her. When Judge Johnson's sealed ruling appointing a special master became public in late October, White House counsel Gregory Craig jumped at another opportunity to lash out at Starr. "This lends credence," said Craig, "to what we have been saying all along. We believe that the Office of the Independent Counsel has been waging a campaign of leaks against the president, in an improper effort to influence public and congressional opinion, and it has done so in direct violation of federal laws safeguarding the confidentiality of grand jury proceedings."

Another Foe Is Stung

The White House proved it would not balk at attacking its own party members if they dared to cross the line against Clinton. Pennsylvania congressman Paul McHale learned this lesson the hard way. Not long after McHale became the first Democratic congressman to call for Clinton's resignation, White House attack dogs turned on him, once again through the vehicle of Geraldo Rivera's *Rivera Live* television program. During a live episode in late August 1998 Rivera announced that he had just received a call from a source very close to President Clinton who reminded him there was a controversy concerning McHale's war record. Rivera continued that McHale claimed to have been awarded a medal higher than the Bronze Star he'd actually received. In fact, McHale had never been awarded a Bronze Star, nor had he boasted of receiving such an award or any higher military honor.

He did have a distinguished service record with the Marines, where he had been a major. McHale referred to the White House smear as "dishonorable. It's consistent with the pattern of personal criticism that emanates from this White House when a person... voices opposition to the president."[44] Embarrassed by the gaffe, President Clinton called McHale to apologize.

To Protect His Family

On August 17, 1998, the day of his grand jury testimony, Clinton finally took to the television airways to admit that he had not been candid with the American people when he denied having had an inappropriate relationship with Monica Lewinsky. He insisted, however, that Paula Jones's deposition was "legally accurate," though he "did not volunteer information." He dismissed the Jones case as a "politically inspired lawsuit." He insisted that his motive had been to protect his family from embarrassment. After an ambivalent apology he launched into a vitriolic attack against Ken Starr. He criticized Starr for investigating his "private life" and noted with satisfaction that "the investigation itself is under investigation." Defiantly, he said that this matter now was between him, his family, and their God, and that it was "nobody's business but ours. Even Presidents have private lives." Clinton implied that Ken Starr, not Bill Clinton, was the cause of all the "personal destruction" and the distraction from the country's "real problems." According to Clinton, Starr was responsible for all the embarrassment that Clinton and the nation had suffered.

Preparing for the Big Battle

As the White House prepared for the delivery of Starr's impeachment referral to Congress, Clinton's aides grew even more combative. After Senator Joseph Lieberman denounced Clinton's behavior as "immoral" on the Senate floor, many other Democrats were urging Clinton to work out a deal with Congress involving a reprimand or censure in lieu of impeachment. Clinton's legal and political advisors, however, rejected that advice and instead geared up for a new round of attacks against Starr. Clinton's strategy would be to characterize Starr's report as nothing more than an X-rated story about sex, with no evidence of criminality on the part of President Clinton. They would continue to portray Starr as a vindictive man obsessed with private lives.[45]

Clinton's lawyer, David Kendall, also challenged Starr's legal right to present his impeachment referral to Congress, despite the unambiguous provision in the Independent Counsel Act requiring that he submit such a report. The law states that "the independent counsel shall advise the House of Representatives of any substantial and credible information which such independent counsel receives, in carrying out the independent counsel's responsibilities under this chapter, that may constitute grounds for impeachment."

Some White House aides were concerned that Clinton had given Starr new ammunition (another perjury charge) when he testified before the grand jury that his testimony in the Paula Jones deposition had been "legally accurate." They were anticipating a "devastating" and "blistering" report. They worried that Clinton's repeated denials that he had sexual relations with Monica Lewinsky would force Starr to go into detail about the sex acts in the White House.

As expected, when Starr's referral was delivered to Congress, Clinton's lawyers submitted a rebuttal calling the Starr Report "pornographic" and "a hit-and-run smear campaign," the legal foundation of which was so shaky "that no prosecutor would present

[it] to any jury."[46] It was Starr, after all, who was the real villain, according to Clinton's team. They accused Starr of "extraordinary overreaching" and "pejorative conjecture." They decried his "tactics, illegal leaking and manifest intent to cause [Clinton] damage." It is wrong, said Clinton's attorneys, for the independent counsel to ask Congress to remove "a fairly elected president" for nothing more than an improper relationship.

While Clinton's lawyers were busy with their legal maneuverings, his propagandists continued their PR assault against the independent counsel. In late September 1998, while discussing the parameters of a possible impeachment inquiry against Clinton, Congress released Starr's documents to the public, including Monica Lewinsky's grand jury testimony. The White House immediately capitalized on Lewinsky's testimony that Starr's deputy prosecutors mistreated her during her initial interview in Room 1012 at the Ritz-Carlton Hotel at Pentagon City. Specifically, Lewinsky testified that when she asked to call her lawyer, they told her that she could face twenty-seven years in prison on possible criminal charges and that calling her lawyer could jeopardize her chances for immunity. She said they threatened to prosecute her mother, Marcia Lewis, and ridiculed Lewinsky for asking to call her. "You're smart, you're old enough. You don't need to call your mommy," said Jackie Bennett, according to Lewinsky.

Clinton's attack squad went into motion, chanting in harmony on television talk shows that Lewinsky was held against her will and terribly mistreated. They also accused Starr of violating Justice Department rules when his deputies discussed an immunity deal with Lewinsky without her lawyer being present. They railed that the prosecutor had taken her into "psychological custody."

But surely they were aware that Lewinsky admitted in her testimony that she was repeatedly told that she was free to leave at any time and that she was permitted to call her mother in private. She had even thanked the deputies "for being so kind and considerate" before she left.

House Impeachment Inquiry: Two "Trials" in One

On October 8, 1998, the House of Representatives voted 258 to 176 to launch an inquiry to determine whether President Clinton committed impeachable offenses, spurring more aggressive countermeasures from Clinton's defenders. Certain congressional Democrats, who were working in tandem with the White House, became more militant in their defense of the president and against his accusers. Their brazen strategy was to turn the congressional impeachment hearings into a trial of Ken Starr.

The congressional Democrats threatened to use their subpoena power to summon witnesses who would accuse Starr of a conflict of interest. Congressman Barney Frank said Starr "should never have been appointed" to investigate the Lewinsky matter because of his relationship with Paula Jones's lawyers. Senator Richard Durbin demanded an investigation to determine why Starr "failed to disclose to the attorney general" his contacts with the Jones attorneys.[47]

One of their key areas of attack was to argue that Starr had improperly failed to disclose to Janet Reno his contacts with Paula Jones's attorneys when he asked her permission to investigate the Lewinsky matter. Starr said his contact with Jones's first attorney, Gilbert Davis, was a matter of public record and that he had even discussed it on television. "Fault my judgment if you will," said Starr, "but it just frankly did not occur to me [to inform

Janet Reno of the contacts]."[48] Clinton's lawyers also alleged that Starr had colluded with Jones's later attorneys to entrap the president in perjury during his deposition in the Jones case. Starr's deputies denied the charge, but it was a complex issue because of innocent and indirect connections between the Jones attorneys and Starr's deputies.

A group of lawyers—Ann Coulter, George Conway, and Jerome Marcus—who came to be known as "the elves," was providing pro bono legal assistance to Paula Jones. (One of the elves, Jerome Marcus, had been recruited by Richard W. Porter, a partner of Starr's in the law firm of Kirkland and Ellis, to assist Paula Jones's legal efforts.) The elves became aware of the Linda Tripp tapes in which Monica Lewinsky revealed her relationship with President Clinton and that Clinton was obstructing justice in the Jones case.

Tripp was confronted with a dilemma. The Tripp tapes would protect her from a perjury prosecution because they would verify that she would be telling the truth to Jones's lawyers. But they might also expose Tripp to criminal liability under the Maryland wiretap statute. How could she arrange for the tapes to be used to protect herself and simultaneously avoid prosecution? Tripp called Starr deputy Jackie Bennett. He was expecting her call.

Earlier, elf Jerome Marcus was having dinner with his law school classmate and Starr deputy Paul Rosenzweig. Marcus told Rosenzweig what he knew about a certain White House intern and tapes held by a Linda Tripp in which the intern described her affair with the president. (Marcus had reportedly learned about the tapes from Lucianne Goldberg, who told him and Porter about them because she was looking for a new lawyer for Tripp.) One Clinton-inspired myth was that the elves were working in collusion on this matter with the Starr team. If anything, the two groups had divergent interests. Indeed, the elves were unlikely to be thrilled about the Office of the Independent Counsel's involvement with the Tripp tapes. Starr might not make timely use of the tapes, thereby destroying any evidentiary value they might have in the Paula Jones case—the elves' bailiwick. But Marcus did happen to know of evidence that the president had committed perjury—and that was the Office of the Independent Counsel's bailiwick. Now, at least, if the Office of the Independent Counsel happened to receive a call from Tripp, they'd know to take her call.

After Marcus told Rosenzweig about the Tripp tapes, Rosenzweig informed fellow Starr deputy Jackie Bennett. Bennett was used to hearing all kinds of bizarre tales, but this one piqued his interest because it also involved White House superlawyer and FOB Vernon Jordan. Jordan reportedly had a role in getting Webster Hubbell a job after he had resigned in disgrace as Clinton's associate attorney general, and he may have played a similar role with Monica Lewinsky. Bennett reported the information to Starr who told him to get word to Marcus that Tripp should come in "the front door" of Starr's office, which meant she should contact Bennett directly.[49] Rosenzweig presumably passed the word to Marcus, who presumably somehow relayed it back to Tripp, because Tripp called Bennett within ten hours of Bennett's telling Rosenzweig to have Tripp contact him.

By the time Tripp had fired her first lawyer and hired a second lawyer, Jim Moody, she had already met with Starr's deputies and given them the lowdown. She had not, however, given them the tapes. That was Moody's only bargaining chip for winning immunity for Tripp from prosecution in Maryland. He successfully negotiated an immunity deal and delivered the tapes to the Office of the Independent Counsel.

Unbeknownst to Starr or his deputies, Linda Tripp was also feeding information to the Jones attorneys, who were preparing for the president's deposition. Starr deputy Rosenzweig acknowledged talking with Jerome Marcus but claimed ignorance of Marcus's connection with Paula Jones. Jackie Bennett assumed Rosenzweig's contact was with someone directly associated with Tripp. "I was unaware on January 9, 1998," said Bennett, "of any connection with the Jones legal team."[50]

Ken Starr appeared before the House Judiciary Committee on November 19, 1998, the first day of its impeachment hearings. As promised, House Democrats made his conduct, rather than Clinton's, the focus of their questioning. Democrats wasted no time challenging Starr's conclusions against Clinton or defending the president's actions. Even the Democrats' chief attorney, Abbe Lowell, conspicuously avoided any discussion concerning the evidence Starr marshaled against Clinton. He reserved his time for berating Starr for his alleged misconduct. The president's lawyer, David Kendall, similarly derided Starr on a litany of grounds, from not being present personally during witness interviews and testimony to the familiar refrain about grand jury leaks. When Chairman Henry Hyde granted Kendall an additional thirty minutes to question Starr, he quipped, "You may want to get into the facts."

During his testimony Starr insisted that he had not been aware that Tripp was talking to Jones's lawyers: "We did not have any information that [Linda Tripp] was, in fact, communicating with the Jones attorneys." Starr also denied any knowledge about the various connections between the Jones attorneys and his private law partners or his deputy prosecutors. Rather, Starr explained that he approached Janet Reno to expand his jurisdiction only when he heard charges that Clinton's friend Vernon

Jordan had helped Lewinsky get a job in exchange for her silence in the Jones case, "a fact pattern that we had seen in the Webster Hubbell investigation."

Starr said that he had never talked with his law partner Richard Porter about the Jones case and was unaware of any involvement Porter may have had with the Jones attorneys.[51] Porter himself testified: "I have no reason to believe that Ken Starr had any knowledge of my discussions with part of the Paula Jones team. I have never discussed Paula Jones or any aspect of her case with Ken Starr."[52]

Starr noted that his investigators "began working almost instantly at cross purposes with the Jones lawyers," which made the argument that they were colluding preposterous. Starr pointed out that he tried to get a court order to limit the Jones attorneys from pursuing the discovery of documents concerning the Lewinsky matter.[53] Finally, the usually unflappable Starr had his fill of Kendall's grilling and responded sharply, "I've chosen until now not to reply [to political criticism from the White House attorneys], but I think the code of silence sometimes in terms of basic fairness gets to come to an end. We have been listening month after month that it's a political witch hunt and that was unfair, but we've learned it goes with the territory."

When Kendall told Starr that no case had been so badly leaked as this one, Starr fired back, "I totally disagree with that. That's an accusation and it's an unfair accusation. I completely reject it.... I don't believe anyone has leaked grand jury information." Starr pointed out that the only information that ever leaked was information available to Kendall, and reminded him that information held exclusively by Starr's people—the DNA test results from the blue stained dress, for example—was not leaked. And the reason this information never leaked into "the public domain," Starr said pointedly, was "because you did not have a witness... you could debrief and tell you."

Clinton's Eclectic Comrades: The Arts and Croissants Crowd and Larry Flynt

While the White House and congressional Democrats were castigating Ken Starr, the arts and croissants crowd decided to weigh in with their brilliance. Ten writers and celebrities, led by Nobel Prize-winning novelist Toni Morrison, demanded that Janet Reno open a Justice Department investigation of Starr. In their open letter published in *USA Today*, they pointed to Starr's "outrageous abuses" and his "biased, incomplete and misleading" report to Congress. They were especially troubled by Starr's "grand jury leaks" and his "conflicts of interest." Next to offer their wisdom were four hundred liberal legal "scholars," who opined that the allegations contained in Starr's referral did not constitute impeachable offenses. Given legal precedent in American and English history, this was manifestly a political rather than a legal conclusion.[54]

Many presidents have had controversial allies—Nixon's Bebe Rebozo, Carter's Bert Lance—but none has been as colorful as Bill Clinton's Larry Flynt, publisher of *Hustler* magazine. As the House Judiciary Committee was preparing for its impeachment inquiry, Flynt seized the opportunity to offer his "expertise" to assist President Clinton. On October 4, 1998, he placed an $85,000 full-page ad in Sunday's edition of the *Washington Post* offering up to $1 million for "documentary evidence of illicit sexual relations" with a member of Congress or other high-ranking government official.

Flynt portrayed himself as being on a crusade to smoke out hypocrisy among the president's accusers. "I feel the people who are going to be sitting in judgment who have not been truthful about similar activities in their own lives should recuse themselves," he said. "What we are talking about is hypocrisy in its highest form. At the least, I want to let them know that it is about sex. People always lie about sex—to get sex, during sex, after sex, about sex. I totally disagree that perjury is perjury. Lying about your private life, even under oath, is totally different."[55] Others believed he was crusading not against hypocrisy but on behalf of his soul mate, Bill Clinton.

In mid-December 1998 Flynt started to get specific by promising to give details about numerous alleged affairs of House Speaker Robert Livingston. "If these guys are going after the president, they shouldn't have any skeletons in their closet. This is only the beginning," boasted Flynt.[56] Congressional Republicans responded vigorously, accusing the White House of orchestrating Flynt's shenanigans. Congressman Dana Rohrabacher said that Clinton's friends "have done everything they could to try to intimidate people. All these women that he's abused, every one of them has been threatened. Every time you turn around they're trying to find any little thing to dig up on somebody. [These are] the worst God-awful tactics that I've ever seen by anybody on the planet." Congressman Brian Bilbray said, "Anyone who is perceived as a threat to the administration is immediately attacked."

Flynt denied that he was colluding with the White House. "I can assure you I've had no contact with the White House. I don't get my marching orders from them."[57] White House press secretary Joe Lockhart weakly responded, "There is no evidence that anyone at the White House had anything to do with this story. Any suggestion to the contrary, without evidence, might be irresponsible." But ABC correspondent Cokie Roberts lent plausibility to a Flynt-White House connection when she reported that a source close to the White House had told her about Livingston's alleged affairs.

Flynt's promise to expose the Speaker of the House led to Congressman Livingston's resignation on the very day Clinton was impeached. When asked about it, Flynt was triumphant and unapologetic. "I'm happy if my efforts had anything to do with it. I think right-wing radical bullies like him are more of a threat to our unique form of democracy than anything else."[58] Livingston was not the first congressman to get burned. Salon.com was preparing to "out" a thirty-year-old affair of Henry Hyde when Hyde went public with it. Salon proudly declared, "Ugly times require ugly tactics." Dan Burton and Helen Chenowith also admitted their indiscretions before reports were released about them in their respective local newspapers.[59]

Flynt's conquest of Livingston emboldened him to threaten further action. "I assure you, there are many others to come.... We intend to take this to the mat, all the way." True to his word, moralist Flynt next turned his sights on Congressman Bob Barr, accusing him of various improprieties. C-SPAN cancelled airing Flynt's press conference on Barr at the last minute, fearing his allegations could expose the network to liability for defamation.

The Landmark Legal Foundation sent a letter to the criminal division of the Justice Department requesting an investigation of Flynt for possible obstruction of a congressional investigation. Republican National Committee chairman Jim Nicholson seconded the demand. Flynt is "the president's favorite pornographer," said Nicholson, who also asserted that obstructing Congress is "a felony punishable by five years imprisonment and a fine of $250,000."

Justice Takes the Baton

Clinton's attorneys led by David Kendall had been pressuring Janet Reno from the beginning to investigate Starr on a variety of charges. At the time of the House impeachment inquiry, Kendall was not only attacking Starr in Congress, he was intensifying his demands that Janet Reno open a Justice Department investigation against Starr and his deputies. Kendall claimed that Starr violated the Independent Counsel Act and Justice Department guidelines by using Linda Tripp as a government witness before the court had expanded his authority to include the Lewinsky matter.[60]

Janet Reno apparently felt so much pressure from the White House to take action against Kenneth Starr that at one point she instructed her aides to research whether she had the legal authority to reprimand or otherwise discipline Starr without firing him. When one of the aides offered his opinion that it would be a mistake comparable to Nixon's "Saturday Night Massacre" firing of Watergate special prosecutor Archibald Cox, she pinned his ears back: "I'm not asking you to make a political judgment. I'm asking you to make a legal judgment."[61]

Marcia Clark, guest hosting for Geraldo Rivera on *Rivera Live*, quoted an anonymous senior Justice Department official as saying, "The revelation of contacts between Starr and the Jones team is breathtaking, unbelievable. The attorney general would never have agreed to expand the jurisdiction if she had known this."[62] In the meantime, the Justice Department was reportedly rifling through Starr's submitted documents to Congress to determine whether there was any evidence to support this conflict of interest claim.[63]

Susan Schmidt and Michael Weisskopf wrote that Janet Reno dropped a bombshell on Starr in a meeting at the Justice Department in mid-November 1998. Just four days before his scheduled appearance at the House Judiciary Committee's impeachment hearings, Reno informed Starr that she planned to investigate his conduct. Reno, apparently aware that Starr believed she was acting as Clinton's pawn, said, "I want to emphasize neither OPR [the Justice Department's Office of Professional Responsibility] nor I have formed any conclusions about these allegations. We're acutely aware that allegations such as those we have received present only one side of the story and that knowledge of your view of them may cast a very different light on them." Starr warned Reno that if her decision to investigate him were leaked it would be "inimical to the appearance of justice." Reno assured Starr that she would be even angrier than he if leaks occurred.

Starr learned after the meeting that *Newsweek* was about to publish a story on Reno's decision to review his conduct—a leak that would obviously undermine his credibility with Congress.[64]

Another very suspiciously timed leak by the Justice Department occurred in early February 1999, around the time the Senate was conducting its final deliberations in President Clinton's impeachment trial. The media discovered (and reported) that in mid-January Janet Reno had written a letter to Ken Starr, advising him that the Justice Department was going to formally investigate the conduct of the Office of the Independent Counsel.

Some of Starr's staff were convinced that Reno was out to get Starr, especially considering Reno's publicly stated policy that she would only investigate the independent counsel if the charges were so serious that they would warrant removal if proven. Moreover, none of the charges of misconduct were new—adding to Starr's suspicions that the timing was politically motivated.[65] Even more disturbing, Reno was graduating her inquiry from an informal review (such as was going on in November) to a formal investigation. An investigation was much more serious because it involved the possibility of subpoenaed witnesses and other investigative techniques not involved with a review.

Among the complaints were that Starr abused his authority to convene grand juries, improperly pressed witnesses, and illegally leaked secret grand jury information.[66] In addition, the Justice Department planned to investigate whether Starr had violated Justice Department rules by discussing an immunity agreement with Monica Lewinsky at the Pentagon Ritz-Carlton Hotel, without her lawyer being present.

Congressman Dan Burton, chairman of the Government Reform and Oversight Committee, complained to Reno about the Justice Department leaks in a letter to her dated February 11, 1999. "Yesterday's article in the *New York Times*, 'U.S. Inquiry on Starr is Seen,' is only the latest in a long line of what appear to be politically motivated leaks emanating from your department," wrote Burton. "While Department of Justice leaks aimed at Judge Starr are not new, the fact that such sensitive information would be leaked to the press in the closing days of the Senate impeachment trial raises the specter of political interference. In November, shortly before Judge Starr's Judiciary Committee appearance, damaging information was also leaked in a partisanly timed manner. As my Senate colleague Senator Domenici noted in today's *New York Post*: 'She's [the Attorney General] not investigating anybody else. I don't know why she's investigating him.'"

Senator Orrin Hatch was so convinced that Justice was responsible for these leaks that he registered his strong objection to the Justice Department's investigating the Office of the Independent Counsel. "The timing of these articles could not be more suspicious.... These press accounts once again call into question the department's integrity, and support the impression many people have that this is a partisan Justice Department," Hatch wrote in a letter to Deputy Attorney General Eric Holder Jr.

Starr also objected to the Justice Department's Office of Professional Responsibility investigating his office. In a letter to Reno he said that it was important to remove the investigation from the Clinton Justice Department to ensure an impartial probe.[67]

There was also disagreement about whether the Justice Department had authority to investigate the independent counsel. Under the Independent Counsel Act, Reno clearly had the authority to remove Starr for cause, but some questioned her authority to investigate. The Landmark Legal Foundation filed a request with the three-judge panel overseeing Starr's investigation to block the Justice Department's investigation. "This initiative by the attorney general—the president's appointee—is clearly calculated to undermine the independent counsel's investigation at a critical stage," wrote Landmark's president, Mark Levin. "[Reno] is attempting to improperly influence and interfere with the independent counsel's investigation." Levin's argument was that allowing the Justice Department to investigate the independent counsel would undermine the purpose of the Independent Counsel law, which was to ensure an independent investigation.

Another Alleged Leak: New York Times

While special master John W. Kern's investigation of the twenty-four alleged leaks remained under seal, the White House accused the independent counsel of another leak of grand jury information. This one was based on a January 31, 1999, *New York Times* article reporting that Starr believed he had the legal authority to indict Clinton while he was still in office. After this article appeared, Starr asked the FBI to help his office conduct an internal leak investigation. While the facts in the *Times* article were not, according to Starr, secret grand jury information, he wanted to discover whether his office had been responsible for the disclosures.

The FBI concluded that Starr's press spokesman Charles Bakaly was the source of the leaks, prompting Starr to refer the matter to the Department of Justice for a criminal investigation. Federal district judge Norma Holloway Johnson promptly ordered both Bakaly and the Office of Independent Counsel to show cause why they should not be held in contempt of court for violating Rule 6(e) concerning leaking grand jury secrets. After further proceedings the court issued an order appointing the Justice Department to serve as prosecutor against Bakaly and the Office of the Independent Counsel for criminal contempt, even though it was clear that Bakaly was the only OIC employee identified with leaking material. To its credit, the Justice Department asked that the court withdraw its referral of the Office of the Independent Counsel for prosecution. The court refused and both parties appealed. In early October 2000 Bakaly was found not guilty of criminal contempt of court for allegedly lying about his role in news leaks during Clinton's impeachment trial. In her written ruling Judge Norma Holloway Johnson said, "The court concludes that the government has not proved its charges beyond a reasonable doubt and therefore the court finds that Mr. Bakaly is not guilty of criminal contempt."[68]

"Starr Told Us to Lie"

While the Justice Department was continuing to investigate Starr's conduct—even after the Senate acquitted the president—Starr was being attacked in another venue. Just as her trial for contempt charges was set to begin in Little Rock, Susan McDougal promised an "all-out fight" against Kenneth Starr. She accused Starr and his prosecutors of a personal vendetta against her because she was refusing to lie about President Clinton, her former partner in the Whitewater real estate investment. McDougal claimed that Starr threatened and punished witnesses who refused to assist him against Clinton. "I fully intend to put Kenneth W. Starr on trial," said McDougal's attorney Mark J. Geragos.[69] The jury later acquitted McDougal on the obstruction of justice charge and deadlocked on the two criminal contempt counts against her.

Elsewhere, another Starr defendant in the U.S. District Court in Alexandria, Virginia, Julie Hiatt Steele, was making similar charges against Starr. Starr had indicted Steele for perjury for denying under oath that her friend Kathleen Willey had told her about being sexually assaulted by Clinton. Steele's attorney, Nancy Luque, argued that her client's indictment was "irreversibly tainted by ethical violations of the Office of Independent Counsel constituting prosecutorial misconduct.... Julie told [Starr] the truth and look what happened to her. He doesn't want the truth. He wants only to punish those who won't go along with his agenda." Kathleen Willey testified in the Steele trial for the prosecution. She depicted Steele as an opportunist and said that she had talked to her "many, many times" about Clinton groping and fondling her in the White House.[70] After Steele's lawyer excoriated Starr in her closing argument, the jury deadlocked and the judge declared a mistrial. A few weeks after the mistrial was declared, reports surfaced that the jury had voted 9 to 3 to convict Steele, and that the foreman of the jury urged Starr to "seriously reconsider" trying her again, saying the evidence against her was "very persuasive."[71]

Starr's Belated Vindication

Starr's enemies made their myriad allegations against him with a ferocious intensity. The press was awash with stories daily about Starr's alleged misconduct. In fact, in many instances media outlets just dropped the "alleged." The media questioned Starr's every step in proving Clinton's culpability but accepted every allegation against Starr. During the heat of this nearly unilateral PR battle—Starr was admittedly inept at public relations—it was difficult for the casual observer to tell who was telling the truth. The people who made the most noise and had the most media support won. Their victory saved Bill Clinton's presidency.

Only after Clinton's fate was determined did the facts begin to come out about the illegitimacy of the charges against Starr. Even then, they were barely publicized. The indisputable truth is that Starr was vindicated on every charge made against him except that one of his deputies had improperly discussed an immunity agreement with Monica Lewinsky without her lawyers being present. But even here, Judge Johnson didn't find any misconduct. She simply chose not to pursue it further. Given her record of exhibiting distrust toward Starr it is a fair inference that had there been any legitimacy to the misconduct claim regarding the immunity deal, Judge Johnson would have followed up on it. In that context it can safely be said that Starr was exonerated across the board.

If Starr was innocent of the charges, then those who made the charges wronged him and the cause of justice and have yet to be held accountable. When it comes to leaks, who but Clinton, his attorneys, and his aides benefited from the leaks? The leaks helped Bill Clinton by dribbling out damaging information that inoculated the public against the president's misconduct when

Starr gave his referral to Congress. It also helped Clinton because it allowed his attorneys to demonize Starr as a politicized prosecutor vicitimizing the president by releasing embarrassing information to the press.

Moreover, Clinton's henchmen knowingly labeled as "leaks" things that were nothing of the kind. The Court of Appeals slammed Judge Johnson for her erroneous interpretation of Rule 6(e). Clinton's lawyers were highly sophisticated litigators who well knew that Starr's statements to the press did not violate grand jury secrecy rules, yet they crucified him anyway. Our adversarial system does not countenance such dishonest advocacy.

What follows is an honest accounting: a summary of how Ken Starr was vindicated—something you won't read in White House memoirs.

Starr's Alleged Mistreatment of Monica Lewinsky: Starr Exonerated

The White House incessantly accused Starr and his deputies of abusing Monica Lewinsky at the Ritz-Carlton Hotel, saying they denied her permission to call her lawyer, held her prisoner in the hotel room, and improperly discussed an immunity deal without her.

In a sealed ruling dated April 28, 1998—but not made public until December 4, 1998, giving Clinton's propagandists nearly two-thirds of a year to misrepresent the facts—federal district judge Norma Holloway Johnson cleared Starr of all but the immunity charge. Even on that charge, she found no reason to take further legal action aside from expressing her disapproval of the tactic, though the Justice Department would later make noise about inquiring into this issue.

Three Ethics Complaints in Federal Court:
Starr Exonerated

After three years, Frank Mandanici finally succeeded in finding a judge to hear his allegation that Ken Starr had a conflict of interest in investigating the president. The conflict was a supposed connection between Starr and Clinton critic Richard Mellon Scaife, who was a contributor to Pepperdine college, which had offered Starr a job. Following Judge Wright's ruling that he lacked standing to bring the case, Stephen A. Smith, a convicted Whitewater defendant, stepped in to fill the breach. On September 17, 1999, Smith adopted Mandanici's complaint, alleging that the Office of the Independent Counsel had tried to control his testimony. "I was provided a written script, containing false testimony, by the Office of Independent Counsel, and this script was to be read by me as my testimony under oath to a federal grand jury," wrote Smith.

On October 12, 1999, Julie Hiatt Steele, whom Starr prosecuted for obstruction of justice to a deadlocked jury, also joined Mandanici in his complaint against Starr. Steele's attorney, Nancy Luque, in her motion to intervene in the Mandanici action, accused Starr of suborning Steele's perjury. On December 21, all seven federal judges in Little Rock recused themselves from the Mandanici-Smith-Steele case. The chief judge then appointed district judge Warren K. Urborn to hear it. When Urborn disqualified himself because of a potential conflict of interest, the chief judge appointed district judge John F. Nangle to preside.[72]

On May 18, 2000, Judge Nangle issued a scathing order refusing to appoint a special counsel to investigate Ken Starr. In dismissing all three ethics complaints by Mandanici, Smith, and Steele, Judge Nangle did not mince words. Concerning the claim that Starr had solicited false testimony, Nangle said, "There is not one shred of support in the hundreds of pages of documents sub-mitted by Mandanici to support these subjective opinions." Judge Nangle referred to the claim that Starr violated the Independent Counsel Act by testifying to Congress as "ridiculous." He said that the abuse of power claims against Starr were "nonsense... absolutely ridiculous." In addressing the many conflict of interest charges against Starr, Judge Nangle used the following language: "very dubious," "the stuff that dreams are made of," "this court has never heard a more absurd argument," "it is totally illogical," and "there is no evidence to support it."[73] Nangle described as "merit-less" and "completely frivolous" Smith's allegations that he had been pressured by Starr to lie. The judge ruled that Ms. Steele presented "absolutely no evidence that the OIC ever directly or impliedly [sic] asked her to lie."

Nangle added, "It is important to remember that not only are prosecutors allowed to be zealous in their positions, they have a duty to be zealous.... The validation of Starr's efforts is evident in his record of 14 convictions in complex, high profile cases, as well as the adoption of the House of Representatives' Articles of Impeachment against the president.... Further, the [independent counsel] prevailed in 17 out of 18 appeals in matters it was han-dling. A record this successful could not have been established on baseless evidence." Judge Nangle also accused Mandanici of violat-ing a gag order concerning the case. "Unlike the inferences and assumptions that formed the basis of Mandanici's complaints about Starr's conduct, Mandanici's three known violations of this court's order merit serious consideration of both discipline and sanctions, matters that this court may consider at a later date," said Nangle.[74]

A week after Judge Nangle's definitive ruling vindicating Ken Starr, an Arkansas Supreme Court panel called for President

Clinton's disbarment for lying under oath and obstructing the judicial process. The juxtaposition of the two rulings concerning the respective ethical allegations against Clinton and Starr prompted the *Washington Post* to comment: "Whatever one thinks of Mr. Starr's investigation, and we have expressed our own reservations, Judge Nangle's opinion offers powerful vindication on some of the leading ethical charges.... But the week's events made pretty clear which of the lawyers in this battle, Mr. Starr and Mr. Clinton, was the one with ethical problems."[75]

Justice Department Complaint by South Carolina Attorney Kendall Few: Starr Exonerated

Lee J. Radek, chief of the Justice Department's public integrity section, found insufficient evidence "for the commencement of a criminal investigation by this office" against Ken Starr for alleged wrongdoing in his representation of General Motors Corporation in 1995.

American Spectator/*David Hale/Richard Mellon Scaife/ Kenneth Starr: All Exonerated*

Judge Shaheen released his 168-page report on July 28, 1999, concluding that most of the allegations, such as payments, were either unsubstantiated or untrue and that there should be no criminal prosecution. "In some instances there is little if any credible evidence establishing that a particular thing of value was demanded [by Hale], offered [to him] or received [by him]. In other instances, there is insufficient credible evidence to show that a thing of value was provided or received with... criminal intent." Curiously, Judge Shaheen presented his report early in the year to the two retired federal judges supervising his inquiry, Arlin Adams and Charles Renfrew, but the judges sat on it. Judge Renfrew, when contacted, declined to explain the delay.[76]

The Twenty-Four "Leaks" Reported by Brill: Starr Exonerated

Special Master John W. Kern had been appointed by Judge Norma Holloway Johnson to determine whether Starr illegally leaked secret grand jury information concerning the Lewinsky scandal to twenty-four media outlets. Within less than a year, Judge Kern submitted his findings to Judge Johnson, completely clearing Starr of leaking secret grand jury information. The judicial ruling was kept under seal, and when it was revealed, it was barely reported by the media. Unsurprisingly, no apologies or retractions emanated from the White House or David Kendall, who had furiously attacked Starr over the alleged "leaks."

New York Times "Leak": Starr Exonerated

On September 13, 1999, seven months to the day after the Senate acquitted President Clinton without an evidentiary hearing, the D.C. Circuit Court of Appeals unanimously overturned Judge Johnson's order that Kenneth Starr face criminal contempt proceedings for allegedly leaking grand jury information to the *New York Times*. The D.C. Circuit held "that the disclosures made in the *New York Times* article did not constitute secret grand jury information covered by Rule 6(e)." Judge Johnson, said the court, applied too expansive a reading to Rule 6(e). "A court may not use Rule 6(e) to generally regulate prosecutorial statements to the press," said the D.C. Circuit. "Prosecutors' statements about their investigations... implicate the Rule only when they directly reveal grand jury matters.... The purpose of the Rule is only to protect the secrecy of grand jury proceedings. Thus, internal deliberations of prosecutors that do not directly reveal grand jury proceedings are not Rule 6(e) material.... The disclosure that a group of prosecutors 'believe' that an indictment should be brought at the end of the impeachment proceedings does not on its face, or in the context of the article as a whole, violate Rule 6(e)."

The White House refused to back off, saying, "We believe that the decision of the panel is inconsistent with the precedents of the Court of Appeals."[77] But now even the *New York Times* felt compelled to criticize the White House: "Mr. Clinton's private lawyer, David Kendall, has indicated he plans to appeal the latest ruling. But at this point it is hard to see what Mr. Clinton stands to gain by seeking to overturn a sound decision on grand jury secrecy—except to add to his pile of unpaid legal fees."[78]

Justice Department Investigation of Starr Leaks: Starr Exonerated

In March 1999, the Special Division of the Federal Appeals Court ruled that the Justice Department could investigate the independent counsel. But Attorney General Janet Reno's only available sanction against Starr would be to remove him for "good cause," meaning deliberate or gross misconduct.[79]

The Justice Department investigation centered on the issue of leaks, but after beginning with a public announcement seeking to discredit Starr, the investigation was eventually put on hold.[80] The *American Spectator*'s Byron York aptly noted that the investigation was not so complicated that it should have dragged on for years. "It seems hard to believe the inquiry is not yet finished. The questions involved are so narrow—this is not the Microsoft trial... that it could have been wrapped up in a few months at most.... For the questions to remain unanswered today is simply outrageous. If anyone on Starr's team was guilty, we should know. If they were not guilty, we should know. And if any of the leaks came from the president's defenders, we should know that, too. And soon."[81] Of course, Mr. York was exactly right, which is why two separate federal courts ruled that no illegal leaks came from the Starr investigation. Rather than come to the same conclusion, the Justice Department merely let its own investigation fizzle out.

Postscript

When Ken Starr appeared before the Senate Governmental Affairs Committee in April 1999, he might have surprised some people when he suggested that the Independent Counsel law should not be extended. Starr used his testimony, however, as an opportunity to set the record straight about the way he had been mistreated by the Clinton administration and the Justice Department's complicity in his abuse.

Starr pointed out that he had never exceeded his authority as independent counsel or violated Justice Department rules or guidelines, and he criticized the White House for trying to undermine his investigation by attacking him and his deputies. "There is a very formidable process of hurling invective at duly constituted law officers, and I think that's bad for the country," said Starr.

He expressed his severe disappointment in Janet Reno for not coming to his defense in the face of White House attacks. "And if the attacks come," said Starr, "if war is declared then against an independent counsel and every move that he or she makes is subject to attack, then the attorney general of the United States has a solemn and weighty responsibility to rally quickly to the side of the independent counsel and to say, 'Call off the attack dogs, and do it now,'" Starr said. "It will not do to have a system, and then to mock the system through constant attacks."[82]

When Starr was appointed, he was one of the most respected jurists in the United States. By the time he resigned, he and his office had been accused by President Clinton, his lawyers, or other Clinton allies of:

- suborning perjury;
- tampering with witnesses;
- conflicts of interest;
- numerous criminal leaks of grand jury information;
- civil and criminal contempt of court;
- entrapping the president;
- being sexual perverts;
- putting partisan interests above the rule of law;
- falsely imprisoning Monica Lewinsky;
- refusing to allow Lewinsky to call her attorney and unethically discussing an immunity deal with her without her attorney being present;
- improper collusion with Paula Jones's attorneys;
- multiple abuses of power.

It was as though the executive branch of our government had been turned over to Abbie Hoffman and the Chicago Seven who decided to terrorize a "straight" prosecutor with every power at their disposal—from pornographers to the Justice Department. Every charge against Starr proved false, and yet at the end of his investigation of the president, it was his reputation that was in tatters, and it was the president—who was manifestly guilty but politically impregnable—whose popularity soared. Trampled on the ground in the politicized Justice Department attacks on Ken Starr was the one thing the independent counsel had fought most zealously to preserve—the rule of law. And yet it appeared that the majority of the American people did not care.

Chapter Five

"A Substantive, Savvy, and Experienced Professional"

B ush White House employee Linda Tripp did not much respect the new Clinton administration and its appalling lack of reverence for the institution of the White House. She was appalled at the lax attitude of the Clintonites—wearing jeans, carrying Walkmans, having dirty hair—their cavalier treatment of permanent White House staff, and the abrupt dismissal of Bush appointees. Initially, Tripp's lack of respect was not reciprocal. Tripp was promoted to special assistant to the counsel to the president and sat outside the offices of White House counsel Bernard Nussbaum and deputy counsel Vincent Foster. Nussbaum, in a June 1993 memo, specifically requested that Tripp be his personal assistant. "As you know, considering the extremely sensitive matters the White House Counsel's office handles on a daily basis, I desperately need a substantive, savvy, and experienced professional to play a leading role on my support staff. Linda Tripp meets this need. She has proven to be a valuable addition to my staff," said Nussbaum.[1]

Tripp's disaffection with the White House grew when she watched administration officials ransack Foster's office after his death, as if they had something to hide.

After Nussbaum resigned, the White House transferred Tripp to the Pentagon to work as a public affairs officer. She was there when she read former FBI agent Gary Aldrich's book about the Clinton White House, *Unlimited Access*, which was a huge whistle-blowing bestseller in 1996. Tripp knew that she had her own whistle-blowing story to tell, if she wanted to, including the story of how White House volunteer Kathleen Willey had emerged from the Oval Office in late 1993 and told Tripp that Clinton had groped her. In the summer of 1996, Tripp called literary agent Lucianne Goldberg. Tripp wanted to write a book comparing her experience in the Bush and Clinton administrations. Goldberg introduced Tripp to conservative columnist Maggie Gallagher as a possible ghostwriter. After submitting to some twenty hours of telephone interviews with Gallagher, Tripp decided to drop the project.[2]

Not long after she abandoned her book, Tripp met fellow Pentagon employee Monica Lewinsky. Tripp became a sounding board and mentor for Lewinsky, and soon Monica was sharing the sordid details of her sexual exploits with Bill Clinton.

In early 1997, Joseph Cammarata, a lawyer for Paula Jones, told *Newsweek* reporter Michael Isikoff that President Clinton had groped a White House volunteer. Isikoff discovered it was Willey. He interviewed her, and she offered Tripp as someone who could corroborate her allegation.[3]

Isikoff contacted Tripp. He finally got her to say that when Willey came out of Clinton's office, her lipstick was smeared and she was "flustered, happy and joyful," at having been approached by the president. Tripp denied that Clinton sexually harassed Willey because Willey appeared flattered by the presidential grope.[4]

As press time approached, Tripp had her attorney request that Isikoff remove her name from the story. Isikoff refused the request and the story ran. The story also quoted Robert Bennett, the president's lawyer in the Jones case, who accused Tripp of lying: "Linda Tripp is not to be believed," he said. Tripp was incensed and determined to vindicate herself. While Clinton's defenders insist that Tripp, Lucianne Goldberg, Paula Jones's attorneys, and the Office of Independent Counsel were locked in a "vast right-wing conspiracy," the insiders say otherwise. Independent Counsel Kenneth Starr claimed that far from acting in concert with Jones's attorneys, he was often working at cross-purposes with them. Likewise, many of the attorneys assisting Jones felt that Starr's investigation was an impediment to their efforts. Lucianne Goldberg completely discounted the notion of a conspiracy. "It was all very formless. We didn't know where it was going, what was going to happen."[5]

After the *Newsweek* story was published, Tripp told Goldberg she was fearful that Jones's lawyers would ask her about the Willey story and that she might be forced, in the course of an interview or deposition, to talk about Monica's trysts with the president. She knew the Clinton administration would crucify her if she talked about Lewinsky.[6] So, according to Goldberg, Tripp's primary motive in getting her story out was self-protection, not exposing the president. "I think that was the main thing that was driving her. To get this out as a story and protect herself by going public," said Goldberg.[7]

Tripp told Michael Isikoff that Clinton was having an affair with a White House intern. At Goldberg's suggestion, Tripp agreed to get Monica on tape, so that she had verification to offer Isikoff. Tripp later told Jones's attorneys about the tapes.

Around the time the Jones's attorneys subpoenaed Lewinsky in December 1997, Goldberg and Tripp suddenly discovered that some of the taping could have been illegal under Maryland's criminal laws. Maryland law (unlike most state laws) prohibits the taping of a phone conversation without the consent of the person being taped. Goldberg referred Tripp to attorney James Moody.[8] Moody offered the tapes to the Office of the Independent Counsel in exchange for an immunity agreement for Tripp. When Starr's office accepted the offer, Moody turned over the tapes.

White House Responds

If Independent Counsel Kenneth Starr was the most unfairly maligned person in the Clinton era, former White House employee Linda Tripp was a close second.

Defenders of the president launched a public relations assault against Linda Tripp, describing her as a turncoat and betrayer of her friend Monica Lewinsky. The White House didn't mention that Lewinsky had tried to convince Tripp to change her testimony—that is, lie and commit perjury—about Willey for the sake of the president, even giving Tripp a "talking-points memo" urging her to submit an affidavit in the Jones case stating that she did not believe, after all, that President Clinton sexually harassed Willey. According to the memo, Tripp would assert, "You now do not believe that what she claimed happened really happened. You now find it completely plausible that she herself smeared lipstick, untucked her blouse, etc."

When Tripp told Monica that she would not lie, especially in court, Lewinsky replied, "I was brought up with lies all the time...

that's how you got along.... I have lied my entire life."[9] But Tripp lost the public relations war to the Clinton spin machine. Monica Lewinsky was portrayed as a victim—not of the president but of Linda Tripp. Democratic leaders in both Howard County and the Maryland General Assembly pressured Maryland state prosecutors to open a felony investigation against Tripp for the unauthorized tapings.[10] Though prosecutor Stephen Montanarelli initially conceded that the case against Tripp entailed "an extremely difficult burden of proof," he convened a grand jury anyway.[11] Tripp and her lawyers were outraged that Mr. Montanarelli decided to announce his grand jury probe just as Tripp was appearing before Kenneth Starr's grand jury in Washington, D.C. "I believe today's announcement is the latest in a series of attempts to intimidate me. This is evident by the fact that this attempt occurs at the very moment I am testifying before the federal grand jury. I am not intimidated in any way. I will continue to testify truthfully and completely, and I urge everyone involved to do the same," Tripp said in a prepared statement read by her attorney Anthony J. Zaccagnini.[12]

Months later, when the court ruled that the prosecutor would not be able to use most of Monica Lewinsky's testimony because of an immunity deal Tripp had entered into with the Office of the Independent Counsel, prosecutor Montanarelli announced that the state was dropping all criminal charges against Tripp.

The media also chimed in against Tripp, assisting the White House in making Tripp, rather than Clinton, the story. Columnist Mary McGrory intoned, "So far only one clear moral has emerged from the maelstrom: Don't get on the wrong side of Linda Tripp. You cross up that lady and she will make you sorry you were born... calling Linda Tripp a whistle-blower is like calling the tornado that flattened Florida recently a high wind."[13] When the House Judiciary Committee released the twenty-two hours of tape-recorded conversations between Tripp and Lewinsky, the *Washington Post* described them as "a sighing, giggling, sobbing soundscape of the American night, and a breathtaking study in betrayal." The *Post* story ends with this dubious moral insight: "At another point, Tripp notes that the president 'has no clue how… lucky he is. I mean, how did he know… that you weren't taping his wacko conversation with you at four in the morning?' Clinton did not know, because he trusted Lewinsky, who trusted Tripp, who hit 'record' and chatted through the night."[14]

Susan Perloff, in a "special" to the *Washington Post*, added, "Linda Tripp gives the word 'girlfriend' a bad name. Of all the bad behavior reported in the unfolding White House melodrama, Tripp's is indisputably treacherous: She betrayed her girlfriend." Perloff quotes a Philadelphia psychologist who said, "Betraying a girlfriend's confidence is unspeakable. Taping her? I can't find a word that fits this taping nonsense. Abhorrent? Repellent? Outrageous? It's against all rules of relationships to engage in such an activity. You have to be pretty disturbed to tape a friend. There's a streak of sadism. It's evil."

Independent Counsel Kenneth Starr got word that the White House had pressured Maryland Democrats to lobby the state prosecutor, Robert Weiner, to bring charges against Linda Tripp for violating Maryland's wiretap statute. Starr later subpoenaed Weiner to determine whether the White House was trying to obstruct his investigation. Weiner vehemently denied that the White House had urged him to make the calls and accused Starr of partisanship and conducting a witch hunt.[15]

Defense Department Abets Its Commander-in-Chief

The *New Yorker*, in its March 23, 1998, issue, reported that Tripp had been arrested in 1969 for larceny. Worse, she failed to report the arrest on her Pentagon security questionnaire. Tripp's attorney, James Moody, said Tripp's arrest at age nineteen was the result of a teenage prank played upon her by friends. The prosecutor reduced the larceny charge to loitering and Tripp pled guilty to it. Loitering under the New York Penal Code at the time was less serious than a misdemeanor and did not appear on someone's permanent record. Kevin Milley, one of Tripp's friends at the time of the incident, confirmed that she was indeed arrested as a result of a "spoof" gone wrong. He said two boys took a watch and some cash from a hotel room and stuck them in Tripp's purse without her knowledge. "She was entirely innocent in this affair," said Milley, who is now a police officer.[16]

More outrageous than the publication of this smear piece was the process by which its author, Jane Mayer, obtained some of her information. After Mayer received the tip about Tripp's brush with the law, she contacted her friend at the Pentagon, Ken Bacon, assistant secretary of defense for public affairs and public spokesman. Mayer and Bacon had been colleagues at the *Wall Street Journal* years ago.

Mayer was already aware of Tripp's arrest; she was after something more. She asked Bacon how Tripp answered a specific question on the national security clearance questionnaire when she was applying for employment in 1987. Had she disclosed to the government that she'd been "arrested, charged, cited or held by Federal, state or other law enforcement or juvenile authorities regardless of whether the citation was dropped or dismissed or you were found not guilty?"

Bacon directed Clifford Bernath, a deputy assistant secretary for public affairs, to check it out. Bernath provided Mayer with her answer: Tripp had failed to disclose the arrest on the questionnaire. Pentagon officials almost immediately announced that they would investigate whether Tripp had lied on her security clearance form and should be penalized.

Defense Department officials told the *New York Times* that they had decided to investigate when they learned about an article in the upcoming issue of the *New Yorker*. They didn't tell the *Times* that they had learned about the article directly from its author and that they supplied her pertinent information for the article. The Pentagon said it would investigate the matter because Tripp held a "top secret" security clearance, and making a "knowing and willful false statement" on a security application is a felony under federal law. "It is a very serious charge," said Clifford Bernath. "We just learned about this matter, and it will be turned over to the investigative services. They will deal with it in their channels."[17]

When the Pentagon started getting questions about the release of this obviously private information, it admitted that it had leaked the information to the *New Yorker*. But Pentagon spokesman Tom Surface said, amazingly, that Tripp's record was public information.[18] The Pentagon also denied that Cliff Bernath had any contact with the White House before releasing the information from Tripp's confidential file.

Congressman Gerald Solomon of New York requested that President Clinton tell him "whether a criminal investigation has been initiated into the unauthorized disclosure of Ms. Tripp's official file.... The integrity of protecting the privacy of all employees of the government is a sacred trust. This covenant has been violated on your watch."[19]

The key to the story was former White House aide Harold Ickes, who was informally managing Lewinsky damage control. In early 1998 he met with Jane Mayer to discuss her plans to write a negative article about Linda Tripp[20] and had a dinner meeting with Ken Bacon during which they discussed the Tripp matter. Ickes denied that the release of Tripp's private Pentagon records was a Bacon-Ickes conspiracy. "Absolutely not. There was totally, absolutely no basis for that whatsoever," said Ickes.[21]

After informing on Tripp to the *New Yorker*, Bernath reportedly deleted documents relevant to Tripp from his computer hard drive. U.S. district judge Royce Lamberth, in a case filed by Judicial Watch, ordered the Defense Department to seize Bernath's computer. "It is highly unusual and suspect" for the computer files to be deleted "when matters relating to Tripp are being investigated" by the independent counsel, said Judge Lamberth. "The Court concludes that it is appropriate to order an examination of Bernath's hard drive and his server." Bernath maintained that none of the deleted documents pertained to Tripp.

In the meantime, Ken Bacon in a press conference issued a quasi-apology about ordering the release of information. "I'm sorry I did not check with our lawyers or check with Linda Tripp's lawyers about this." Bacon continued to maintain that the White House was not involved in his decision to cooperate with Jane Mayer.[22]

In an apparent effort to distance itself from the White House, the Pentagon took the official position that a career government employee (Bernath), as opposed to political appointee (Bacon), provided the information to Mayer. The problem with that story was that Bernath did so on the orders of Bacon.[23] Bacon said, "I was certainly aware that he was doing it and did nothing to stop it."[24] Bacon admitted that he talked with Mayer personally. "She knew me, she called me." But he insisted that he didn't treat Mayer differently from other reporters.[25] He explained that he didn't believe the information would be harmful to Tripp because she indicated on the form she hadn't been arrested. It would have been different, he said, had they disclosed that Tripp had been arrested.

Bacon's explanation made no sense because Mayer already knew Tripp had been arrested; she was trying to prove that Tripp had lied about it on the form. That's why she asked Bernath whether the questionnaire pertained to arrests or convictions and what the consequences would be if Tripp had lied on the questionnaire.

Greg Caires, a military reporter for *Defense Daily*, denied that the Defense Department readily shares personnel files with the media. Caires said the Pentagon is so sensitive to security concerns that it is extremely difficult for reporters to get the records of military employees even if they've been dead for thirty years. "Listen, it took me two years just to get a permanent pass to get into the Pentagon. Believe me, it's very odd," said Caires.[26]

Former Clinton advisor Dick Morris, in a column for the *New York Post*, pointed to Bacon's close connection to the White House. "Ken Bacon's background indicates that he's a man the White House can turn to. He's the one who hired former White House intern Monica Lewinsky when the White House needed to move her out of Clinton's range but still keep her on the reservation."

The Pentagon determined, upon review, that Linda Tripp had not given inaccurate information on her security background application form. Ken Bacon said, "I can tell you that the investigation is complete and that as a result of the investigation, she has been told that she will retain her security clearance." The Pentagon promised further investigation of whether Tripp's privacy had been violated.

Meanwhile, in his sworn deposition testimony, Bacon confessed that he orchestrated the release of information from Tripp's personal file and had related to Jane Mayer that there might be a Privacy Act problem with releasing the information.

Bernath testified that Bacon gave him explicit orders to comply with Mayer's request. "I didn't do it on my own," said Bernath and specified that Bacon made clear that providing Mayer the information was a "priority." Bernath did not remember Bacon ever raising the Privacy Act as a concern, as Bacon had claimed.[27]

Mayer was indignant that questions were being raised about the propriety of the release of the information. She referred to a *Washington Times* story on the issue as a "piece of [foully odoriferous sewage]" and slammed a reporter for "making such a stink over how people get their information." "You spent all this time trying to figure out whether Ken Bacon broke a law. I haven't seen you spend any time on Linda Tripp. Did she break a law?"[28]

According to the *Washington Times*, "numerous current and former high-ranking officials in the Pentagon's sprawling public affairs operation said Mr. Bacon's leak was an extraordinarily blatant breach of privacy regulations." Even more significant, "those regulations are routinely taught to all public affairs officers—both military and civilian—at a special school under Mr. Bacon's purview."

One unnamed official, who had worked in Bacon's office, said, "Mr. Bacon knows the Privacy Act. But he also knows that he's a political appointee who is ultimately serving the White House. I mean, who's the No. 1 master—the Privacy Act or the White House?"[29] A former longtime Pentagon public affairs officer agreed: "Nobody at his level at the Pentagon would ever in a gazillion years take it on himself to release such information on his own. Couldn't happen, didn't happen, no way, no how. Remember, everyone who comes into public affairs is told Privacy Act rules. You don't release someone's confidential information—to anyone, much less the media. This is Public Affairs 101. And Bacon is perpetrating a shameful lie. Any professional in the building will tell you the same thing."[30]

Also lending credence to the White House connection was the fact that despite clear evidence that Bacon broke the law, Clinton didn't fire him. In 1992, during the presidential campaign, Clinton berated the Bush administration for rifling through his passport file to see if he'd tried to renounce his U.S. citizenship (Passportgate). Clinton vowed to fire anyone who committed similar breaches of privacy in his administration. "If I catch anybody doing it, I will fire them the next day.... [We] won't have to have an inquiry or rigmarole or anything else," he said.

When Ken Starr summoned Bacon before the grand jury, certain grand jurors were skeptical about Bacon's story. One asked, "What would make you think that it would be all right to release that kind of information... knowing that it was a confidential question in files that were locked up?" Defense Secretary William Cohen admitted that the leak was "certainly inappropriate, if not illegal." Cohen, perhaps aware of the uncomfortably close connection Bacon had with both Jane Mayer and the White House, tried to assign the primary blame to Bacon's assistant, Cliff Bernath. Even after further facts were revealed and Bacon's role was made obvious, Cohen failed to correct the record.[31] Linda Tripp struck back in September 1999, filing a civil lawsuit against the White House and the Pentagon for violating her privacy and subjecting her to "extreme public embarrassment, humiliation, anxiety, and ridicule." Tripp alleged that the unlawful disclosure of her confidential records was designed to spread "embarrassing or damaging information... for partisan political purposes." Tripp's complaint charged that the White House conspired with Defense Department officials to smear her once she emerged as a potential witness against Clinton.[32]

Justice Department Facilitates Injustice

On April 6, 2000, the Justice Department announced that it would not prosecute Bacon and Bernath. A Justice Department official, speaking anonymously, said the Privacy Act requires proof that the perpetrator knowingly and willfully intended to violate the law. The Justice Department's Criminal Division eventually concluded there was insufficient evidence to prosecute.

Senator James Inhofe was outraged. "What does it say to citizens who want to serve in government that their most private confidential personnel file can be leaked to the press in clear violation of the law, the perpetrators can be caught, and yet nothing is done—no one is held accountable?" he asked.

Inhofe was fuming that the Justice Department had sat on the investigation for twenty months. As early as the summer of 1998, the Defense Department had told Justice that the release of information from Tripp's private personnel file "constituted a clearly unwarranted invasion of her privacy." But the Justice Department made no comment until April 2000, and then only to announce its decision not to prosecute.

These disclosures prompted Inhofe to allege "an ongoing corrupt cover-up." Inhofe said the matter would now be in the hands of Defense Secretary Cohen. "It is his job to ensure some semblance of justice in this case. Like in so many other cases, the American people simply can no longer trust the decisions of the Clinton administration's sad excuse for a Department of Justice,"

Inhofe said.[33] Senate Republicans were not seriously considering
the option of bringing Janet Reno before them to testify yet
again, because, "We get Janet Reno up here and she goes into her
act... a well-practiced drill that rarely ends with any questions
being answered."[34]

Cohen Slaps Wrists

On May 25, 2000, Defense Secretary William Cohen criticized
Ken Bacon and Cliff Bernath for releasing information from
Tripp's personnel file to the media. In a Defense Department briefing that same day, Rear Admiral Craig Quigley explained that "You
always do a balancing act between the Freedom of Information Act
and the Privacy Act—you do a balancing test, I should say. And in
this case... the inspector general's report found that the Privacy Act
was violated in this case, and recommended to the secretary that he
take appropriate action to Mr. Bernath and Mr. Bacon."

Quigley said that Secretary Cohen, in his letter, expressed disappointment in Bacon's and Bernath's "serious lapse in judgment."
"But on the other hand," said Quigley, "it also points out that
there was no criminal intent or intent to harm Ms. Tripp; that
there was no influence of any outside party in their decision to
release the information." Incredibly, Quigley said that Bacon and
Bernath "both made a strong case that in the balancing test they
think they did the right thing." Cohen's letter cited other "miti-
gating circumstances"—namely, that Bacon and Bernath only provided information in response to a reporter's inquiry and had
"otherwise exhibited" a " very high quality of performance...."

Quigley announced that with the delivery of his letters to the
men, Cohen considered the matter closed. He revealed that the
letters would not become a part of the men's personnel files. They

were not letters of reprimand but "official letter[s] expressing the secretary's disappointment in judgment by both men."

One persistent reporter pointed out that these letters amounted to "non-action" because there was a finding that the men had violated the Privacy Act, which is punishable by law. Quigley began to vacillate about whether the Privacy Act had been violated, even while admitting that the inspector general's report concluded that it had. Quigley said, "Whether or not the Privacy Act was violated is a matter for the courts to decide.... This needs to be addressed separately as part of the ongoing litigation," which meant the civil suit by Linda Tripp. Following receipt of Cohen's letter, Bacon issued a statement saying he respected Cohen's decision but insisted that "I believe that ultimately my conduct will be found lawful." Separately, Bernath defiantly disputed the inspector general's finding that he had violated the Privacy Act.

Linda Tripp's attorneys issued a harshly worded press release condemning Secretary Cohen's failure to "take appropriate disciplinary action" against Bacon and Bernath. In the statement, the attorneys alleged that the release of Tripp's private information was "not simply an innocent release of information in response to an inquiry by a reporter." Bacon and Bernath knew, said the attorneys, that the requested information would be used to smear Tripp. The president and his supporters, they said, turned their public relations machine against Tripp to divert attention from the president's illegal conduct and to undermine Tripp's credibility. Then came the punchline: "Today, Secretary of Defense Cohen, through his refusal to properly protect a federal witness and his failure to ensure that the laws protecting whistleblowers are enforced, has sent the wrong message to the entire federal work force. The bottom line is simple: High level presidential appointees and their managerial cronies can harass, intimidate and destroy whistleblowers—even by illegally releasing confidential government information."

The Importance of Linda Tripp

Linda Tripp was the most important whistle-blower in the vast array of Clintonian scandals. Without her tapes, President Clinton would likely never have been impeached. The Clinton administration recognized her importance, which is why it unleashed its spin dogs to destroy her reputation.

But what does it say about the political and judicial system when the president of the United States can, with impunity, publicly humiliate and defame, trample on the privacy rights, and lobby for the prosecution of the main whistle-blower against him? How ironic that Clinton's defenders cite the right to privacy as the driving principle behind Linda Tripp's prosecution by Maryland authorities.

The Justice and Defense Departments' decision not to take action against Bacon and Bernath would have been bad enough if the release of Tripp's file had been inadvertent. But this was a case of deliberate leaking of the private file of the employee who had—with enormous publicity—implicated the president of the United States in serious wrongdoing. Even if the two Pentagon employees had been innocent of any malicious intent, Bacon and Bernath should have been fired on the spot for simple incompetence. They blatantly ignored Tripp's right to privacy, but worse became complicit in trying to discredit her as a witness who was cooperating with the independent counsel on charges that everyone knew could lead to the impeachment of the president of the United States. That they were allowed to get away with it—while Tripp's reputation lies in tatters, shredded by the White House—speaks volumes for the status of the rule of law and justice in Clinton's America. The Clinton machine knew it could use political power to smear and destroy. Its politicized Justice Department ensured there would be no consequences.

Chapter Six

Presidential Privilege

Throughout his scandal-ridden tenure President Clinton used various tactics, legal and otherwise, to withhold information from the courts and Congress. He frequently invoked legal privilege claims to prevent his aides and others from testifying before the grand jury and congressional committees.

Clinton's favorite stonewalling tool was "executive privilege." The Constitution did not expressly create "executive privilege." The courts established the privilege based on the Constitution's separation of powers to exempt members of the executive branch in certain cases from being compelled to disclose documents or other information to Congress or the courts.

Evolution of a Presidential Right

President Eisenhower coined "executive privilege" in a May 7, 1954, letter denying information to a Senate subcommittee.[1] President Kennedy also invoked "executive privilege" to refuse information to a Senate subcommittee, though he qualified its scope.[2] Kennedy said his goal was to "achieve full cooperation with the Congress in making available to it all appropriate documents, correspondence, and information."[3]

President Nixon asserted the privilege when he refused to turn over White House tapes to the special prosecutor during the Watergate scandal. In 1974, in *United States v. Nixon*, the Supreme Court set the parameters of executive privilege.[4] Nixon's lawyers argued that the privilege was absolute so as to entitle the president not to disclose any communications between himself and his advisors. The Court affirmed the president's constitutional right to assert the privilege but qualified it to apply only when military, diplomatic, or national security secrets were involved. Such privileges against disclosing evidence, held the Court, must be narrowly construed because "they are in derogation of the search for truth." In the absence of those applicable situations, the president's interest in keeping his communications confidential is outweighed by the interest of the courts in administering justice in criminal cases. Since none of those situations applied, the Court ordered Nixon to produce the tapes.

In a footnote, the Court made clear that its ruling applied only to claims of executive privilege in the context of criminal cases, not in civil litigation or congressional inquiries—subjects the Court had not been called upon to address.[5]

Abusing the Privilege

Presidents Ford, Carter, and Bush each invoked executive privilege only once.[6] President Reagan asserted it three times in eight years. But President Clinton invoked it more than ten times to deny information to grand juries and congressional investigators, not to mention his numerous assertions of other privilege claims. Clinton asserted executive privilege many times during the

Lewinsky investigation. He used it to block the grand jury testimony of his secretarial assistant Nancy Hernreich, which was particularly frivolous since his secretary Betty Currie had already testified extensively.[7] When Independent Counsel Kenneth Starr challenged Clinton's refusal to allow Hernreich to testify, Clinton withdrew the privilege, proving that he was using it as a delaying tactic. White House aide Sidney Blumenthal refused to testify before the grand jury on the basis of executive privilege, as did White House lawyer Bruce Lindsey, who also invoked attorney-client privilege. Attorney General Janet Reno announced that she would not represent the White House on its executive privilege claims because of her possible conflicts of interest. Yet she filed a vigorous amicus curiae (friend of the court) brief in support of Lindsey's attorney-client privilege claim even though she had no less a conflict of interest problem in opposing the independent counsel on that issue.[8]

Kenneth Starr viewed these executive privilege claims as specious. So did the ordinarily liberal New York Times editorial page, which referred to them as "an alarming attempt to extend presidential power."[9] Even former Clinton advisor George Stephanopoulos said the White House "cannot win this fight on executive privilege. It has been tried before in the Whitewater case and eventually they turned over the documents." In fact, in 1994, President Clinton's former White House counsel Lloyd Cutler had stated in a memo: "In circumstances involving communications relating to investigations of personal wrongdoing by government officials, it is our practice not to assert executive privilege either in judicial proceedings or in congressional investigations and hearings."

The district court eventually rejected the White House's executive privilege claims for Lindsey and Blumenthal, as well as

Lindsey's attorney-client privilege claim. In her thirty-two-page opinion, Judge Norma Holloway Johnson ruled that executive privilege was qualified, not absolute. The independent counsel's interest in obtaining information for the grand jury to determine whether a crime had been committed outweighed the president's interest in preserving the confidentiality of White House discussions that did not involve military, diplomatic, or national security secrets. Kenneth Starr convinced the court that the contested testimony was essential because there was no other way for him to obtain that evidence.

Judge Johnson disallowed the White House's attempt to assert the attorney-client privilege for government lawyer Bruce Lindsey because he was a government-paid lawyer rather than President Clinton's private attorney. As such, Lindsey owed no duty of confidentiality to Bill Clinton personally. The White House appealed the rulings concerning Blumenthal and Lindsey. When Kenneth Starr requested an expedited appeal directly to the Supreme Court, White House counsel Charles F. C. Ruff abandoned the White House's executive privilege claims for Blumenthal and Lindsey and said they wouldn't be invoking executive privilege to block aides from testifying in the future.[10]

"We have no intention of asserting the privilege, executive privilege, in any situation that I'm aware of," he said.[11] Ruff pressed forward, however, with the appeal of the attorney-client privilege claim. In due course the court of appeals affirmed Judge Johnson's ruling in rejecting the privilege. It wasn't even a close call.

"To state the question is to suggest the answer, for the Office of the President is a part of the federal government, consisting of government employees doing government business, and neither legal authority nor policy nor experience suggests that a federal government entity can maintain the ordinary common law attorney-client privilege to withhold information relating to a federal criminal offense." The court noted that when Judge Robert Bork—solicitor general during the Nixon administration—was invited to join the Nixon's legal defense team during Watergate, Bork replied: "A government attorney is sworn to uphold the Constitution. If I come across evidence that is bad for the president, I'll have to turn it over. I won't be able to sit on it like a private defense attorney."[12] That, according to the court, was an honest reading of the law.

"In sum, it would be contrary to tradition, common understanding, and our governmental system for the attorney-client privilege to attach to White House counsel in the same manner as private counsel. When government attorneys learn, through communication with their clients, of information related to criminal misconduct, they may not rely on the government attorney-client privilege to shield such information from disclosure to a grand jury."

The Prevaricator-in-Chief

Throughout these legal imbroglios President Clinton pretended to be out of the loop. During a state trip to Africa, the press asked him about his use of executive privilege. "You should ask someone who knows.... I haven't discussed that with the lawyers," Clinton said, denying any involvement, though fully aware that executive privilege can only be invoked by the authority of the president.[13] Indeed, the president's counsel, Charles F. C. Ruff, was on the record saying that he specifically discussed the privilege issue with the president, who ordered that the privilege be asserted.[14]

It later became clear why Clinton abandoned his executive privilege claim with respect to Lindsey in the appellate court. He knew that he would lose the case and that an unfavorable ruling would prevent him from asserting it for other aides. Thus, an invaluable delaying tactic would be foreclosed. Sure enough, to Starr's surprise, Clinton invoked the privilege again for White House attorneys Lanny Breuer, Cheryl Mills, and, believe it or not, Bruce Lindsey.[15] The president had employed the same tactic of asserting, then withdrawing, the privilege in August 1996 to prevent White House attorneys from producing documents regarding their communications with Hillary Rodham Clinton. He pulled the trick again to prevent Thomas "Mack" McLarty from testifying fully in 1997 about his efforts to obtain employment for Clinton's former assistant attorney general Webster Hubbell.[16]

When Clinton testified before the grand jury, the independent counsel, at the request of a juror, asked Clinton why he had asserted, then withdrawn, executive privilege. Clinton responded that he felt that it was important in principle to assert the privilege at the trial level, but he felt strongly that they shouldn't appeal it when they lost. Only four days after so testifying, he appealed Judge Johnson's rejection of Lanny Breuer's executive privilege claim.

In addition to asserting executive privilege liberally, the White House crafted another novel legal theory to prevent key grand jury testimony from Secret Service agents. One of the agents, who usually worked outside the Oval Office on weekends, had reportedly expressed concerns to a White House staff member about Lewinsky's visits to the White House. The next day, Lewinsky was transferred to the Pentagon.[17] Starr said that he had received numerous and credible reports that Secret Service agents had evidence relevant to the Lewinsky investigation.[18] During depositions as part of grand jury proceedings, certain of these Secret

Service agents refused to answer questions from the independent counsel, asserting a "protective function privilege."

The Office of the Independent Counsel filed a motion with the district court to compel the agent's testimony. The Secret Service is part of the Treasury Department, whose legal counsel is the Justice Department, which entered the case on behalf of the Secret Service and Treasury. President Clinton again played this childish game of denying that the White House was behind the Secret Service's refusal to testify. "With regard to the Secret Service, I literally have had no involvement in that decision whatever." But when Kenneth Starr called Clinton's hand by requesting that he order the agents to testify, Clinton refused, effectively endorsing the agents' assertion of this illusory privilege. The Justice Department argued that the special relationship between presidents and the Secret Service would be permanently damaged if agents were forced to testify about things they witnessed while on duty. Justice insisted that if presidents believed their private conversations could someday be publicly disclosed, they might keep agents at a distance and expose themselves to danger, including assassination.

The Office of the Independent Counsel countered that there was no legal basis for "protective function privilege." As sworn law enforcement officers, Secret Service agents have an obligation to assist criminal investigations.[19] Kenneth Starr warned that allowing the Secret Service to refuse to testify before a federal grand jury would turn the agency into an imperious "Praetorian guard" around the president, leaving him free to engage in criminal activity.[20] Starr emphasized that the testimony of certain agents was "highly relevant to the questions of whether one or more persons may have engaged in criminal activity, including perjury, obstruction of justice, and intimidation of witnesses."[21]

The district court agreed, rejecting the argument that such testimony would drive a wedge between the Secret Service and the president. "When people act within the law, they do not ordinarily push away those they trust or rely upon for fear that their actions will be reported to a grand jury."

Further, "The claim of the Secret Service that 'any presidential action—no matter how intrinsically innocent—could later be deemed relevant to a criminal investigation' is simply not plausible." Secret Service agents, as law enforcement officers, have a duty to report criminal activity. This duty constitutes a "persuasive policy reason in favor of compelling grand jury testimony."

An indignant President Clinton reacted by accusing Starr of being insensitive to security considerations. "At least, it will have a chilling effect, perhaps, on the conversations presidents have and the work they do and the way they do it.... There's a serious possibility that that could occur." He said that this particular privilege had not been established yet because "no one ever thought that anyone would ever abuse the responsibility the Secret Service has to the president."[22]

The Justice Department appealed the decision, arguing that "The court provided no explanation for rejecting the uncontradicted conclusions of the Secret Service directors and President Bush," who had written a letter advocating the establishment of the privilege. But four former U.S. attorneys general, Edwin Meese III, Dick Thornburgh, William P. Barr, and Griffin B. Bell, filed friend of the court briefs supporting the Office of the Independent Counsel. They ridiculed the notion that the denial of the privilege would increase the likelihood of the president's assassination. "Such hyperbole has no place in a federal appellate brief." The extreme rhetoric, they said, proved that the agency's arguments were untenable.[23]

Clinton's Tool

The Justice Department's appeal was unsuccessful, but the Secret Service case illustrated the extent to which Janet Reno's Justice Department had become President Clinton's tool. Regardless of Janet Reno's personal views concerning the propriety of Secret Service agents testifying, it was highly improper for her to pit the Justice Department against the Office of the Independent Counsel on this issue, as well as others. The Office of the Independent Counsel derives its powers from the Justice Department and therefore stands in its shoes as to those matters over which the court grants it jurisdiction.

Judge Lawrence Silberman, in his concurring opinion, excoriated the Justice Department for injecting itself into the Secret Service case. By law, once an independent counsel is appointed he acquires the full investigative and prosecutorial functions and powers of the Justice Department. Judge Silberman noted that the appellate brief in the Secret Service case did not identify the appealing party. There was a good reason for that. The Justice Department was aware that only the Office of the Independent Counsel could represent the United States in the case, so Attorney General Reno just left Justice's name off the pleadings. Despite that, Silberman pointed out, she nevertheless claimed to represent the government on the first page of her brief. The judge said that this meant that two opposing lawyers were representing the same named party (the United States), which he said was "analytically impossible."

Silberman also explained that the entire purpose of the Ethics in Government Act, which governed the independent counsel, would be defeated if the independent counsel were not allowed freedom to conduct his investigation without interference from the Justice Department. The act, he said, greatly reduces the number of options available to the attorney general. Litigating against the independent counsel is certainly not among them. Indeed, the act affirmatively requires the Justice Department to provide assistance to the independent counsel.

On the last page of his opinion Silberman offered a stinging critique of the Clinton administration and the Justice Department. "I am mindful of the terrible political pressures and strains of conscience that bear upon senior political appointees of the Justice Department when an independent counsel (or special prosecutor) is investigating the president of the United States. Those strains are surely exacerbated when the president's agents literally and figuratively 'declare war' on the independent counsel (can it be said that the president of the United States has declared war on the United States?)."

At a minimum, the president's repeated attempts to block the independent counsel amounted to a series of frivolous law suits of the kind that are routinely thrown out of court, sometimes with penalties attached for wasting the court's time. That the Justice Department was a party to such law suits can only be described as a corruption and politicization of its purpose. Indeed, Reno and the Justice Department were fully aware that the protective function privilege had virtually no chance of being adopted by the courts. As Susan Schmidt and Michael Weisskopf point out in *Truth at Any Cost*, Deputy Attorney General Eric Holder admitted to one of Starr's deputies, Jackie Bennett, that Justice had no better than a 5 percent chance of prevailing on the Secret Service privilege claim. "DOJ's point man on this issue, Jonathan Schwartz," wrote Schmidt and Weisskopf, "was even less charitable. He told Starr deputy Bob Bittman that he feared DOJ's advocacy of the 'protective function privilege' would be seen as a political exercise. The department's veteran lawyers, he said, thought it 'wrongheaded.'"

Clinton's egregious misuse of the various privilege claims constituted an abrogation of his constitutional duty to faithfully execute the laws. So flagrant were Clinton's perversions of presidential privilege that Ken Starr included them as a separate ground for the president's impeachment in his referral to Congress.[24]

The House managers and their counsel, David Schippers, later decided not to include the assertion of phony privilege claims as a basis for impeachment. It is difficult to determine why they omitted that count. It could be that they knew that it would be politically difficult to sell the idea that a president ought to be punished for using all available legal tactics in his effort to resist impeachment.

Regardless of whether Congress should have included this particular abuse of presidential power as a ground for Clinton's impeachment, it is clear that Clinton exploited the privilege claims. It is also true that Janet Reno, in assisting the president with such claims, used the taxpayers' Department of Justice in contravention of its constitutional and statutory duties. Once the independent counsel was appointed it was Reno's duty to assist the Office of the Independent Counsel with its investigation. Instead, at every turn, not only did she not assist Starr, she tried to thwart his investigation. Rather than treating his office as an extension of the Justice Department, she, as Judge Silberman observed, assisted President Clinton in declaring war on the independent counsel. That was tantamount to declaring war on the Constitution itself. She turned her department into a glorified legal defense firm for a felonious president. The two highest law enforcement officers of the land, President Clinton and Janet Reno, worked in concert to obstruct rather than enforce the law, setting an unpunished precedent that is the greatest domestic abuse of executive power since the Watergate scandal.

Chapter Seven

The Mother of All Scandals

Of all the innumerable scandals of the Clinton administration, none is more shocking and disturbing than the
campaign finance scandal. None is more far-reaching
or complex. Of all the examples in this book detailing the complicity of the Clinton-Reno Justice Department in furthering the
administration's political and personal ends, none is more glaring
and shameful than its role in the campaign finance scandal.
Though this Byzantine scheme of events and the investigations
concerning it are difficult to grasp, there are recurring issues, as
Charles La Bella, the supervising attorney for the Justice
Department's Campaign Finance Task Force, observed in his
Interim Report. "There run through each investigation certain
common themes," wrote La Bella, "the desperate need to raise
enormous sums of money to finance a media campaign designed to
bring the Democratic party back from the brink after the devastating congressional losses during the 1994 election cycle, and the

calculated use of access to the White House and high level officials—including the President and First Lady—by the White
House, DNC and Clinton-Gore '96, as leverage to extract contributions from individuals who were themselves using access as a
means to enhance their business opportunities."

President Clinton and the Democratic Party were desperate to
ensure Clinton's reelection and to recapture some of the ground
they lost in Congress. They needed huge amounts of money to
fund an advertising blitz to recast Clinton's image and that of his
party. President Clinton began meeting with his advisors in early
1995 to develop a plan aimed at securing his reelection by "pulling
out all the stops" in campaign fund-raising.[1] Political consultant
Dick Morris, who joined the Clinton-Gore effort in mid-1995,
estimated that the essential advertising campaign would cost
upwards of $1 million per week. Morris convinced Clinton and
Gore that they were going to be defeated in the absence of
Herculean fund-raising efforts. One important Democrat said that
Morris was "pushing the hell out of the president and vice president. He was saying the polling in early 1995 showed that Gore
was likely to be a defeated vice president and his career would be
over.... They were scared to death. People were panicked. The
vice president was panicked."[2]

Apparently, the White House was willing to go to any lengths,
including compromising the security interests of the United States,
to obtain the money necessary to hold on to power. In the process,
the president, vice president, and first lady literally sold access to
themselves and to the institutions of the presidency and the White
House. Donors were rewarded with access in direct proportion to
the size of their contributions. Fund-raisers who raised $100,000
and individual donors who gave $50,000 became managing trustees

of the Democratic Party, entitling them to special privileges. Among those perks were opportunities to rub elbows with the first and second families, special seating at Democratic National Committee functions, access to White House coffees, and trips on Air Force One and Air Force Two. Other special privileges included sleepovers in the Lincoln Bedroom, seats in the President's Box at the Kennedy Center, use of the White House pool and tennis courts, tickets to DNC events, participation in trade missions, membership in party committees, and participation in other high-level White House meetings.[3]

President Clinton—the quintessential campaigner with his eye always on the big ball—became utterly obsessed and preoccupied with raising money. According to the Senate Governmental Affairs Committee report, Clinton spent "enormous amounts of time during the 1996 election cycle raising money. In the ten months prior to the 1996 election, President Clinton attended more than 230 fund-raising events, which raised $119 million. The President maintained such a pace for over a year before the election, often attending fund-raisers five and six days each week." (That must have been what he meant when he repeatedly stated that he had to get back to work for the American people.) "According to Presidential campaign advisor Dick Morris," the Senate report continued, "President Clinton would say, 'I haven't slept in three days; every time I turn around they want me to be at a fundraiser.... I cannot think, I cannot do anything. Every minute of my time is spent at these fundraisers.' This frenzied pursuit of campaign contributions raises obvious and disturbing questions. Can any President who spends this much time raising money focus adequately upon affairs of state? Is it even possible for such a President to distinguish between fundraising and policymaking?"[4]

While the Democratic Party has since made a great deal of noise about the impropriety and sordidness of soft money contributions in the political process, Clinton and Gore set a new standard for the creative uses of soft money funds. Campaign finance laws limit the amount of money that individuals and corporations can donate directly to political candidates and their campaigns (hard money) and such limits have been upheld by the United States Supreme Court against challenges that they violated the First Amendment. The Supreme Court has been unwilling to countenance statutory limits on soft money, however, based on the First Amendment guarantees. Soft-money contributions are those contributions made to the political parties—as opposed to the political candidates—for party-building activities. Clinton and Gore consistently abused the soft money exception by directing that contributions to the party be used to finance advertising buys for specific political campaigns. Such use of party money could hardly be construed as being in furtherance of party building, but Clinton and Gore figured they would only have to deal with the consequences of their illegal activities if they got caught, which would be safely after they and their comrades had been reelected.

President Clinton attempted to distance himself from complicity in these scandals by saying he had no control over the soft money of the Democratic National Committee and concerned himself only with the expenditures of funds from the Clinton-Gore reelection campaign. But in practice Clinton recognized no such distinction between the two sets of funds and asserted control over the Democratic National Committee's funds too. Clinton purposely blurred the distinction between soft money and hard money so he could get around the legal limitations on hard-money contributions.

The Senate Governmental Affairs Committee's report clearly set out the situation:

> Indeed, no one has done more to erode this very distinction than the President himself, who with his staff effectively seized control of DNC operations and ran all Democratic party campaign and fundraising efforts out of the White House. During the 1996 campaign, the DNC was the alter ego of the White House.... The Clinton-Gore and DNC advertising campaigns were also virtually inseparable, constituting a seamless web of White House-directed campaigning that employed all the same consultants, pollsters, and media producers. Ultimately, in fact, the President himself exercised total control over the DNC advertising. Having reduced the DNC to an arm of the White House, President Clinton and Vice President Gore are responsible for the actions it undertook in their names and at their direction....[5]
>
> Extensive DNC fundraising occurred because the President and his advisors... decided that the party's massive advertising campaign would cost more than could possibly be provided by the "hard" money in the President's "official" campaign treasury. To fill the gap, they turned to unregulated "soft" money even though such monies could not by law be used to help a candidate's campaign for office. Unlike official "campaign" contributions, however, DNC "soft" money could be raised from wealthy donors in unlimited quantities. By diverting DNC funds to campaign advertising controlled by the White House, the Democrats had the best of all possible worlds: de facto "hard" money from key donors in unlimited quantities.[6]

The public's first exposure to the scandal was in the latter part of 1996, when reports began to surface about the involvement of foreign money in the United States political system. The *Los Angeles Times* reported on September 21, 1996, that the Democratic National Committee had been forced to return a $250,000 contribution from Cheong Am America, Inc., a recently formed subsidiary of a South Korean electronics firm. The new company was seeking a site for a manufacturing plant in Los Angeles County but had yet to generate any revenue, which meant that its political donation necessarily came from its foreign parent. The problem was that federal law prohibits foreign nationals and companies from contributing to United States political campaigns.[7]

The illegal foreign contribution was made worse by the revelation that the chairman of the parent and subsidiary, John H. K. Lee, attended a Democratic fund-raiser in April where he personally met Bill Clinton and promised the contribution. David Eichenbaum, the DNC communications director, implied that this had been an isolated incident. He said that the party's standard procedure to ensure the propriety of donations from foreign-owned companies had broken down in this case. Eichenbaum said that the DNC was led to believe that the company's principals were either U.S. citizens or permanent residents. The now familiar figure John Huang was involved in the incident. Huang at the time was serving as the Democratic Party's national finance committee vice chairman specializing in handling Asian American donors.[8] Huang was formerly an executive with the Lippo Group, a large Indonesian conglomerate involved primarily in banking and finance. Its main company, Lippo Ltd., showed assets of $3.6 billion in 1995.

Lippo Plants Its Seeds

Mochtar Riady, whose son James Riady was to figure heavily in the Clinton-Gore campaign finance scandals, founded the Lippo

Group. The Riadys were ethnic Chinese living in Indonesia. The Lippo Group was the company that hired Clinton's disgraced assistant attorney general Webster Hubbell, between his resignation and his jail sentence in 1994, and paid him $100,000 without requiring any appreciable work from him. Investigators suspected that the $100,000 was hush money to procure Hubbell's silence about the various Clinton scandals, including Bill Clinton's notorious 1992 meeting with James Riady.

Some argue that Clinton's first foray into illegal foreign contributions didn't begin with the 1996 election but the 1992 one. They say that although his desperation for cash was real following the 1994 Republican victories, his means of collecting money during the 1996 campaign was nothing new. He was simply resorting to tricks that he and his colleagues developed during his first presidential campaign. He had worked with the Riadys then too.

Clinton's association with the Riady family began in the early eighties in Little Rock. When the Riadys purchased a controlling interest in a major bank in Arkansas, James Riady settled in Little Rock to run the bank. He began to associate with Bill Clinton shortly thereafter. Riady reportedly visited the White House some twenty times after Clinton was elected in 1992. At one of those meetings Riady encouraged Clinton to expand trade with China.[9]

A very important meeting between Clinton and James Riady took place in August, during the heat of the 1992 campaign. Clinton's handlers arranged for Clinton to meet with Riady at a fund-raiser in a large Chinese restaurant in Little Rock. Clinton met Riady and the two rode together to Clinton's next meeting. The upshot of the Clinton-Riady conversation was enormous. A Clinton campaign memo turned over to the House Government Reform and Oversight Committee and the Justice Department revealed that Riady had flown from Indonesia (where he was then based) to give $100,000 at the fund-raiser and that he would be giving much more in the future. The Lippo companies, in fact, became the single biggest donors to the Clinton campaign. Some of Lippo's donations were thought to have been laundered through individuals (called straw donors) to conceal that Lippo was the actual donor.[10] These types of gifts were known as illegal conduit contributions.

John Huang

Lippo official John Huang was also to become a key figure in the Clinton foreign fund-raising network. He had first met James Riady in the early eighties when Governor Clinton was the featured speaker at a financial seminar that Riady was attending. When Riady became president of the Worthen Banking Group in Little Rock owned by his family, he hired Huang. As he grew in the Worthen position and began to commute between Little Rock and Worthen's Bank in Hong Kong, Huang developed business and social relationships with many friends and associates of Bill and Hillary Clinton.[11] In the mid-eighties James Riady encouraged Huang to become active in Democratic politics.

In 1988 Riady hosted a fund-raiser for the Democratic Senatorial Campaign Committee, from which he raised $110,000. At the same time, he was lobbying senators to pressure Taiwan to permit Asian American banks, such as those owned by his family, to open offices in their country. Huang came to be an important fund-raiser for the Democratic Senatorial Campaign Committee and became acquainted with several senators at the time, including John Breaux and Al Gore. In 1992 Huang hosted a fund-raiser for Clinton's presidential campaign.

Not long after Clinton won the election, Huang started angling for a job in the new administration. In 1993, his efforts paid off when the White House offered him a job in the Commerce Department. Lippo gave Huang $450,000 in severance pay when he left Lippo for Commerce. Not everyone was pleased with Huang's appointment. One undersecretary of commerce considered Huang to be "totally unqualified."[12] Once at Commerce, Huang was put in charge of Asian trade matters.

Interestingly, when Huang completed his standard federal employment form seeking the position at Commerce, he was required to state his "reason for wanting to leave" his current employer. His answer for giving up his $205,000-a-year Lippo banking position was "to have the opportunity to serve the country through this administration." (Notice he didn't specify which country.)[13]

Within a month of his appointment and in preparation for his new job at Commerce, Huang acquired a top secret security clearance, which, according to a Commerce official, was necessary "due to his critical need for his expertise... [by Commerce] Secretary [Ron] Brown." Huang enjoyed this security clearance while still straddling the private sector; he didn't leave the Lippo group until July 1994, over six months after Clinton appointed him.

During Huang's tenure as a midlevel official in the Commerce Department, he had extraordinary access to President Clinton.[14] He attended many high-level briefings in which classified information was discussed. Commerce officials estimate that Huang attended more than seventy such meetings in 1994 and thirty-nine in 1995. Secret Service logs confirmed that between July 1, 1995, and October 3, 1996, Huang visited the White House seventy-eight times. (The White House tried to downplay the meetings by saying that only three of them took place in the Oval Office and two of those were social meetings. Administration officials refused to explain Huang's seventy-five other White House visits.) Huang also saw more than two dozen intelligence reports. At the same time he maintained very close ties to the Lippo Group, even after he formally left their employ. Phone records later released show that he often called Lippo (some seventy times) shortly after intelligence briefings.

Toward the end of 1994 Clinton had an important task for Huang. The administration was engaged in an intense campaign to renew Most Favored Nation (MFN) trade status for China. China's human rights abuses had many congressmen wary of closer American-Chinese cooperation. The administration sent Huang to lobby four congressmen and within one day Huang delivered commitments from all four to support MFN renewal for China.[15]

Welcome to the DNC

A new chapter in the unfolding campaign finance saga began at a critical meeting at the White House on September 13, 1995, between Clinton, John Huang, James Riady, and others. At the meeting Clinton personally arranged for Huang to be transferred from the Commerce Department to an important position in the Democratic National Committee.[16] In fact, several officials said that Clinton asked DNC finance chairman Marvin Rosen at the time, "Where does it stand with John Huang?" White House press secretary Mike McCurry insisted the president "didn't recall" having said that, "but would not rule it out."[17] The Senate Governmental Affairs Committee was certain that Clinton arranged for Huang's placement at the DNC. "Two things are clear about Huang's obtaining a job as a DNC fundraiser," said the committee report. "First, it would not have occurred but for the President's personal interest and recommendation. Second, it took place even though Huang had already engaged in illegal fundraising from foreign sources while at the Commerce Department, and despite the DNC's awareness of clear indications that Huang would continue to raise funds illegally as the DNC's Chairman for Finance."[18]

Ostensibly because of a bureaucratic error, Huang retained his top secret clearance after he left the Commerce Department for the DNC. Before he was transferred to the DNC to raise money, Huang occupied a very important position in the Commerce Department dealing with trade policy. It should be noted that the Lippo Group, whose United States operations Huang once headed, benefited from at least $1 billion in trade deals that were negotiated through the Commerce Department.[19]

Once Huang got settled in at the DNC, Al Gore sent him a warm thank you letter in which he said, "I value your friendship... and I am grateful for your backing and encouragement. The President and I will need your help and active support to succeed and to continue our efforts in the years to come."[20] Huang was indispensable to the Democratic effort. He had established an impressive network of friends and acquaintances through the years. In 1996 he developed an ambitious plan to raise $7 million from Asian Americans. His main sales pitch to them was that they could acquire clout through their donations.[21] Huang organized a fund-raiser with important Taiwanese businessmen, one of whom was a billionaire. The group dined with Clinton and paid him collectively almost $500,000.[22] Republicans later charged that as a result of that meeting, the Democratic Party changed its platform to be more favorable to Taiwan.[23]

The DNC based Huang's compensation on how much he raised: an incentive bonus plan. It worked. Altogether while at the Democrat National Committee Huang raised nearly $3 million for the party, approximately half of which was illegal foreign money that had to be returned. Many suspected that Huang was serving as an "agent of influence" for the People's Republic of China, channeling Chinese money into the Democratic Party.[24] In any event it seems likely that Clinton put Huang in the Commerce Department in order to raise illegal Chinese funds. When James Kleindienst, a former banking colleague, asked Huang how he got his job in the Clinton administration, Huang smiled and said, "FOB," meaning Friend of Bill Clinton.[25]

Indonesia: The Wiriadinatas

The next news of illegal foreign contributions to the Democratic National Committee again came from the Los Angeles Times in October 1996, less than a month before the election. While the first report (in September) had involved South Korean money, this one concerned Indonesian contributions. Arief Wiriadinata, a landscape architect, and his wife Soraya, were legal immigrants living in Virginia. In late 1995, they suddenly began making large contributions to the DNC. Their first such payment was a $15,000 contribution in November 1995. In December they contributed an additional $100,000 by way of six separate checks. Although they left the United States and returned to Indonesia they continued to pour cash into the DNC. By mid-1996 they had contributed a whopping $450,000 to Bill Clinton's party.

These major contributions from a foreign, middle-income family raised many questions, particularly as to whether the Wiriadinatas were a front for foreigners who were legally precluded from making such contributions. Federal election law permits permanent resident aliens (green-card holders), such as the Wiriadinatas, to contribute money to political campaigns provided they are still living in the United States (and provided the money is actually coming from those residents). Once the Wiriadinatas returned to Indonesia, the contributions that followed were illegal. But the story that emerged was even more troubling. Mrs. Wiriadinata's father, Hashaim Ning, was associated with the Lippo Group, as a business partner of Mochtar Riady, the patriarch of the Riady family. It looked as though the Indonesian contributions to the Clinton campaign were meant to influence Clinton's Indonesia policy. When Clinton campaigned for president in 1992 he castigated Indonesian president Suharto for waging an "unconscionable" war against the natives of East Timor, a former Portuguese colony that had been seized by Indonesia in 1975 and brutalized ever since. Once elected, however, Clinton began making trade deals with Indonesia, suspended an investigation of possible Indonesian human rights violations, and even considered selling it nine F-16 jet fighters. Republicans were concerned about a March 1993 letter from Mochtar Riady to Clinton, advocating that America resume relations with Vietnam. Clinton in fact normalized relations with Vietnam in 1994.[26]

The Clinton administration, seeking to prove that it had not altered its policy toward Indonesia in exchange for the contributions, protested that it had been tougher on the Indonesian government than had former Republican administrations. It released confidential documents to prove that Clinton had challenged Indonesia on a number of issues.[27] In response to Newt Gingrich's call for a congressional inquiry, Vice President Al Gore uttered his now familiar refrain, "There have been absolutely no violations of any law or regulations."[28]

Once again John Huang—still in charge of Asian American donors for the DNC—was at the center of these contributions. Just as with the $250,000 South Korean contribution, he personally handled the Wiriadinatas' contributions. Huang knew Mrs.

Wiriadinata's father, Hashaim Ning, through their mutual contacts with the Riadys and the Lippo group. Huang told the *Los Angeles Times* that the Wiriadinatas "expressed an interest in supporting the Democratic Party, and the president and I suggested they contribute to the DNC." The DNC and the White House both claimed that the enormous political contributions were the Wiriadinatas' way of saying thank you to President Clinton for writing get well letters to Mrs. Wiriadinata's father, Mr. Ning, who had had a heart attack while visiting Virginia in 1995. The depth of their gratitude is curious given the admission by Mark Fabiani, associate White House counsel, that the letters Clinton sent were form letters signed by an auto-pen. Nevertheless, DNC national chairman, Don Fowler, insisted that the letters moved the Wiriadinatas to make the contributions.[29]

New allegations of corruption unfolded almost weekly. Newspaper editorials began to probe John Huang's relationship with Bill Clinton and the Democratic Party. The *Sacramento Bee* asked, "Who was Huang primarily serving at Commerce: the American public, his former employers at Lippo or party bosses at the DNC? Most important: Were U.S. trade, foreign and human rights policies in any way compromised by Huang's alleged conflict of interest? The administration owes the country an explanation."[30]

A bizarre addition to the fund-raising scandals was the reappearance, via check, of Cheong Am American, Inc. The Democrats had already had to return $250,000 in illegal contributions from the firm. Now it was discovered that the chairman of the company, Kyung Hoon (a.k.a. John) Lee, had donated an additional $10,000, which the DNC was forced to return. Cheong Am, however, had vacated its California offices, and John Lee had disappeared.

The Buddhist Temple

On October 18, 1996, the *Washington Post* reported that John Huang had been responsible for organizing another fund-raiser—this one in April 1996 at the Hsi Lai Buddhist Temple close to Los Angeles where Vice President Al Gore was the main attraction. The DNC records of the event revealed that many of the donors, who contributed anywhere from $2,000 to $5,000, were monks and nuns from the Fo Kuang Shan Buddhist Order, a sect with close ties to the Taiwanese government. The monks and nuns had taken vows of poverty and didn't have that kind of money to donate. Seven of the contributors who gave addresses close to the temple were listed in Federal Election Commission reports as having made contributions to the DNC the preceding February and at the temple event totaling $37,000. Altogether, the DNC raised $140,000 at the temple, not counting the unreported $15,000 cost the temple absorbed in sponsoring the event. One donor said she was approached by a Democratic activist at the temple who gave her $5,000 in small bills and asked her to write a $5,000 check to the DNC. It is against federal election law to make a contribution in someone else's name. In another hint of illegality, DNC records listed a $2,000 contributor from the temple neighborhood, but the resident at the given address had never heard of the contributor.[31] Al Gore, for his part, denied any knowledge that the Buddhist Temple event was a fund-raiser and described it as a "community outreach event."

It later became clear that Huang had quarterbacked the fund-raiser, convincing twenty Buddhist followers to write $5,000 checks each to the Democratic National Committee, assuring them they would be reimbursed by the temple. Bank records reveal that such reimbursements followed.[32]

Helping Huang organize the Buddhist Temple fund-raiser was Maria L. Hsia, a longtime friend of Al Gore, as well as a DNC fund-raiser, immigration advisor, and spokeswoman for the temple.

Republicans stepped up their condemnation of the DNC's illegal foreign fund-raising activities. House Speaker Newt Gingrich predicted that this would turn into the largest scandal in American history "because it involves foreigners being directly involved in the American political system, the American government, the American criminal justice system." Republican presidential nominee Bob Dole charged that Democrats were laundering foreign money. "They've got their own laundromat pumping out money. Now they are out raising money at Buddhist temples where they take a vow of poverty," said Dole.[33]

With this string of damaging revelations, the DNC, hoping to implement some degree of damage control for President Clinton during the heat of the campaign, announced that it had suspended John Huang's fund-raising duties "as part of a downsizing." It also announced that it would return $15,000 to the Buddhist temple to reimburse it for its costs connected to the fund-raiser. The committee would not agree, however, to return the $140,000 it had raised at the temple event, even though it was abundantly clear that much, if not all, of the money had come from monks and nuns who were almost certainly being used as a cover for illegal campaign contributions. The DNC admitted that it was a mistake to have held a fund-raiser at the temple because federal law prohibits such activities by tax-exempt organizations.

Meanwhile, the White House sought to create distance between itself and the DNC. White House chief of staff Leon Panetta, who was traveling with President Clinton at the time, said that the White House was "concerned" about the apparent problems with DNC contributions, especially involving Asian donors. The White House, he said, had asked the DNC for an explanation.[34]

At the same time, the White House began to do what it did best when under attack: counterattack. Clinton campaign press secretary Joe Lockhart said, "If Bob Dole wants to talk about campaign money-laundering, he should check in with his own campaign fundraisers." He then proceeded to deliver a summary of three federal investigations into questionable fund-raising by Republicans.[35]

Vice President Al Gore on *Meet the Press* issued more denials of wrongdoing. "Number one, we have strictly abided by all of the campaign finance laws, strictly. There've been no violations.... There have been no violations of law, no violations of regulations. We've strictly complied with every single one of them," said Gore. Even more amazing, though, was Gore's brazen defense of the $450,000 worth of contributions by the Wiriadinatas. The Wiriadinatas, insisted Gore, were "legal residents of the United States who comply with all the laws, live here, work here, et cetera." Their contributions, he said, were "perfectly legal."[36]

The Indian Connection

The next illegal foreign contribution to the DNC to be exposed was from a great-grandnephew of Indian spiritual leader Mahatma Gandhi. Yogesh Gandhi, of California, had his driver's license revoked for failing to pay traffic fines, had been assessed $10,000 in back taxes, had two civil judgments rendered against him in court for unpaid bills, and was indebted to friends. Despite that financial resume, Gandhi donated $325,000 to the DNC at a fund-raising event in Washington, D.C., in May 1996. His donation came in the form of buying thirteen tickets to the event for $25,000 each. His gesture allowed him to be photographed while presenting the Mahatma Gandhi World Peace Award to President Clinton. Notably, the White House had previously rejected Gandhi's offer to present Clinton the award but agreed after Gandhi's contribution of $325,000.

Again, John Huang was the solicitor of the funds. Though Gandhi had testified under oath in small claims court in August 1996 that all of his money came from his family trust in India, he changed his story in October when asked about the contributions. He said that his business had experienced an upturn because of technology transfer deals he had made with domestic and foreign companies.

The White House claimed that Gandhi's contribution was legal because he was a green-card holder—a permanent resident permitted to make campaign contributions. White House officials failed to explain how the impecunious Indian obtained his new-found wealth. They offered no reason why this man, who had no appreciable background in politics, decided to part with all of his newly acquired money. They denied that it was Gandhi's contribution that entitled him to a private audience with Clinton.

Not long after the DNC defiantly defended Gandhi's contribution, it had to eat its words. It announced on November 6, 1996, that it was returning the $325,000 donation because it could not verify that Gandhi was the source of the funds. The explanation by DNC spokeswoman Amy Weiss Tobe was revealing. She noted that "the donation was lawful on its face." But after the *Los Angeles Times* questioned its legality, she said, "We did our own investigation and ascertained that the check needed to be returned because there were so many unanswered questions."[37] Which begs the questions: Why didn't this enormous contribution from a destitute Indian-American, regardless of whether it was lawful on its face,

raise the DNC's antenna? Would it have ever questioned the donation had the *Los Angeles Times* not acted as campaign finance police?

Indeed, the *Los Angeles Times* observed that Gandhi's refund
was just one in a series of donations that had been returned only
after press inquiries exposed their dubious nature. "It fuels criti-
cisms that the [DNC] exercised little, if any, oversight of foreign
contributors in its rush to keep pace with Republicans." The
Democrats, noted the *Times*, had returned more than $700,000 in
"questionable or unlawful" donations in the six weeks preceding
the election. The *Times* exposé also led California's assistant attorney general, Carole Ritts Kornblum, to announce that as a result
of the *Times*'s inquiries, the state's Charitable Trust Section would
open an audit of Gandhi's organization, the Gandhi Memorial
International Foundation, to determine whether it had violated its
charitable exemption status.[38]

Several years later, in March 1999, Gandhi was arrested and
entered a plea of guilty to mail fraud, tax evasion, and arranging a
$325,000 illegal foreign contribution to the Democratic Party.

Republicans Cry Foul and Democrats Stonewall

Controversy exploded when the Democratic National
Committee failed to file its final preelection campaign finance
report with the Federal Election Commission. At a news conference in late October about a week before the election, Republican
National Committee chairman Haley Barbour charged that "This
refusal shows the Democrats' utter contempt for the law, for the
Federal Election Commission, and more important, their contempt for the public's right to know where the Democrats get their
money and how they spend it.... The most obvious question is,
what are Bill Clinton and the Democrats hiding?... Now, let's be

clear about one thing, the DNC's refusal to file its campaign finance report, as law requires, is not a casual act or a bureaucratic snafu. This is a coldly calculated act by very sophisticated political operatives who fully understand that they will take political heat, have a political firestorm for violating disclosure laws. Clinton and his DNC appointees have decided that whatever it is they're hiding is even more damning than openly breaking the law of public disclosure." Barbour announced that the Republican National Committee would seek a restraining order to freeze all DNC assets until the report was filed.[39]

Republicans demanded an accounting by the Democrats, but the White House and the Democratic Party continued to stall by denying wrongdoing and making reciprocal allegations against Republicans. Clinton also began to divert attention from his campaign's fund-raising illegalities by calling for new campaign finance laws. In effect Clinton was saying, "What we did was wrong but not illegal. Let's pass new laws to make our conduct illegal to prevent future candidates from engaging in the type of unethical behavior we engaged in." Four days before the election, Clinton said that it was "time for action" on bipartisan legislation limiting special interest money. He called for tightening up the laws pertaining to foreign campaign contributions. Clinton refused to apologize for his or his party's behavior. The nation's chief law enforcement officer said, "We have played by the rules. But I know and you know we need to change the rules."[40]

Of course, the idea that Clinton and his party had played by existing rules and laws was preposterous and outrageous. Clear violations of existing law were going unpunished, and the Justice Department was deliberately putting a lid on any serious investigation, including the appointment of an independent counsel. The other culprit, the Federal Election Commission, was also doing precious little to enforce the existing laws. Without question, President Clinton, Vice President Gore, and the Democratic National Committee broke the spirit, if not the letter, of the law by spending an unprecedented $35 million in soft money for their 1996 advertising campaign (this was hardly for purposes of party building per se, unless one defined the party as Bill Clinton and Al Gore's reelection effort). Campaign finance reform crusader Fred Wertheimer observed that Clinton was personally involved in circumventing campaign finance laws. Clinton and the DNC unmistakably violated the laws with respect to the large-scale solicitation and receipt of illegal foreign campaign contributions.

Just a few days before the presidential election, which Clinton/ Gore now had safely in hand, the Democratic National Committee chairman, Senator Christopher Dodd, publicly proposed that Democrats and Republicans agree, "as of today," to accept no more contributions from non-Americans (even if they were permanent residents) and ban soft-money donations from corporations. Republican chairman Haley Barbour pointed out that the Democratic proposal was malicious posturing because, while pretending to offer reform, Dodd's proposal would permit unlimited contributions from big labor, while cutting off those from big business. Barbour also pointed out that the Democrats were obscuring the fact that they had already grossly abused the law with massive illegal soft-money and foreign-money contributions. "They're trying to change the subject," said Barbour. "The subject here is they're violating the law as it exists now."[41]

The Democrats' claim that their campaign fund-raising violations were bureaucratic snafus was undercut by Democratic spokeswoman B. J. Thornberry, who confessed that the DNC allowed its standards to slide because it was "so desperate to keep up" with the Republicans' campaign funds.

Why were the Democrats so hard up for money? Ironically, it was because the Democrats, for decades, had relied on big business for their campaign contributions, despite their relative unfriendliness to corporate America. As a practical matter, big business had no choice because the Democratic Party had a monopoly on Congress for decades. Big business supported the Democrats, hoping to avoid being punished with even more stifling taxes and regulations. When Republicans captured Congress in 1994, corporations suddenly felt free to donate to the party of free enterprise, and the Democrats, for the most part, would have to look elsewhere.[42]

Because the labor unions couldn't make up the shortfall by themselves, the Democrats were desperate for a new source of funds and had to rely on the only card they had—Bill Clinton and Al Gore. While the president and the vice president have little direct power, by themselves, over American businesses, the president can wield enormous power on foreign policy. In the Clinton White House, Al Gore was given a leading role in foreign affairs, especially with regard to Russia, international environmental treaties, and other matters. White House initiatives here could have a major effect on foreign businesses. That power, and President Clinton and Vice President Gore's willingness to use it and sell it, is the most likely explanation for the Democrats' all-out rush on foreign donors. To attribute these innumerable and bizarrely interconnected foreign contributions to accident or coincidence requires an unparalleled suspension of disbelief.[43]

Some Democrats weren't buying the party line. Jerome Zeifman, chief Democratic counsel to the House Judiciary Committee during the Watergate impeachment inquiry, denounced his fellow Democrats. "In some ways, this is a lot worse than Watergate, because the Democrats in my party are marching in lockstep in support of a corrupt president," he said.[44] Democratic senator Russell Feingold also broke ranks, joining House Speaker Newt Gingrich in calling for the appointment of an independent counsel to investigate the foreign contributions to the DNC.

Connections to Iraqis, Russians, and Drugs

On October 21, 1996, the DNC hosted a Detroit fund-raiser organized by Chaldeans, members of an Iraqi Christian minority who were anxious to persuade President Clinton to end the economic embargo against Iraq. Clinton personally attended the fund-raiser, where the party netted some $800,000. Julie Danou, the niece of the event's organizer, said that the president was receptive to the idea of relaxing sanctions. "It was to help Iraq, to help the people there, to open sanctions," said Danou. Clinton, she said, seemed responsive and promised to work toward "lifting the embargo and help send food and medicine to the kids and the Iraqi people." Danou, whose family members were Iraqi natives, estimated that her family contributed between $400,000 and $500,000 to the DNC at the event. Clinton campaign press secretary Joe Lockhart vehemently denied any improprieties connected with the fund-raiser. "The gentleman is an American citizen. The contributions are legal," said Lockhart.[45] In any event, the Chaldeans were given a lesson in Clintonism: he felt their pain, pocketed their money, and then forgot about them, allowing his secretary of state Madeleine Albright to keep the screws on Iraq.

Another interesting fund-raiser involved Grigory Loutchansky. *Time* magazine described him as "the most pernicious unindicted criminal in the world." He had attended a fund-raising dinner for the president in October 1993 but was reportedly turned away from a Democratic fund-raiser in July 1995 when the party discovered that Nordex, his Vienna-based company, had been established by the Russian KGB and was suspected of helping transfer nuclear materials to North Korea and Iran.[46] President Clinton's former CIA director R. James Woolsey was shocked that Loutchansky had even been invited to the 1995 event, let alone the 1993 event, as his reputation was well known. "Next to Loutchansky," he said, "the Lippo syndicate looks like the Better Business Bureau. At a bare minimum, any DNC invitation to Loutchansky in 1995 would show a severe lack of scrutiny and appalling judgment. It would be unwise in the extreme for there to be any ties between the U.S. government and Loutchansky or Loutchansky's company, Nordex."[47]

But the Clintons and the Democratic Party did not seem very particular where their money came from. They even invited a Miami drug kingpin to the White House for Christmas dinner after he donated $20,000 to the Democratic National Committee. At the Christmas party he was photographed with first lady Hillary Clinton. The DNC returned the $20,000 when the matter became public. His record, too, was no secret. He had been imprisoned in the 1980s on narcotics charges. He was arrested again in January 1997 during a Miami drug bust that yielded three tons of cocaine. He pled guilty to one drug count, and his attorney said that the $20,000 contribution to the Clintons was not intended to buy protection for drug smuggling; it was a business investment. "He had a lobster and stone crab fishery in the Keys and felt that the contribution might promote that future course," said the attorney.[48]

The Justice Department's First Dodge

After the election, the DNC promised reforms of its fund-raising apparatus, including database searches to verify the legal status of donating corporations and individuals. DNC chairman Donald Fowler said, "It is truly difficult for me to express the disappointment that I feel personally at the turn of events of the past few weeks. Mistakes were made, and we have set out to correct them." Donald Simon, executive vice president of Common Cause, a vocal critic of the campaign finance violations, implied the DNC's reforms were meaningless window dressing. "This is a little bit like rearranging the deck chairs on the Titanic to make sure they're all aligned when the ship hits the iceberg," said Simon.[49]

On the Friday following the election, which offered White House spinmeisters a convenient weekend news hiatus, the administration quietly admitted that Mark Middleton, a former White House employee and a friend of John Huang, had abused his White House access to impress business clients. Middleton, like Huang, had been implicated in illegal fund-raising activities for the Democratic Party.[50]

Under growing pressure from Republicans (and a few Democrats) to appoint an independent counsel, Attorney General Janet Reno finally announced, in mid-November, safely after the election, that she would not do so. Instead, she turned the matter over to a special task force of the Justice Department's Criminal Division, Public Integrity Section. The task force would have the power to prosecute cases or recommend referral to an independent counsel. Around the same time, the Commerce Department said that it would conduct its own investigation into the activities of John Huang.

A few months after the Justice Department Task Force was formed, it issued more than forty subpoenas. One of them went to John Huang.

The Thai Connection

With Clinton-Gore reelected, the Democrats let their guard down a bit. A few weeks after the election the DNC stated that it had returned $253,000 more in campaign contributions—this time from a Thai businesswoman, Pauline Kanchanalak, who was a permanent U.S. resident. She had illegally fronted a donation for her Thai mother-in-law, who, oddly, was also a permanent U.S. resident and could have made a legal donation herself. Why, then, the illegal front? Perhaps because, as DNC press secretary Amy Weiss Tobe conceded, the ubiquitous John Huang had raised $135,000 of the money. And there were other dubious strings attached. Pauline Kanchanalak was president of Ban Chang International, a Washington business-consulting company specializing in recruiting American investment for Thailand. The company was connected to the Thai conglomerate the Ban Chang group.[51] Kanchanalak was a regular visitor to the White House during the presidential campaign (she made twenty-six trips to the White House), and she had worked with John Huang when he was at the Commerce Department. Just as troubling, this brought the total DNC refunds of illegal contributions to more than $1 million.

The Lums

At the end of November the *Chicago Tribune* reported that Gene and Nora Lum had been "hosts and sponsors" of a presidential gala in August 1996 that had raised $2.5 million for the Democratic Party. The problem was that federal authorities had been investigating the Lums for more than a year. It was suspected that their political fund-raising was intended to buy access to the Commerce Department and influence it to advance their business interests. In 1991, then-DNC chairman Ron Brown had appointed Nora Lum to be executive director of APAC, the Asia Pacific Advisory Council (a new Democratic Party office), whose responsibility was to raise money and enlist support among Asian

Americans for the Clinton-Gore ticket. The *Tribune* disclosed that three of the employees working in APAC's Torrance, California, office estimated that APAC raised between $250,000 and $1 million in contributions but had filed no reports concerning those contributions with the Federal Election Commission. DNC spokeswoman Amy Weiss Tobe said that the DNC could find no records concerning the Torrance office, and no contributions or costs for APAC's rent, utilities, or phone bank were listed on the DNC's disclosure forms.[52]

The House Government Reform Committee announced that if the Lums would testify about a scheme to funnel foreign money to Democratic campaigns in 1992, the committee would try to get them legal immunity. The Lums claimed to know details about a foreign donor giving $50,000 to the Democratic Party in 1992 in exchange for a Clinton-Gore campaign letter endorsing the leader of an Asian nation—a letter the Lums said had been signed by a campaign official in then-governor Clinton's name. The Justice Department strongly opposed the immunity, saying it "would cause serious and irreparable harm to the ongoing criminal investigation" of the Lums.[53]

Charlie Trie and the Chinese Embassy

In late December a report surfaced that Wang Jun, the head of a weapons-trading company owned by the Chinese military and the head of a major investment conglomerate owned by the Red Chinese government, had been invited to a Clinton White House coffee earlier in the year. Another close friend of President Clinton, Charles Yah Lin Trie, a restaurateur from Little Rock, was responsible for inviting Jun to the coffee. Trie was a naturalized American born in Taiwan. Trie's name had been in the news earlier for having raised $640,000 in illegal foreign money for the president's legal defense fund. Trie had visited the White House some thirty-one times in 1994 and 1995. During 1996, he worked very closely with John Huang in fund-raising for the Democratic Party. Republican congressman Jerry Solomon, chairman of the House Rules Committee, which was considering whether a special or standing committee should investigate the Democratic fund-raising scandals, said, "It's one thing for the President of the United States to look the other way when China arms nations hostile to us, when it isn't too busy flooding our markets with cheap, slave-labor goods. But it's another thing to smile and shake hands with China's number one arms supplier, right at the White House. What is this administration thinking? And how can Congress conduct the people's business, including our security, when we can hardly keep up with the new revelations every day?"[54]

A few months later the Justice Department began to investigate allegations that the Chinese embassy in Washington, D.C., had tried to direct money to the Democratic National Committee for the 1996 election. Watergate-famed reporter Bob Woodward broke the embassy story on the front page of the *Washington Post* on February 13, 1997. Woodward said that his sources "declined to provide details about the scope of the evidence" or to specify what foreign contributors were solicited but that "the new evidence now being scrutinized is serious."[55]

The FBI in 1996 had warned six members of Congress that China had targeted them for illegal contributions to be funneled through foreign corporations. One of the six, Senator Dianne Feinstein, at the time sat on the East Asian and Pacific Affairs Subcommittee of the Foreign Relations Committee, which oversees relations between the United States and China. Feinstein had written an editorial in the *Los Angeles Times* in support of permanent Most Favored Nation status for China, arguing that it would be a mistake to condition China's trade status on its human rights record. According to the FBI, "We have reason to believe that the government of China may try to make contributions to members of Congress through Asian donors." Feinstein shortly thereafter was embarrassed to have to return $12,000 in contributions she had received from contributors connected with the Lippo Group.

More alarming was the FBI revelation that it had acquired "conclusive evidence" that the Chinese government transferred monies into the United States and laundered it for use in political races. Intelligence sources were certain that the Chinese government was intending to influence U.S. policy—specifically targeting congressional votes to grant China Most Favored Nation trade status in the spring of 1995. Intelligence also showed that in early 1995 the Chinese had planned to spend some $2 million to buy influence in the Clinton administration and Congress.[56]

Some of the intelligence information came from electronic eavesdropping by federal agencies. The report contained the obligatory denial by a Chinese embassy spokesman who said the Chinese government did nothing to improperly influence the administration. The White House, through press secretary Mike McCurry, also issued its denials. "To the best of my knowledge," said McCurry, "no one here had any knowledge of" the allegations. The information was taken seriously enough, however, that the Justice Department increased the number of FBI special agents working on the Justice Department Task Force investigation from a few to twenty-five. According to the report, the Chinese government had been trying to win influence with the Clinton administration since Clinton first took office. During the campaign,

Clinton had criticized President Bush for coddling Beijing and giving China Most Favored Nation trade status after the 1989 crackdown in Tiananmen Square.[57]

The Reform Diversion

As the new year began and reports of illegal contributions kept pouring in, President Clinton and the Democrats continually tried to divert attention from the scandal by stepping up their calls for campaign finance reform legislation. Their public relations offensive led willing media voices to blame the system, rather than the Democrats, for fund-raising abuses. "The current system has indicted itself: apparently illegal foreign contributions in the presidential campaign, television attack ads that traffic in character assassination, lavish corporate and labor contributions to political parties, each argues for swift and sweeping reform," wrote one news service, completely discounting any Democratic culpability.[58]

Congressional proponents of reform played into this "broken system theory" because by avoiding partisan blame, they hoped to win bipartisan support for changes in the law. The scandal, said reporters picking up on this angle, was not illegality but loopholes. "Campaign-finance laws have bigger, more imaginative loopholes than the Internal Revenue Code," wrote two reporters. "They are easier to cheat on, and not get caught, than Medicare. And just like the gold-plated congressional pension system, they are designed to serve incumbents."[59]

Later, the Federal Election Commission, in testimony before Congress, also attributed the scandals to problems with the system. The commission insisted that to be an effective watchdog it would require a substantial boost in funding. The commission was created in 1974 following Watergate.[60]

These efforts at scapegoating the system led to renewed enthusiasm for the McCain-Feingold campaign finance reform bill. The bill proposed banning political action committee (PAC) contributions to all federal candidates and imposing severe restrictions on soft-money contributions, among other things. President Clinton gladly jumped on the reform bandwagon, opportunistically pledging his support of the bill. Clinton also praised the DNC's announcement that it would no longer accept contributions from legal immigrants or from U.S. subsidiaries of foreign corporations and would limit single contributions to $100,000. Clinton applauded the new policy as "sound and necessary" and "the first steps in the reforms we need." Democratic National Committee chairman Steven Grossman chimed in, "We're taking steps way beyond the current law in order to show good faith." Vice President Al Gore agreed. "Take this step with us, walk with us side by side," said Gore. "We're putting our money where our mouth is."

Less than a week later, Clinton, almost predictably, lashed out at Republicans, saying, "They raise more money, they raise more foreign money, they raise more money in big contributions, and we take all the heat. It's a free ride." A day after the charge, White House officials were still scrambling to provide a shred of documentation to support the president's outlandish claim.[61]

Clinton's enthusiasm for the Democratic Party's pledge to police itself quickly waned. Toward the end of February he attended a New York fund-raiser for the Democratic Senate Campaign Committee (DSCC), which was estimating total collections of $1 million, a good portion of which would be soft money. When asked about Clinton's apparent change of heart after having endorsed the party's self-imposed restrictions, White House press secretary

Mike McCurry brushed it off, saying that the DSCC doesn't play by the same rules as the DNC and the president's campaign committee. "Candidates will have to raise money and some committees will not have the same view we do about soft money," said McCurry.[62]

Within a few short months, the Democrats not only reversed themselves on their policy not to accept contributions from legal immigrants or U.S. subsidiaries of foreign corporations but actually targeted legal immigrants for campaign contributions and as foot soldiers for the party. Shamelessly, the DNC chiefs announced on May 3, 1997, the formation of a new committee to reach out to "citizens-in-waiting"—16.5 million resident aliens. "While we don't excuse the practices that were wrong and corrupt," said newly appointed Democratic Party chairman Roy Romer, those Asian Americans who made illegal campaign contributions "ought not to be used as a characterization of a whole community."[63]

More Revelations

Under intense pressure the Democratic National Committee conducted an internal audit and discovered more potentially illegal contributions. Prior to the audit, reported in late February 1997, the DNC had returned $1.6 million of illegal or questionable contributions. A White House official said that as a result of the audit the Democratic Party would have to return an additional $1 million worth of contributions. Meanwhile, Roy Romer reiterated calls for Congress to enact stricter campaign finance laws. Apparently, without new laws, the Democrats would find it impossible to respect the old ones. But Romer did admit that President Clinton should not have held fund-raising coffees in the White House.[64]

The problem, however, wasn't limited to the White House. Federal Election Commission records showed that Keshi Zhan, who was connected to Charlie Trie and Thai businesswoman Pauline Kanchanalak, made illegal foreign contributions to the campaigns of House minority leader Richard Gephardt and Senate minority leader Tom Daschle.

Chapter Eight

The Mother of All Scandals
Moves to Congress

In early December 1996, Senate majority leader Trent Lott announced that the Senate would open a probe of the campaign finance scandal. The Senate Governmental Affairs Committee, under the leadership of Senator Fred Thompson, would conduct the investigation. The Senate Rules Committee approved $4.35 million for the investigation, about two-thirds of the $6.5 million requested, but higher than the $3 million proposed by the Democrats. Senator Thompson said he could live with the reduced funding because the FBI agreed to contribute $800,000 for its agents assisting with the probe. At the heart of the FBI's inquiry would be a closer look at three of the principal fundraisers associated with illegal foreign contributions: John Huang, Charlie Trie, and Pauline Kanchanalak.

To keep the proceedings bipartisan, Senate Republicans eventually capitulated to the Democrats' demand that the investigation cover the general need for campaign finance reform and not focus exclusively on criminal violations of existing laws. Senator Joseph

Lieberman said the Republican surrender was "the best sign yet that we may yet pass some campaign finance reform." Left unsaid was that by commingling the issues of reform with specific acts of illegality, the Democrats hoped to dilute and confuse the congressional hearings.

Senate majority leader Trent Lott then acquiesced to another Democratic demand and imposed a December 31, 1997, deadline on the investigation. Thompson warned that the deadline would give the White House an incentive to stonewall and to withhold requested documents.[1] Thompson's prediction was born out. His committee's postinvestigation report made this observation: "The imposition of the December 31, 1997, deadline virtually invited witnesses to engage in obstructive tactics, perhaps none more than the DNC and the White House. This obstruction, combined with the sheer complexity of the investigation, made this deadline the single greatest obstacle faced by the Committee's inquiry."[2]

House Begins Hearings

On the other side of the Capitol, Congressman Dan Burton, who chaired the House Government Reform and Oversight Committee, began the House's campaign finance scandal probe by issuing more than one hundred subpoenas. But, at the beginning of the investigation, Burton lost a tactical decision to limit the scope of the investigation, just as had happened in the Senate. Certain Republicans, fearful that they would otherwise be viewed as too partisan, joined with Democrats in agreeing to widen the parameters of the probe to include allegations of Republican campaign finance misconduct. "Once we get into an investigation, it shouldn't be limited. It should be open to all aspects," said Congressman Benjamin Gilman. "We'll go without reference to party," added Congressman Steven LaTourette. It was left to Congressman John McHugh to observe, "I don't want to prejudge where we'll go, and I'm not ruling anything out, but the preponderance of evidence is substantively about the White House."[3]

When the White House failed to turn over all the records subpoenaed by Burton's committee, Burton threatened contempt proceedings against it. Burton asked White House counsel Charles F. C. Ruff to appear on Capitol Hill and explain why the White House hadn't supplied all the documents, accusing the administration of "stonewalling." "Rather than produce the documents essential to a complete investigation, the president continues to withhold these records based on novel claims of exemption and purely political complaints about the committee's document security protocol," said all twenty-two Republican committee members in a statement.[4]

Ultimately the House committee faced incredible obstacles to its investigation, far beyond the inevitable stalling by the White House and the DNC. One hundred and twenty subpoenaed witnesses either fled the country or pled the Fifth Amendment.

Al Gore: Solicitor-in-Chief

Vice President Gore was at the center of the Democratic Party's fund-raising efforts for the 1996 election. Both he and Clinton received weekly reports of the DNC fund-raising meetings. Both men micromanaged strategies to acquire more funds. Clinton personally reviewed "mind-numbing campaign budget minutia on a weekly, and sometimes daily basis." Clinton and Gore were also well aware that their activities were illegal. In a memo from Harold Ickes reporting that the DNC would have to set aside $1.5 million for audit costs and another $1 million for potential fines from the Federal Election Commission, Clinton scribbled in the margin, "Ugh"—clearly revealing his awareness that they were breaking the law.[5]

Gore made personal phone calls, soliciting big donations in what was described as a heavy-handed and offensive manner. It was unprecedented for a vice president to inject himself into direct solicitation, but because Clinton didn't like to make the calls, Gore had to. He soon acquired the moniker "solicitor-in-chief." One person commented that Gore sounded more like the DNC finance director than the vice president of the United States. In at least one case, Democrats admitted there was an uncomfortable connection between the solicitation of funds and government action. After Secretary of Commerce Ron Brown helped a Texas telecommunications company acquire a $36 million contract in Mexico, the firm contributed $100,000 to the Democratic National Committee. Gore personally called an executive at the company to thank him for the donation.

In addition to his phone solicitation, Gore made many personal appearances at fund-raising events during the campaign. He was the featured draw in thirty-nine events outside the White House that raised $8.74 million for the DNC. He was the principal attraction at twenty-three White House coffees, accompanied Clinton at eight more such gatherings, and opened up the vice president's residence for other fund-raising parties. All together, Gore was responsible for raising $40 million of the DNC's $180 million take during the election cycle.

Some of Gore's targets were offended by his high-pressure approach. One, who was supposedly a longtime Gore friend and supporter, described his tactics as "revolting." Another donor who wrote a $100,000 check to the DNC under pressure by Gore, said,

"There were elements of a shakedown in the call. It was very awkward. For a vice president, particularly this vice president who has real power and is the heir apparent, to ask for money gave me no choice. I have so much business that touches on the federal government—the telecommunications act, tax policy, regulations galore."

Gore spokeswoman Lorraine Voles vigorously disputed the notion that there was anything untoward about Gore's direct participation in the process. "There is nothing inappropriate about the vice president calling people for money."[6]

After four months of silence—and after watching White House press secretary Mike McCurry fumbling to explain Gore's level of involvement in the mounting fund-raising scandals—Gore called a press conference. He insisted he had broken no laws, but said he would no longer make fund-raising calls from his office. Gore said that he was "very proud" of the millions of dollars he had raised through his fund-raising efforts. During the twenty-four minute conference, Gore resorted seven times to answering allegations of illegality with the statement: "My counsel advises me, let me repeat, that there is 'no controlling legal authority' that says that any of these activities violated any law." He protested that he had used a Democratic National Committee credit card when making his phone solicitations, presumably to demonstrate that his calls were for soft money and not hard money, the latter of which would have been illegal.

When confronted with a 1995 memo from then White House counsel Abner Mikva ordering White House employees not to make fund-raising calls or send mail solicitations from the White House or other federal buildings, Gore said the memo didn't apply to him or President Clinton. Gore denied reports that his solicitation calls had amounted to a shakedown of donors. "Well, I cannot explain to you what some anonymous sources want to say," said Gore. "I can tell you this, that I never, ever said or did anything that would have given rise to a feeling like that on the part of someone who was asked to support our campaign. I never did that, and I never would do that." Gore added, "I never did anything that I thought was wrong. If there had been a shred of doubt in my mind that anything I did was a violation of law, I assure you I would not have done that."

If Clinton and Gore treated their own campaign funds and DNC funds as one giant pot, that in itself had legal ramifications because, when the Clinton-Gore campaign decided to accept $62 million in public funds for the 1996 campaign, it expressly agreed to abide by the proposed spending limits. Gore denied the funds were mixed, saying, "No, there was a clear distinction" between the DNC and the Clinton-Gore campaign. "There was a separate message. There were separate legal requirements," said Gore.[7]

Round Two from the Justice Department and the Independent Counsel Act

In the spring of 1997, Janet Reno once again rebuffed Republican demands for an independent counsel to investigate the Democrats' campaign finance improprieties. She said the Justice Department's special task force would continue to handle the probe "vigorously and diligently" and added that the allegations against Clinton and other top administration officials were not specific and credible enough to trigger the independent counsel act.

In a letter to Senate Judiciary Committee chairman Orrin Hatch, Reno said, "I can assure you that I have given your views and your arguments careful thought, but at this time, I am unable to agree, based on the facts and the law, that an independent counsel should be appointed to handle this investigation." Senator Lott accused Reno of a "clear conflict of interest" and bemoaned the "politicization of the Clinton Justice Department." House Judiciary chairman Henry Hyde's reaction was even more pointed. "It is reasonable to assume that she is under enormous pressure from the White House," he said.

The controversy centered on Reno's interpretation of the Ethics in Government Act—a.k.a. the Independent Counsel Act—enacted in 1978. The law was written because the attorney general is an executive department employee under the president's command. In the case of allegations against the president or other high-ranking officials in the executive branch, the attorney general has an inherent conflict of interest. How can one be free to investigate one's boss?

The relevant part of the law required the attorney general to conduct a thirty-day review to see if further investigation was warranted. If within that thirty-day period she determined that there was specific and credible information that the president or any other top official may have violated federal criminal law—other than certain types of misdemeanors or other minor infractions—she was required to conduct a ninety-day preliminary investigation. The purpose of the preliminary investigation was to determine whether there were reasonable grounds to believe that further investigation was warranted (with respect to any alleged violation of criminal law). If so, she was required to apply to the Special Division of the District of Columbia Court of Appeals for the appointment of an independent counsel.

In her letter to Senator Hatch, Reno maintained that there was insufficient evidence that campaign contributions were illegally solicited on federal property with either the White House coffees or the Lincoln Bedroom overnights, because the private presidential residence at the White House was not considered "federal property" under the law. She discounted Gore's alleged fund-raising calls from the White House because he supposedly used a Democratic National Committee calling card, which was a "nongovernment credit card." (Reno was embarrassed—but not enough to alter her decision about an independent counsel—by the later revelation that Gore had actually placed his calls on a Clinton-Gore calling card, rather than a DNC card.) Reno also said that Gore was raising soft money, which she said was legal by virtue of a 1979 law. She denied that there was any evidence that any person covered by the statute had been involved in foreign efforts to influence United States policy. Reno made a special point of emphasizing that she had relied on "career professionals" at the Justice Department to advise her as to the applicability of the independent counsel law.[8]

The Republicans responded by publishing an open letter to President Clinton that read, in part, "The evidence of Democratic fundraising improprieties continues to mount, day after day. Among those charges: soliciting and accepting foreign funds, laundering money, cash for government favors, influencing a union election in return for campaign contributions and, not least, the possibility of espionage…. With so many senior officials of your Administration and your party under this dark cloud, it is impossible to expect officials from your Administration's Department of Justice to conduct a credible and independent investigation."[9]

The Republicans' Turn

Time magazine reported that the Republican National Committee had received illegal foreign contributions in both the

1994 and 1996 elections. Democrats on Senator Thompson's Governmental Affairs Committee called for an investigation of the charges. The allegation involved Young Brothers Development of Hong Kong and its U.S. subsidiary in Florida, Young Brothers Development, Inc. Democratic aides "wasted no time in drafting subpoenas for presentation to Chairman Fred Thompson, who agreed to issue six of them...."[10] Democrats also asked the Federal Election Commission to investigate the charges, and the Democratic National Committee's general counsel, Joseph Sandler, alleged that the "RNC actually used the National Policy Forum as a means to hide illegal contributions to the RNC."

In several hours of testimony before the Senate committee, former RNC chairman Haley Barbour made an obvious good-faith effort to meticulously rebut every charge, with charts and graphs showing how the Republicans had ensured the contributions came from a domestic company, so that there could be no question as to the facts, no ambiguity about "controlling legal authority." Not only was the allegation about illegal foreign campaign contributions to the RNC "outright false," said Barbour, but the National Policy Forum, which the Democrats had alleged was a shadow donor, was, in fact, a "siphon" of RNC funds, not a contributor, and actually owed the RNC $2.5 million.[11] That shortfall occurred because Barbour had founded the National Policy Forum with seed money from the Republican National Committee.[12]

But Barbour's charts, graphs, and eloquence were punctured in May 1997, when the Republican National Committee discovered that Young Brothers Development in Florida was, indeed, a shell company for the parent corporation in Hong Kong. The Republican National Committee immediately returned $102,400 that had been donated to it by Young Brothers. The RNC's new chairman, Jim Nicholson, said that the party had had no previous reason to believe the contributions were illegitimate but had acted as soon as it discovered otherwise. [13]

Democrats could barely contain themselves. "For months Republicans have piously proclaimed their purity on campaign finances. But the truth is now out—they have deliberately concealed receipt of foreign contributions," said DNC general chairman Roy Romer. RNC chairman Nicholson tartly replied, "As much as the Democrats would like to spread the blame for their own fundraising scandal by claiming 'everybody does it,' the facts—including the facts about this case—verify that everybody doesn't do it. Not only did the Democrats engage in an orchestrated effort to solicit illegal contributions from foreign individuals and foreign sources, they went so far as to send their own fundraisers overseas to get the money."[14] Nicholson ordered an internal audit of all Republican National Committee contributions of $5,000 or more, from 1994 forward, to determine whether any further improper contributions were made.

While Democrats insisted Republicans were equally guilty of fund-raising abuses, the Democrats ultimately were forced to return some $3.2 million—more than thirty times the amount returned by Republicans.

Nevertheless, both Congressman Burton and Senator Thompson issued subpoenas to further investigate the Young Brothers donations to the RNC. Neither man wanted to be accused of partisanship.

The White House and Democrats Orchestrate a Cover-up (With a Little Help from Their Friends at Justice)

Haley Barbour's willingness to testify was in sharp contrast to the roadblocks thrown in front of Senator Thompson by the Democratic Party. In a letter to DNC chairman Roy Romer,

Thompson said that Democratic officials were relying on attorney-client privilege to dodge inquiries, especially regarding key fund-raising figure John Huang. He said that the DNC "attorneys are blocking those inquiries in what seems to be a very calculated and selective process." The attorneys, said Thompson, were relying "on privilege claims (ranging from attorney-client privilege to work-product privilege to a common defense assertion with the White House) in order to prevent witnesses from answering relevant questions." In addition, more than forty-five witnesses had already either fled the country or refused to cooperate by asserting the Fifth Amendment. When the committee appealed to President Clinton to persuade these witnesses to cooperate, he took no action. Newspapers reported that Thompson was considering granting immunity to "lower-level players" in order to secure their testimony and cooperation with the investigation. Democrats warned Thompson that immunity could only be granted by a two-thirds majority vote of the committee.

True to their threat, Senate Democrats initially refused to grant immunity to eighteen key witnesses who had volunteered to testify. To grant immunity, Thompson needed at least two of the seven committee Democrats to break ranks, but none did initially.

Fifteen of the eighteen witnesses were Buddhist monks and nuns who, in some cases, contributed up to $5,000 at the Buddhist Temple fund-raising event. David DeBruin, an attorney for several of the witnesses, informed the committee that his clients would testify about whether "political contributions were solicited by persons outside the Temple" and whether "individuals were reimbursed for the contributions they made"[15]—in other words, about whether the penniless monks and nuns were straw contributors, fronting for the actual foreign contributors. The Justice Department prevaricated about whether immunity should be granted, first telling Senator Thompson's chief counsel, Michael Madigan, yes, and then telling Democratic senators they should oppose the immunity grants.[16] The Democrats advised that as long as Senator Thompson refused to investigate the involvement of the Christian Coalition and the National Rifle Association in Republican campaigns, they would oppose all immunity deals.

Thompson accused the Democrats of orchestrating a cover-up. Thompson—who had been the minority counsel for the Senate Watergate Committee—reminded the senators that "We should have learned from history that cover-ups do not work. They occasionally work for a while, but they never work forever. Too many people know too many things. We will stay at this task until we have peeled away the diversions, the distractions and the irrelevancies."[17]

The monks and nuns appealed to the Justice Department to grant them immunity, but Janet Reno refused. Yet at the same time Reno asserted that she didn't need to appoint an independent counsel because her prosecutors were aggressively pursuing the case.[18] Eventually Thompson's committee voted to confer immunity on nine witnesses, five of whom testified.

Opening Shots

The Senate hearings began on July 8, 1997, with opening statements. Senator Thompson said his committee's investigators had found evidence of a Chinese plan "designed to pour illegal money into American political campaigns" with the purpose of "subvert[ing] our election process" in the 1996 presidential campaign. He said that "high-level Chinese government officials" were involved with "substantial sums of money." Their effort to influence American politics by illegal activities "continues today." "There apparently was a systematic influx of illegal money in our presidential race last year," said Thompson. "We will be wanting to know: Who knew about it? Who should have known about it? And was there an attempt to cover it up?" Republican senator Pete Domenici addressed the ongoing conflict between those who wanted to investigate illegal conduct and others who were hoping to use campaign finance reform as a means to obscure violations of existing laws. "Some would suggest... we really don't need these hearings, we only need to reform the campaign laws," said Domenici. "But reforming the laws will not solve the problem if officials are already ignoring or violating those already on the books."[19] Democratic senator Carl Levin best articulated the Democrats' position. He argued that the intricate web of Democratic illegalities was no more than improper conduct, permitted by loopholes in the law. The real urgency was to reform the existing laws. "The vast majority of what we're going to hear about and the bulk of the activity that creates concern and has the largest effect on the campaign process right now is what's legal—it's what's allowed by loopholes—and most of it involves so-called soft or unregulated money."

Ranking minority member John Glenn's remarks were noteworthy for signaling the Democrats' one-upmanship approach to the hearings. He made it clear that he intended to match every charge of Democratic corruption with an equal charge of Republican corruption. "The abuses have been bipartisan, and our investigations must be bipartisan," said Glenn. [20]

Senator Glenn also said that John Huang had agreed to testify provided he be given limited immunity. Previously, Huang had said he would assert the Fifth Amendment privilege not to incriminate himself. [21]

On the second day of the hearings, Senate investigators produced a March 1994 letter from California State Senate Democratic staffer Maeley Tom to then-DNC chairman David

Wilhelm. In the letter, Tom described a plan by James Riady to funnel illegal campaign contributions from Asian business leaders to the Democratic Party. Tom saw Riady's plan as a "vehicle to raise dollars from a fresh source for the Democratic National Committee." Tom later became a consultant for Riady, a position reportedly arranged by John Huang. Tom noted that Riady had asked her to "consider working for them on a contractual basis to put together the business leaders from East Asia with the administration for meetings and education purposes." Republican senator Thad Cochran said that in her letter, Tom was clearly signaling that she was ready to raise money from East Asian business leaders for the DNC to support Clinton's reelection campaign.[22]

As the hearings continued Republicans and Democrats tussled over several issues. Was Gore aware that the Buddhist Temple event was a fund-raiser? Had John Huang actively solicited foreign contributions? Were any of the 103 White House coffees illegal fund-raisers? Had Clinton and the Democrats sold overnight stays (938 people during Clinton's first term alone) in the Lincoln Bedroom in exchange for contributions to the party? Many of the guests were friends of the Clintons; others were major contributors, donating as much as $10 million to the Democratic Party. Later, internal documents revealed that Clinton had indeed hatched a plan to exploit the White House and the trappings of the presidency for fund-raising. President Clinton personally scratched a note across one fund-raising memo saying, "Ready to start overnights right away."

At the hearings, Democrats portrayed Huang as an honorable man. But Richard Sullivan, former DNC finance director, had admitted in an interview with Senate investigators that DNC officials had been nervous about associating with Huang because of the possibility that he might solicit illegal foreign campaign contributions.

Johnny Chung

The committee produced evidence of another figure allegedly involved in soliciting foreign contributions: Johnny Chung. Chung reportedly contributed more than $360,000 to the DNC and visited the White House some fifty times. He allegedly received a wire transfer of $150,000 from the Bank of China around the same time he gave Maggie Williams, Hillary Clinton's chief of staff, a $50,000 check, presumably for President Clinton's reelection campaign. Chung allegedly made the donation in exchange for access for himself and five Chinese businessmen to a Clinton radio address. That access was granted despite the protests of former DNC finance director Richard Sullivan. [23]

Hip Hing Holdings and the 1992 Campaign

A week into the hearings senators presented evidence of a $50,000 contribution to the DNC Victory Fund on behalf of Hip Hing Holdings of Los Angeles, a subsidiary of the Indonesian conglomerate, the Lippo Group. Because Hip Hing's only asset was a $10 million tract of real estate in Los Angeles (a vacant Chinatown parking lot), Republicans charged that it was Lippo's shell company, existing for the sole purpose of laundering money to the Democratic Party. The senators had a genuine "smoking gun" on this contribution, in the form of a memo from the president's friend John Huang to Lippo, requesting that Lippo "please kindly wire" the money to cover the contribution. The memo explicitly earmarked the funds for the DNC. The money was wired that day from Lippo's Jakarta headquarters to Hip Hing's U.S. bank account. Republicans also produced the check from Hip Hing to the DNC Victory Fund.

Hip Hing bookkeeper Juliana Utomo testified to the committee that she had authorized the $50,000 check to the DNC but was "unaware that the initials stood for the Democratic National Committee." Even Senator Joe Lieberman had to acknowledge that "There's a pretty clear document here requesting a reimbursement for a $50,000 donation to the DNC Victory Fund, which certainly looks like the movement of foreign money into an American campaign in 1992."[24] The Democratic National Committee responded by announcing that it would return the $50,000 contribution.

Republicans reported that the Lippo Group had subsidized three other unprofitable businesses that had made political contributions to the DNC. Juliana Utomo, the company's bookkeeper, said that Hip Hing showed annual losses of more than $400,000 in the early 1990s with less than $40,000 of income being generated from the company's Los Angeles parking lot. Utomo testified that the company survived only because of regular infusions of cash from Lippo's headquarters in Jakarta, Indonesia. (Under federal election law, U.S. subsidiaries or affiliates of foreign companies can only contribute to U.S. political campaigns money they directly produce.)

As the hearings continued, the committee presented further evidence that the seeds of the 1996 campaign corruption began in 1992, with John Huang being the constant figure. "Obviously Mr. Huang has been willing to put illegal foreign money into the United States longer than we first knew," said Senator Thompson.[25]

Enter the Red Chinese

Another bombshell exploded when Republican senators produced evidence that Eric Hotung, a Hong Kong businessman with ties to the Red Chinese government, promised to contribute $100,000 in 1995 to the Democratic Party in exchange for a meeting with White House National Security officials to discuss the administration's China policy. Shortly after this disclosure, the White House admitted that Hotung had in fact met with then-deputy national security advisor Sandy Berger on October 4, 1995, but insisted that it was not linked to any money pledge.[26]

White House counsel Lanny Davis said, "Mr. Berger had no knowledge of any contributions or promise of contributions by Mr. Hotung." On October 12, eight days after the meeting, Eric Hotung's wife, Patricia, wrote a $20,000 check to the DNC and the next day she wrote another one for $79,000. White House aides insisted that the meeting between Hotung and Berger and the Hotungs' subsequent contributions to the DNC did not result in a change in United States policy toward Taiwan. Senator Thompson viewed it differently. "The documents," said Thompson, "set forth pretty clear evidence that a foreign citizen, I think through his wife, offered to make a $100,000 contribution in exchange for assistance in arranging a meeting with a top official."

Huang/Lippo/China Resources/Red Chinese Government

Republican senator Susan Collins of Maine produced documentary evidence establishing that John Huang had made some four-hundred telephone calls to his friends at the Lippo group while he was working at the Clinton Commerce Department. The committee also heard testimony from Thomas Hampson, a business intelligence expert, that Lippo was connected to a company called China Resources, which was "an agent of espionage" completely controlled by the Chinese government. Hampson said Lippo had dozens of joint ventures with similar firms that were owned by the Chinese government. Hampson characterized Lippo as a Communist Chinese-Indonesian joint venture. Evidence was introduced to show that Lippo's ties to the Red Chinese had increased over the last five years.

The Democrats rushed forward a member of the board of directors for the Lippo Bank in San Francisco who described John Huang as "a very fine, honest" man.[27] But it became clear that the Riady family had orchestrated the effort to install John Huang at the Democratic National Committee. There was indisputable evidence that James Riady had lobbied both Donald Fowler—who was then chairman of the Democratic Party—and President Clinton himself to bring Huang to the DNC as a fund-raiser.[28]

As the damning evidence accumulated, the White House spouted its usual lines: "This is old news." "Everyone does it." "The Republicans are just as guilty." "We did nothing wrong." "The laws need to be changed." The administration, however, offered no explanations for its refusal to encourage witnesses, such as Charlie Trie, John Huang, or Pauline Kanchanalak to cooperate with investigators. It didn't explain why witnesses to Democratic corruption were taking refuge in foreign countries, eluding investigators.

Charlie Trie

Senate investigators also produced evidence that Ng Lap Seng (a.k.a. Mr. Wu), a Chinese developer who served on a Chinese Communist government advisory commission, had illegally given more than $750,000 over three years to the Democratic Party through Bill Clinton's old friend Charlie Trie. During that same period Trie passed along more than $1.4 million in donations to the Democratic National Committee and Clinton's legal defense fund, all of which had to be returned. Before Clinton's presidential campaign in 1992, Charlie Trie had never contributed more than $100 to any political campaign. But Trie, his wife, and his company together gave $202,000 to the Democratic Party between 1994 and 1996. Trie was allegedly tied to both fellow fund-raiser John Huang and the Lippo Group. Trie would not testify because he fled to China and refused to respond to subpoenas.[29]

Still, the committee discovered that Trie was involved in another money laundering scheme. Two Chinese women who were green-card holders testified under grants of immunity that they were asked by a friend of Charlie Trie to write checks from their personal checking accounts to the DNC. They said Trie and Ng Lap Seng then reimbursed them. One of the ladies made out two checks for a total of $20,000 and was reimbursed with one $20,000 check. The other lady wrote a $5,000 check for a Democratic National Committee fund-raiser and was also immediately reimbursed.[30]

FBI agent Jerry Campane testified that Trie's business had never cleared more than $30,000 per year and couldn't possibly fund these donations. Yet bank accounts he controlled received wire transfers totaling $905,000 from Ng Lap Seng. A substantial portion of that money made its way into the coffers of the Democratic National Committee.

As it turned out Charlie Trie was one of the most substantial contributors of illegal foreign funds to the Democratic National Committee, perhaps second only to John Huang. The DNC ultimately returned more than $2 million in contributions from Trie and Huang alone.

Vice President Gore's White House Phone Calls

Documents presented to the Senate committee showed that Vice President Gore, using his White House office telephone, sought contributions of between $25,000 and $100,000 from a minimum of forty-six people between November 1995 and May 1996. Gore's fund-raising efforts—including his calls—eventually brought in almost $3.7 million. [31]

More than $120,000 of the money Gore solicited over the phone went into a Democratic National Committee hard money account within days or weeks of the calls. Though soft money must be reported, there are no contribution limits on it. Hard money is subject to limits and other regulations and cannot be solicited from federal property. Some of the calls were charged to government phones at the White House, prompting the DNC to reimburse the U.S. Treasury $24.20. But Gore raised another problem for himself with the language he used in some of the thank-you letters he sent to contributors. In one typical letter, Gore wrote, "President Clinton and I thank you.... We appreciate your dedication to our Administration." If a solicitation contains a reference to a federal candidate or a federal election, the money is subject to federal election laws.[32]

Gore maintained that he had not expressly solicited hard-money contributions and was unaware that any money from his phone calls had ended up in hard-money accounts. Amy Weiss Tobe, a spokeswoman for the Democratic National Committee, explained that the soft money was inadvertently placed in the hard-money account. A review of the records, however, indicated that something other than inadvertence was involved. Routinely, when a contribution exceeded $20,000—the legal limit for a hard-money contribution—the excess was placed into a soft-money account. [33]

These revelations finally forced Reno's hand. On September 3, 1997, the Justice Department issued a statement that it was "reviewing allegations to determine whether the vice president illegally solicited campaign contributions on federal property [that] should warrant a preliminary investigation under the Independent Counsel Act."[34]

Buddhist Temple Fund-raiser

The White House was now worried that further senatorial investigation of Gore's fund-raising might "kill his presidential campaign." So it focused on the Buddhist Temple event and released a slew of internal documents to demonstrate that Gore was unaware it was a fund-raiser. One e-mail message from Gore said he was scheduled to attend a fund-raising event in Los Angeles. The date was the same as his Buddhist Temple appearance, but aides said it was referring to a different event.[35]

The administration tried to shift the responsibility for the "mistake" from Gore to his aides. "This is a story of mid-level Gore staff people not communicating what they had learned," said an administration official. Another said, "This is a shot across the bow. Anyone who suggests the slightest knowledge by Al Gore of the illegal reimbursement scheme we will not permit to go unchallenged."

But the documentary evidence against Gore was more convincing than the denials. One memo from John Huang to Gore's scheduling director Kimberly Tilley about the event was titled, "Fund-raising lunch for Vice President Gore." Another internal e-mail message referred to the event as a "DNC funder for lunch." Finally, a draft schedule of one Gore aide referred to the contribution amounts: "DNC Luncheon in LA/Hacienda Heights: 1000-5000 head."

DNC finance officials delivered Gore a briefing memo telling him that his role was to thank the Asian American donor council members that would be attending the event for their past support and to "inspire political and fund-raising efforts among the Asian Pacific American Community."[36]

Two nuns testifying before the Senate committee told about their frantic effort to conceal the Buddhist Temple's level of involvement in fund-raising for the Democratic National Committee. They were panic-stricken when they read newspaper stories about Gore's presence at the event. They described how the temple reimbursed eleven different contributors for the $5,000 each had given to the Democratic Party immediately after the gathering. One nun testified that she threw away a list of attendees and the amounts of their contributions to avoid embarrassment to the temple.[37]

The Senate committee's final report concluded that Vice President Gore "was well aware" that the Democratic Party event in April 1996 at the Buddhist Temple "was designed to raise money for his party." The committee criticized Gore for his "lack of candor" about the event. "While there are obvious reasons for the vice president to wish to distance himself from the temple event by claiming that he had no idea fundraising was involved, such a claim is improbable." The committee based its conclusion on two primary facts: first, that Gore knew the event's organizers, Maria Hsia and John Huang, specifically as key fund-raisers with the DNC; second, the numerous memoranda and White House e-mails that repeatedly referred to the event as a fund-raiser.[38]

Roger Tamraz and the National Security Council

Another unlikely contributor to the Democratic National Committee was Roger Tamraz, an Egyptian-American oil financier.

A shady character, Tamraz was wanted in Lebanon on embezzlement charges. During the 1996 election cycle he contributed $300,000 to the Democratic Party and its candidates. Tamraz wanted to construct an oil pipeline from the Caspian Sea region of Central Asia to Western markets, and was hoping his donations to the DNC would win White House support for his project. For his contribution, he was permitted to attend a White House coffee with President Clinton—even though the National Security Council objected, and White House security had not cleared him for access.

Sheila Heslin, a former aide for the National Security Council, testified before the Senate committee that officials of the Central Intelligence Agency, the Energy Department, and the Democratic National Committee separately pressured her into approving Tamraz's access to President Clinton and other top administration officials.

One of those who applied pressure, said Heslin, was Energy official John Carter. He told her that Clinton advisor Mack McLarty was interested in the pipeline project and wanted Tamraz to meet Clinton. Carter added that Tamraz had given $200,000 to the DNC and would give another $400,000 if he could get a personal audience with the president. Heslin described the call from Carter as unpleasant. "He was pressuring me," said Heslin. "I'd never had a conversation with Jack like that before or since. He is a gentleman and he wasn't very gentlemanly during that talk. He said that Mack was also representing this because the president wanted him to do this."

Heslin, who described the Carter call as her "worst in government," was unmoved. She told Carter that she would ask senior National Security Council officials to intervene if Carter continued to pursue a Tamraz-Clinton meeting. Carter said she "shouldn't be such a Girl Scout."

McLarty denied having spoken to Carter about Tamraz, and Carter denied to Senate investigators before the hearing that he pressured Heslin or that he said that Tamraz's donations to the DNC were contingent on a meeting with Clinton. Yet Heslin's contemporaneous handwritten notes after Carter's call contained the words, "Roger Tamraz-DNC" and "$400,000-$200,000" and "Pres want." Tellingly, when Carter testified under oath, he did not contest Heslin's version of their conversation. White House records showed that Tamraz attended six Clinton social events at the White House between 1995 and 1996.

Heslin also testified that a CIA agent—described only as "Bob of the CIA"—gave her misleading information about Tamraz. At Bob's request, Heslin met with Tamraz in June 1995. Bob called her four times after that, "lobbying on behalf of Roger Tamraz."

When Heslin stood her ground and continued to block the meeting, Tamraz went to DNC chairman Don Fowler. Fowler then called Heslin two times and informed her that "Bob" would ease her apprehensions about Tamraz. "I tell you I was shocked" by the Fowler calls, said Heslin. Fowler claimed to have no memory of such contacts.[39]

Following Heslin's testimony, a defiant Roger Tamraz made no apologies for using his money to buy access to President Clinton. He admitted that the only reason he contributed $300,000 to Democrats during the 1996 election cycle was to gain influence with the president. When Senator Lieberman asked Tamraz if he got his money's worth, Tamraz responded, "I think next time I'll give $600,000."

The DNC and the Teamsters—Contribution Swaps

The Senate Governmental Affairs Committee reported that labor unions and their political action committees spent more than $119 million during the 1996 election cycle on political contributions—to federal candidates, on political and issue advertising, and other arguably campaign-related activities. This was made possible only by an aggressive, coordinated effort by the White House, the Clinton-Gore campaign, and the DNC to entice labor to contribute unprecedented sums. In the process, the Democratic fundraising apparatus and certain labor unions engaged in a variety of illegal and improper acts.

The Teamsters supported Republican presidential candidates in the 1980, 1984, and 1988 elections. But in 1992, under new leadership, they shifted their allegiance to the Democratic Party and strongly supported Bill Clinton in his first presidential campaign. Across the board in 1992, the Teamsters contributed to the Democratic structure, including state campaigns, the DNC, the Clinton-Gore campaign, congressional campaigns, and various other efforts. The union also supplied an enormous amount of manpower to assist in the campaigns.[40]

After 1992 the union was undergoing internal strife and much of its energy and resources were being devoted to expenditures on internal politics. As a result, the union failed to contribute to the DNC in 1993 or 1994. Its problems continued into 1995 because union president Ron Carey faced a tough reelection challenge in 1996 from Jimmy Hoffa Jr. In 1995, as the Clinton-Gore campaign machine geared up for the president's reelection effort, the White House began to devise ways to reinvigorate the Teamsters' enthusiasm for the Democratic cause. The White House, largely under the leadership of aide Harold Ickes, arranged for the president and other administration officials to develop closer contacts with labor leaders. Many meetings took place where the White House offered assistance to the union on various policy initiatives.

In one White House document, entitled "Teamster Notes," the administration emphasized the importance of altering substantive policy as a means of generating the union's political loyalty. In the document, under the section "Recommendations," the administration telegraphed its plan. "It is in our best interest to develop a better relationship with Carey.... Carey is not a schmoozer—he wants results on issues he cares about. The Diamond Walnut strike and the organizing effort at Pony Express are two of Carey's biggest problems. We should assist in any way possible." The administration acted on the recommendations. Harold Ickes met with important union officials concerning the Diamond Walnut Strike, the Pony Express issue, and other matters. Based on the meetings, the Clinton administration agreed to take action that could help the Teamsters in these policy areas.

The White House strategy paid off. William Hamilton, the Teamsters' government affairs director, in a memo dated March 14, 1996, acknowledged President Clinton's hands-on policy assistance on countless issues and recommended the Teamsters endorse Clinton. Hamilton wrote, "It's also a fact that we ask for and get, on almost a daily basis, help from the Clinton Administration for one thing or another. In the absence of a better candidate, it doesn't make sense to complicate our ability to continue doing so." Hamilton's memo grew more specific. He continued:

> But let's understand each other. We need Bill Clinton and Bill
> Clinton needs us. Every day we get help in small ways from Bill

Clinton—he makes a phone call, he uses the veto threat, he makes an appointment. In the last few months [he]:

- Stopped the NAFTA border crossings.
- Told his negotiators to open up Japanese airports to UPS planes, competitively disadvantaged to FedEx there. (We asked him to do it.)
- Killed a provision that Dole wrote into the budget bill to make it easy for newspapers to contract out our work.
- Guaranteed a veto on Davis-Bacon repeat.
- His NLRB has changed the rules to make it easier to get hearings and decisions toward single-cit [sic] unit determination.
- He stood up against cuts in OSHA, job training.
- He promised to veto the TEAM Act and FLSA changes.[41]

Though Clinton had certainly rekindled the Teamsters' spirit of loyalty for his effort, it was going to be very difficult for the union to support him to the extent it had in the past. The union's internal political battles continued to compete for resources and the White House brain trust would have to design innovative solutions if it expected to restore Teamster support to its former levels.

To remedy the situation the DNC arranged for a quid pro quo with the Teamsters. They would each indirectly funnel monies to the other in what the Senate committee referred to as a "contribution-swap scheme." The DNC would arrange for a major donation to Ron Carey's reelection campaign and in return the Teamsters would direct $1 million to state Democratic parties.[42]

Ultimately, the scheme resulted in criminal convictions for three of Teamster president Ron Carey's top campaign aides who entered pleas of guilty on September 18, 1997, to criminal fraud and conspiracy charges connected to the Teamsters' arrangement with the DNC. The scheme involved the DNC arranging for the transfer of illegal cash payments from other labor unions and foreign citizens to Carey's reelection campaign. The three defendants detailed a plan whereby the Teamsters agreed to contribute huge sums to the Democratic Party in exchange for the DNC directing a foreign citizen to contribute $100,000 to Carey. The foreign citizen wanted to contribute money to the DNC, but the DNC convinced him to divert his funds to the union leader. The Teamsters then pledged hundreds of thousands of dollars to the Democratic Party.[43]

Wherever investigators dug, they found new tunnels of DNC-Clinton-Gore corruption. The piles of illegal money had now grown so tall that even Janet Reno couldn't ignore the scandal.

Chapter Nine

The Mother of All Scandals and the Justice Department

J anet Reno admitted on September 5, 1997, that her Justice Department task force first learned that much of the money solicited by Vice President Gore from his White House office went into hard-money accounts from a *Washington Post* story. When Reno sought an explanation from the task force, officials confessed that records had been in their possession to show the hard-money deposits, but no one had examined them. This embarrassment partially contributed to her decision to reorganize the task force and bring in new people to direct it. She appointed Charles G. La Bella as chief prosecutor to replace Laura Ingersoll. La Bella was head of the U.S. Attorney's office in San Diego and had extensive experience in public corruption investigations. The task force would help Reno determine whether to request an independent counsel and/or to pursue criminal charges. Reno made the changes to the task force in the middle of a thirty-day review of Gore's fundraising activities that was scheduled to end October 3, 1997.[1]

In addition to having reopened a review into Gore's phone solicitations, Reno began a review of allegedly similar calls by

Clinton. Call sheets revealed that Clinton was requested in February 1996 to call musician Frank Zappa's widow to solicit a contribution. Several months later she contributed $30,000 to the DNC, of which $20,000 ended up in a hard-money account. Clinton was also suspected of calling Robert Meyerhoff, a Maryland businessman, from the Oval Office. Meyerhoff made a $100,000 contribution to the DNC. White House spokesman Lanny Davis said, "We are confident no laws were broken."[2]

Contrary to Reno's assertion that her original task force had done "a very professional, very fine job," the investigation was nearly immobilized with internal disagreement among its members. The FBI officials strongly objected to the approach that the Justice Department was taking, believing it to be much too narrow, restrictive, and focused on newspaper accounts rather than interviewing senior administration officials and Democratic National Committee staff. The FBI believed that the procedure was almost assured to insulate "covered persons." "The FBI wanted to investigate the president and the vice president," said one Justice Department lawyer, but the agents were instructed not to seek out evidence of crimes by "covered persons." They were merely to flag such evidence and take it to Reno if they happened on it. "You can't ask someone whether a covered person committed a crime," said the Justice lawyer. More than that, according to a Justice attorney, the task force was to avoid investigating new information of Democratic fund-raising scandals. The FBI and Justice task force deadlocked even over routine matters, which were referred to their supervisors who sometimes were equally divided.[3]

The original task force didn't allow FBI agents to interview senior administration officials for eight months into its investigation. Reportedly, even the White House was incredulous that they had escaped stricter scrutiny. "It was something of a mystery to us," said one senior White House official who added that neither the Justice Department nor the FBI had even asked to interview witnesses concerning the main issues being investigated. Speaking of the Justice Department's unwritten prohibition against interviewing top administration officials, one Justice Department prosecutor observed, "You don't tell the FBI that in this particular investigation—unlike any other—you don't seek a full explanation of what happened. You follow the facts and let them lead where they may." The refusal of the Justice Department to permit the interviews was strong proof of Reno's conflict of interest, the prosecutor explained. "If they said we're not going to look into this because it might lead to a covered person... it's prima facie evidence of proof of conflict of interest. If they were restraining the agents, if they curtailed the manner in which questions could be asked, that should have been the moment when they appointed an independent counsel," said the attorney. Terry Eastland, a former Justice Department official under Ronald Reagan and an expert on the Independent Counsel Act, said, "If you feel that constrained that you can't interview anybody... you've already bumped up against the statute, and you ought to hand it off" to an independent counsel.[4]

Regardless of what was motivating her, Reno, at least outwardly, seemed hamstrung by her interpretation of the Independent Counsel Act. It involved a catch-22. She apparently didn't believe that she could home in on a covered person without specific and credible evidence that he had committed a crime. Yet she wouldn't allow her investigators to do the necessary footwork to determine whether such a covered person may have committed a crime. It was later revealed that Charles La Bella complained about this catch-22 in his memo. He said that the task force was never allowed to conduct a comprehensive investigation because "an inquiry can only be conducted pursuant to a preliminary investigation under section 591 of the Act. However, we have been told that we can only commence a preliminary investigation if there exists specific and credible evidence that a potential criminal violation has occurred. That is, you cannot investigate in order to determine if there is information concerning a 'covered person,' or one who falls within the discretionary provision, sufficient to constitute grounds to investigate. Rather, it seems that this information must just appear." The result was that investigators were placed in the extraordinary position of being in a passive, rather than an aggressive, role. One senior Justice Department official warned that Reno's restructuring of the task force would result in no change in its investigative approach—primarily because Reno's philosophy had not changed. "The overall strategy has not changed," he said. "The idea is to investigate a criminal case, piece by piece, and be alert at all times for any evidence that triggers the [independent counsel] statute."[5] As it turned out, those were prophetic words.

Reno Declines Independent Counsel for Clinton and Gore

After the Justice Department completed its ninety-day preliminary investigations, Janet Reno announced on December 2, 1997, that she would not recommend the appointment of an independent counsel to investigate Clinton or Gore. She emphasized that she personally made the decision, denying that politics or any other outside pressure had influenced her. "They should know that we have worked as hard as we can to do the right thing," said Reno.

Reno determined that there was no reasonable basis to believe that Clinton or Gore violated the law against fund-raising on federal property. She said the White House calls variously were made from residential quarters, did not involve direct solicitations, or did not raise actual campaign money. "Evidence found by the investigators shows that the vice president solicited only soft money in these calls, not hard money," said Reno. Reno formally advised the three-judge panel of the D.C. Court of Appeals of her decision that there were no reasonable grounds for further investigation.

Republicans criticized Reno's decision, pointing to a recommendation by FBI director Louis J. Freeh that Reno should seek an independent counsel. Freeh stated publicly, "Lawyers and investigators can and often do disagree. I and all of my colleagues in the FBI respect her decision and understand fully that it is the Attorney General's by law to make." Outside forces criticized Reno, too. Common Cause president Ann McBride, within mere minutes of the announcement of Reno's decision, denounced the attorney general for "turning a deaf ear" to Louis Freeh, head of the nation's top law enforcement agency.

When word of Freeh's recommendation came out, White House officials privately denigrated Freeh, calling him a disloyal subordinate. News of Freeh's dissent led the House Government Reform and Oversight Committee to issue a subpoena for Freeh's memorandum. Reno had refused to volunteer the memo, saying that to release it would compromise her investigation—without explaining how it would do so. Gore said, "I am pleased by the decision. Now that there has been a full and independent review, the issue of the phone calls can be put behind us." Clinton said, "The attorney general made her decision based on a careful review of the law and the facts and that's as it should be."

Reno did not dismantle the special task force, however, saying that it should "pursue every lead, explore every avenue, interview witnesses and ask any question.... Today's decisions represent, if you will, a snapshot, not an ending. Our investigation continues, and no allegation will go unexamined."[6]

Charlie Trie Indicted

On January 28, 1998, the Justice Department persuaded a federal grand jury in Washington, D.C., to indict President Clinton's longtime Arkansas friend Charlie Trie for arranging illegal foreign contributions to the Democratic Party. According to the fifteen-count indictment, Trie had engaged in a "straw donor" scheme. Trie allegedly collected funds from foreign citizens and then laundered those funds into the coffers of the Democratic Party and President Clinton's legal defense fund. Together, the Democratic National Committee and Clinton's legal defense fund returned $1.2 million that Trie had raised. The essence of the indictment was that Trie purchased access to high-level United States government officials (including Clinton and Gore) by contributing and soliciting contributions to the DNC. Trie and his Asian business associates attended many exclusive political events including White House coffees and presidential galas. Trie's primary source of funds was Ng Lap Seng, a hotel and casino owner living in Macao.

At the time of the indictment Trie was still in China, having been there since 1996 when his name first surfaced as one who had been involved in the White House and DNC fund-raising scandals. Soon after being indicted, however, he returned to the United States and entered a plea of not guilty on the federal criminal charges. Trie was also accused of destroying documents that were subpoenaed by the Senate Governmental Affairs Committee.

Trie's attorney, Reid H. Weingarten, said, "He never intended to corrupt the American political system. Any effort to make him the heavy in this political scandal will fall of its own weight."[7]

Trie's case lingered until late May 1999 when it finally went to trial. On the fourth day of trial on obstruction of justice charges, Trie agreed to enter a guilty plea to two federal election law violations in exchange for his cooperation and potential testimony in cases arising out of the campaign finance investigation. Trie's Little Rock office manager, Maria Mapili, was the chief witness against him, testifying that he had ordered her to destroy business records that were under subpoena by Senate investigators and federal prosecutors.

The facts concerning the destruction of evidence were damning, as they implicated the Justice Department. Reporter Carl Cameron of Fox News broke the story that the Justice Department had intervened in July 1997 to prevent investigators from seizing the documents that Trie's secretary, Maria Mapili, was shredding. Columnist Robert Novak reported that the FBI had pressed for a search warrant but was forestalled by Justice Department orders from Washington.[8] House Government Reform Committee chairman Dan Burton subpoenaed Justice Department records on the incident, but the department ignored the subpoena.

Not only was evidence destroyed, but the Justice Department's indictment was botched. Trie pled guilty to one felony conviction and one misdemeanor conviction. Astonishingly, prosecutors did not reach an agreement in advance on the substance of Trie's testimony.[9] In November 1999 Trie was sentenced to three years probation and two hundred hours of community service work—which was incredibly lenient.

Maria Hsia Indicted and Convicted

On February 19, 1998, a federal grand jury indicted Democratic fund-raiser Maria Hsia for laundering illegal campaign contributions to the Clinton-Gore reelection campaign in connection with the Buddhist Temple event. Upon entering a not guilty plea to a six-count indictment, Hsia maintained her innocence. "I have done nothing wrong, and I am prepared to fight," said Hsia. The thrust of the charge was that Hsia defrauded the Federal Election Commission by soliciting temple monastics to act as straw donors. Gore again denied involvement. "It had nothing to do with me," he said. And Hsia's attorney, Nancy Luque, denied a link to Communist China. "She is certainly not an agent of the Chinese government," said Luque. Hsia's trial was slated to begin April 27, 1998.[10]

On September 10, 1998, the federal judge presiding over the case dismissed five of the six felony charges against Maria Hsia, in which she had been accused of causing the DNC and the Clinton-Gore campaign to file false statements about the temple event with the Federal Election Commission. But Judge Paul Friedman declined to dismiss the essence of the indictment, which was that Hsia had conspired to launder illegal foreign campaign contributions. The maximum punishment for the conspiracy charge was five years in prison.[11]

It was not until February 2000 that the government finally brought Hsia to trial. The trial took three weeks. Twenty-seven witnesses, including John Huang, testified against her. The result: Maria Hsia was convicted of channeling more than $100,000 in illegal contributions to Democratic candidates in 1996, including $65,000 from the Buddhist Temple fund-raiser. Hsia's compatriot, Vice President Gore, was safely visiting a kindergarten in Manhattan when he learned of the verdict. "The jury has rendered a verdict. It's a hard day for her," he said. "She's been a friend and a political supporter. But since this is a matter still in the courts I won't comment on it." Republican National Committee chairman Jim Nicholson said, "If Al Gore was a victim of Maria Hsia, then

Clyde Barrow was a victim of Bonnie Parker." House Government Reform Committee chairman Dan Burton stated, "There is no doubt that the vice president and the DNC were not victims. The vice president just hasn't leveled with the American people."[12]

Johnny Chung Indicted

Democratic fund-raiser Johnny Chung was indicted in Los Angeles on March 5, 1998, in another straw donor scheme. Chung, according to the indictment, arranged for illegal foreign contributions to the Democratic Party by his friends and employees, who were later reimbursed. Chung entered into a plea agreement in exchange for his cooperation with investigators. He informed the government that Lieutenant Colonel Liu Chao-ying, an officer in China's People's Liberation Army and an executive for a Chinese government-owned aerospace company, gave Chung $300,000 to donate to the Democratic National Committee. The aerospace company sold and launched rockets and satellites. This was a breakthrough in establishing a direct money trail from the Chinese government to the Democratic Party. Liu had appeared with Chung at a presidential fund-raiser in Los Angeles in 1996 where Liu had her picture taken with President Clinton. Between 1994 and 1996 Chung's personal and corporate donations to the DNC totaled $366,000, all of which the DNC was forced to return. In a 1997 interview with the *Los Angeles Times* Chung commented, "I see the White House is like a subway: You have to put in coins to open gates."[13]

The White House responded to Chung's revelations by denying any knowledge of the source of Chung's funds or the background of Liu Chao-ying. Liu Chao-ying was the daughter of Liu Huaqing, a retired, once-powerful general in the Chinese army. Senator Fred Thompson proclaimed that "the new information shows that the 'China Plan' the [Senate] committee investigated last year was carried out in some form." Senator Arlen Specter added, "This really is a very big matter. The need for an independent counsel to investigate the campaign finance scandal has been clear for some time, and this puts the icing on the cake."[14]

Once Chung "turned state's evidence" he alleged that the Democratic National Committee was not an innocent victim in the fund-raising donations he had arranged. He said that then-DNC finance director Richard Sullivan personally asked him for a donation of $125,000 in April 1995 for a fund-raiser at Hollywood director Steven Spielberg's home. At that time, Sullivan allegedly was aware that Chung was a suspected intermediary for Chinese businessmen who had made illegal contributions to U.S. political campaigns. Nevertheless, the Justice Department refused to make Sullivan or other DNC officials "targets" of its investigation.[15]

Chung also disclosed to investigators that both Clinton-Gore and DNC officials knew that he was bringing foreign guests to a Los Angeles fund-raiser in September 1995. Though campaign officials rejected Chung's check for $20,000 that evening because it violated the legal limit of $1,000 per person, they accepted twenty checks from Chung's friends for $1,000 apiece the very next day. Chung admitted that he subsequently reimbursed the twenty contributors.[16]

When Chung testified to the House Government Reform Committee he reiterated his claim that the illegal foreign contributions he had arranged were intended to influence the 1996 election. Chung denied, however, that he personally acted as an agent for the Chinese government. He also repeated that Democratic officials "were fully aware" that he was trying to open doors for Chinese businessmen with the illegal foreign contributions he arranged.

In an interesting twist, however, Chung said that Liu Chao-ying was not the source of the $300,000 contribution. Though Liu had promised Chung the money, she ended up introducing Chung to another important person in the Chinese military instead. Chung met General Ji Shengde, the chief of China's military intelligence, who offered, and contributed, the $300,000. "We really like your president," said Ji, who told Chung he could "give [the $300,000] to your president and [the] Democrat Party." When Chung discussed Ji's offer with Liu Chao-ying, Liu told him she wouldn't have to use all the money for campaign contributions. Eventually, congressional investigators traced between $20,000 and $35,000 as going to the Democratic Party.

Chung also testified that he had been threatened because of his cooperation with the investigation. He said that Robert Luu, a California businessman, had approached him following his guilty plea and told him, "If you keep your mouth shut, you and your family will be safe."[17]

House Government Reform Committee chairman Dan Burton later alleged that the Justice Department obstructed the Chung investigation for at least two years by failing to follow up on information it had concerning Liu Chao-ying's $300,000 wire transfer to Chung.[18]

Satellite Exports Investigation

The Justice Department presented information to a grand jury that two American companies illegally provided China with satellite technology, enabling the Communist government to accelerate its nuclear missile program. The two companies were Loral Space and Communications of Manhattan and Hughes Electronics, a General Motors subsidiary based in Los Angeles. The charges against Loral were particularly sensitive because its chairman and CEO Bernard Schwartz was the largest individual contributor to the Democratic National Committee the previous year, 1997, and had donated almost $1 million to the Democrats since 1995.

The investigation was based on a 1996 incident in which Loral and Hughes reportedly shared secret information with the Chinese while investigating why a Chinese rocket carrying a Loral satellite had crashed. The information allegedly included sensitive rocket-guidance technology. This guidance technology is transferable to ballistic missiles that could be used against the United States.[19] Reportedly, a 1997 classified Pentagon document concluded that the security of the United States "has been harmed" by the incident.[20]

While the grand jury was investigating this matter, President Clinton approved—over the opposition of the Justice Department—Loral's request to export the same type of technology to China, along with another satellite and expert American assistance. Clinton's top advisors warned him that his granting of the waiver might be seen as letting Loral's space subsidiary "off the hook on criminal charges for its unauthorized assistance to China's ballistic missile program."[21] If President Clinton formally approved the sharing of this technology with China, how could the government make a credible case that the companies had committed a serious criminal violation?[22]

White House internal documents later revealed that Clinton's decision to approve the Chinese launching of the American satellite was a calculated political move. Clinton's staff persuaded him that the economic and diplomatic advantages in the decision outweighed the security risks and the opposition of federal prosecutors. Of course, Clinton denied that his decision had been influenced by the fact that the Democratic Party's largest contributor, Bernard Schwartz, had pressured him to grant the waiver. "I think the decision was the correct one," said Clinton. It "was based on what I thought was in the national interest and supportive of our national security."

While Clinton insisted that the waiver was a routine act, White House records showed that it was anything but routine— that Clinton, in fact, rushed the waiver through so that Loral would suffer no financial penalty from a delay. Clinton's motive was not to protect national security, but to protect one of his largest contributors. Just four weeks before Clinton approved one of Loral's waiver applications in early July 1996, Schwartz donated $100,000 to the Democratic Party.[23]

White House press secretary Mike McCurry denied that Clinton's action had contributed to Chinese military capabilities because Loral had agreed to "stringent standards" to avoid the sharing of unauthorized technology. Clinton's waiver allowing the transfer of technology contained the ironic statement that it was being granted in furtherance of the national interests of the United States. "We are more engaged with China," said McCurry. "One area of that engagement has been commercial satellite technology, which we perceive to be in our interests as well as that of China's."[24] Senate and House Republicans, unpersuaded by Clinton's rhetoric, lambasted the president for placing his donors' commercial interests above national security.

As Senate and House Republicans investigated Clinton's waiver, Senate majority leader Trent Lott and House Speaker Newt Gingrich wrote in a joint letter to Clinton: "To date, the administration has refused to provide so much as one document to refute the evidence put forward in press accounts" of the incident. Republicans were exploring whether there was a provable causal relationship between the large donations of Bernard Schwartz and Clinton's technology waivers.[25]

One House Democrat, Nancy Pelosi, criticized President Clinton for granting the waiver over the Justice Department's objections. She also found it ironic that Clinton was purporting to be acting in the national interest "while at the same time China was planning to sell weapons-of-mass-destruction technology to Iran, in spite of signing another agreement not to do so in October 1997."[26]

As the investigation continued Loral admitted that one of its top executives had helped draft a report to the Chinese on the causes of its rocket crash. Though the report touched on sensitive technology issues, the executive had not cleared his action with federal officials. The company denied, however, that it had either acted illegally or compromised United States national security. Loral's denial was contradicted by a classified Pentagon study that concluded that China's missile-guidance capabilities had been enhanced to the detriment of U.S. security.

The Chinese military benefited from Clinton's waiver, but so did a Chinese business, China Aerospace, because its rockets were permitted to launch American satellites. This fact was some evidence that Clinton's Chinese donors were rewarded for their healthy contributions to the DNC. The chairman of the company, Liu Chao-Ying, was responsible for arranging thousands of dollars of donations to the DNC during the summer of 1996 through Johnny Chung. China Aerospace was also the parent company of China Great Wall Industry, a company that the State Department sanctioned in 1991 and 1993 for selling missiles to Pakistan.[27]

Clinton had justified his waiving of restrictions on technology sales to Communist China because the technology was being used solely for civilian purposes. This was also Clinton's primary argument for transferring decision-making concerning technology sales from the State Department to the Commerce Department.

But the Chinese military was clearly an additional beneficiary of the sales, as was demonstrated to the American public in shocking detail by *Washington Times* reporter Bill Gertz in his 1999 *New York Times* best-selling book *Betrayal* and its year 2000 follow-up, *The China Threat*. The Clinton administration was obviously aware that China's military was exploiting American satellite sales to Asian companies. A Chinese army newspaper reported that its officers used to "[cry] themselves hoarse" or run to distant post offices to send urgent messages over the military's outdated communications system. "Those phenomena are now history," said the article, pointing out that (American) satellite communications had changed all that. Confronted with these facts, Clinton maintained that it was impractical for the United States to force companies that buy American communications satellites to certify that they would be used only for civilian purposes. But many exporters, who were not "Friends of Bill," managed to do it.[28]

In time more evidence was uncovered revealing that the Clinton administration had deliberately ignored national security concerns voiced by some of its highest officials, including Secretary of State Warren Christopher, when it stripped the State Department of its licensing authority over commercial satellites. Ron Brown's Commerce Department was demonstrably more sympathetic to satellite exporters. A line in an internal administration memorandum from Anthony Lake, the national security advisor, and Laura D'Andrea Tyson, head of the National Economic Council, revealed the crassness and recklessness of the administration's approach. "Industry should like the fact that they will deal with the more 'user friendly' Commerce system," said the memo.[29]

A classified Pentagon report provided more information on the activities of Democratic contributor Hughes Space and

Communications. Hughes scientists, said the report, helped Chinese engineers improve highly sophisticated mathematical models that enhanced China's rocket-launching capabilities. Hughes denied any wrongdoing. Further, it said its actions had been approved by the Clinton Commerce Department. Evidence emerged that the CIA "killed a report" by one of its scientists that Hughes had provided ballistic missile technology to China. The scientist, Ronald Pandolfi, however, was correct. As it turned out the Chinese did adopt the recommendations contained in the Hughes report.[30] Another interesting fact about Hughes was that it hired the son of the Chinese general who oversaw China's military satellite programs.

Charles La Bella, the Justice Department's Special Task Force chief, finally concluded that there was insufficient evidence to prove that Schwartz or Loral had broken the law. In the addendum to his initial memo, La Bella wrote, "This was a matter which likely did not merit any investigation." La Bella reportedly regarded Bernard Schwartz as a victim of overreaching by the Justice Department, which relied on "a wisp of information" to justify its inquiry.[31]

However, if La Bella was ultimately charitable to Loral, he was the opposite to the president concerning his relationship with Schwartz and Loral. In his initial memo, La Bella wrote, "If in fact there is anything to investigate involving the Loral 'allegations,' it is—as set out in the Task Force's draft investigative plan—an investigation of the President. The President is the one who signed the waiver, the President is the one who has the relationship with Schwartz; and it was the President's media campaign that was the beneficiary of Schwartz's largess by virtue of his own substantial contributions and those which he was able to solicit." In the addendum to his memo, La Bella indicated that the focus was still on President Clinton. "Finally," said La Bella, "to the extent we are pursuing the Loral investigation, the President is at its center. This fact alone is sufficient under the ICA [Independent Counsel Act] to trigger a preliminary investigation."

Regardless of La Bella's conclusions about the complicity of Schwartz and Loral, the "Cox Report" issued by Republican con- gressman Chris Cox of California, after the most extensive congressional investigation of the matter, concluded that there was evidence of transfers of technology that could endanger the national security interests of the United States. As one columnist who read the report noted, "The question of whether the presidential waiver was influenced by Schwartz's political contributions is separate from the question of whether Loral and Hughes Electronics Corp., the other large satellite maker, have transferred vital missile and satellite technology to China. That question was investigated by the Cox committee. Its unanimous report found that there was evidence of transfers that could endanger both our security and our commercial interests. La Bella was not investigating that; he was following the money."[32]

Pauline Kanchanalak Indicted

The Justice Department on July 13 announced a twenty-four count indictment against Pauline Kanchanalak and her sister-in-law, Duangnet Kronenberg, for using illegal foreign campaign contributions (exceeding $690,000) in exchange for access to top administration officials, including President Clinton. The two were also charged with obstructing justice by destroying computer files and other documents. The Justice Department reportedly was optimistic that it could work out a deal with Kanchanalak whereby she would give it critical information about John Huang, the main player in the entire campaign finance saga. Kanchanalak was indicted when she refused to cooperate. This was the Justice Department's fourth major indictment in the campaign finance scandal in six days. Kanchanalak allegedly used her mother-in-law and Kronenberg, who were permanent residents (and who could therefore legally contribute their own money to U.S. political campaigns), as straw donors. Kanchanalak arranged for them to contribute to the DNC and other state Democratic Party organizations. They were then reimbursed with foreign monies. Kanchanalak's industriousness paid off. She became a member of the DNC's finance board of directors and attended numerous White House events, including President Clinton's fiftieth birthday party. Her most egregious violation occurred in June 1996, when she accompanied three Thai corporate officials to a White House coffee where President Clinton, DNC cochairman Don Fowler, and John Huang were present. Within days of the event, she and Kronenberg channeled more than $450,000 in illegal donations to the DNC and other Democratic organizations.[33] On July 29, Kanchanalak pleaded not guilty to the charges.

Almost two years later, in July 2000, Pauline Kanchanalak agreed to plead guilty to a plan to funnel in excess of $690,000 in illegal foreign campaign contributions to the Democratic Party in exchange for access to President Clinton and other administration officials. As part of the deal, Kanchanalak agreed to cooperate with the Justice Department in its investigation.

Dissension in Justice Department over Independent Counsel

Not everyone within the Justice Department agreed with Attorney General Janet Reno that specific and credible evidence did not exist to warrant the appointment of an independent counsel to investigate Democratic campaign finance abuses. In the fall of 1997 Justice Department Special Task Force chief Charles La Bella urged Reno to request appointment of an independent counsel to investigate President Clinton and Vice President Gore, concerning their fund-raising calls from the White House. Despite having placed La Bella in charge of the reorganized task force, Reno flatly rejected his advice.

On June 19, 1998, FBI director Louis Freeh (a former federal judge) briefed Senate committee chairman Fred Thompson and ranking Democrat John Glenn on the contents of a twenty-seven-page legal memorandum he had delivered to Janet Reno. In the memo, Freeh advised Reno that she was misreading the law in refusing to recommend an independent counsel. Freeh's words were pointed: "It is difficult to imagine a more compelling situation for appointing an independent counsel.... It's a conflict for the attorney general to investigate her superiors."

Much of Freeh's memo focused on Vice President Gore's White House phone solicitation calls. He was upset that the Justice Department was "relying almost exclusively on the vice president's own statements to draw inferences favorable to him even where those statements are contradicted by other reliable evidence." In his memo Freeh said, "In the face of compelling evidence that the vice president was a very active, sophisticated fundraiser who knew exactly what he was doing, his own exculpatory statements must not be given undue weight." Freeh urged Reno to reorient her investigation toward the major players. He maintained that the investigation's preoccupation with bit players was unproductive. Freeh tried to persuade Reno to pursue a top-down investigation starting with President Clinton and a "core-group" of his aides because "most of the alleged campaign abuses flowed directly or indirectly from the all-out efforts by the White House and DNC to raise money."

Just a month later the *New York Times* came out with an even bigger bombshell. Special Task Force chief Charles La Bella again recommended that Reno seek the appointment of an independent counsel. This time, La Bella wasn't just recommending an independent counsel for Gore's White House phone solicitations. In his memo, La Bella argued that Reno had misinterpreted the Independent Counsel Act by requiring an artificially high standard to trigger the appointment of an independent counsel. La Bella concluded that there was sufficient evidence for appointment of an independent counsel on both the mandatory and discretionary provisions of the act. Attorney General Reno, maintained La Bella, had no choice but to recommend the appointment of an independent counsel.

La Bella contended that the Justice Department had examined the evidence of alleged misconduct separately and in isolation, when it should have viewed the conduct of all the actors in concert. He referred to this myopic approach as "stovepiping." As La Bella wrote, "the campaign finance allegations do not present the typical criminal matter. Rather, they present the earmarks of a loose enterprise employing different actors at different levels who share a common goal: bring in the money."

La Bella called for a comprehensive investigation into "the entire landscape" of campaign finance allegations. He said that there were schemes "conjured up by sophisticated political operatives to circumvent" election finance laws during the 1996 presidential campaign. La Bella contended that there was sufficient evidence to warrant the appointment of an independent counsel for the following persons: President Clinton, Vice President Al Gore, first lady Hillary Rodham Clinton, and former White House aide Harold Ickes. With respect to Hillary Clinton, La Bella said that an independent counsel should investigate the extent of her knowledge about the illegal foreign fund-raising activities of Johnny Chung and Charlie Trie. Both La Bella and Freeh argued that the Justice Department didn't sufficiently investigate whether Bill Clinton had, in essence, controlled the Democratic Party's advertising campaign and used it and its funds in support of his reelection effort.

"It is hoped that this report will place in context the abuses uncovered in our investigation: a system designed to raise money by whatever means, and from whomever would give it, without meaningful attention to the lawfulness of the contributions or the manner in which the money was spent," La Bella wrote. "The intentional conduct and the 'willful ignorance' uncovered by our investigations, when combined with the line blurring, resulted in a situation where abuse was rampant, and indeed the norm. At some point the [Clinton-Gore reelection campaign] was so corrupted by bloated fund raising and questionable contributions that the system became a caricature of itself."

He maintained that his Justice Department superiors were "intellectually dishonest" and practiced "gamesmanship" to avoid an independent counsel investigation. "The contortions that the Department has gone through to avoid investigating these allegations are apparent." At one point, La Bella suggested that the department was so intent on protecting the president that it had made its decision and then tried to apply its reasoning retrospectively. "In Loral avoidance of an ICA was accomplished by constructing an investigation which ignored the President of the United States—the only real target of these allegations. It is time to approach these issues head on, rather than beginning with a desired result and reasoning backwards."

La Bella also complained that the Justice Department applied a different standard ("two distinct thresholds") to trigger the Independent Counsel Act between covered and noncovered persons. He basically said that while there was a built-in catch-22 impeding the triggering of the act for covered persons, "the Task Force has commenced criminal investigations of noncovered persons based only on a wisp of information."

Former Watergate special prosecutor Henry Ruth said, "The failure of Reno to listen to La Bella seems to me to put a cloud on the impartiality at the top of the Justice Department in what was supposed to be the most ethical administration in the history of the United States. I can't remember... someone at that level, plus the FBI, saying 'go' and the attorney general vetoing it without satisfactory explanation."

As reports about the Freeh and La Bella memos surfaced, Senate and House investigators requested, and then subpoenaed, copies of the memos, but Janet Reno adamantly refused to turn them over. Finally, the House Government Reform and Oversight Committee voted to hold Reno in contempt of Congress for refusing to comply with the subpoenas.

La Bella "Rewarded" for His Diligence

When he concluded his duties with the Special Task Force, La Bella was planning to return to San Diego as interim United States attorney. He was in line for a permanent appointment and was earnestly seeking it. But just fifteen days after he recommended an independent counsel, Democratic senator Barbara Boxer, related by marriage to Hillary Clinton, rejected him for appointment. Even the *New York Times* editorial board registered outrage. "Democrats," wrote the *Times*, "have added a new tactic to the campaign to protect President Clinton from an independent investigation of White House fund-raising during 1996. The tactic is to punish the truth-tellers.... [This] will send a chilling message to assistant United States attorneys throughout the country. Democratic fund-raising is a no-go area for Federal law enforcement, and if you push too hard, the President's Congressional allies will make you pay."[34]

Another Gore Investigation Begins (and Ends)

On August 26, 1998, Janet Reno announced that she had ordered a ninety-day preliminary investigation into another potential criminal violation by Vice President Gore—that he lied to Justice Department investigators. On November 12, 1997, Gore told investigators that he believed the Democrats' 1996 media effort was to be financed solely with soft money. Gore said his White House phone solicitations were for that soft money effort. Yet handwritten notes on a DNC memo by Gore's former deputy chief of staff, David Strauss, indicated that the decision to finance the media campaign with both hard and soft money was discussed at a meeting on November 21, 1995, that Gore had personally attended. President Clinton, White House deputy chief of staff Harold Ickes, and several DNC officials were also present. None of them admitted that the issue of hard or soft money was discussed. But Strauss's notes contained the incriminating inscription, "65% soft/35% hard." These percentages just happen to parallel the federal guidelines for the financing of advertising.[35]

At the end of the ninety-day period, Janet Reno unsurprisingly decided again not to seek the appointment of an independent counsel against Vice President Gore. In her report to the three-judge panel Reno wrote, "Taken altogether, I find the evidence fails to provide any reasonable support for a conclusion that the Vice President may have lied." Reno added, "While the vice president was present at the meeting, there is no evidence that he heard the statements or understood their implications, so as to suggest the falsity of his statement two years later that he believed the media fund was entirely soft money." Reno referred to the case against Gore as "weak circumstantial evidence." Reno reportedly was of the opinion that Gore's misdescription of the financing methods was a mistake rather than a lie.

Some Justice Department attorneys strongly disagreed, as did FBI Director Louis Freeh and Justice Department Task Force chief Charles La Bella, who said, "The fact is that Gore, using a Clinton-Gore [hard money] credit card, placed several calls from the White House to pitch soft money contributions. The Vice President denied that he was aware that the soft money contributions were routinely being split upon receipt by the DNC between soft and hard accounts. He stated in his interview that he did not recall the Ickes memos directed to him on the issue or the discussions at the regular Wednesday night meetings about this point. The Vice President's failure to recall reading the memos sent to him is reminiscent of his claim not to have read the April 1996 memos advising him that an event he was to attend at the Hsi Lai Temple in Hacienda Heights, CA, was in fact a fundraiser arranged in part by Maria Hsia."[36]

Internal Justice Department documents later revealed that during these many earlier investigations of Bill Clinton and Al Gore's questionable fund-raising conduct, Justice officials never questioned them about certain things. They never asked Gore about the Buddhist Temple fund-raiser. They never asked Clinton about John Huang. Neither was asked about James Riady. House Government Reform Committee chairman Dan Burton asked, "Did they forget? Did they think it wasn't important? Did someone tell them not to?"

Harold Ickes Investigated

A week after she ordered a preliminary investigation into whether Gore had lied to investigators, Reno launched a ninety-day preliminary investigation into whether White House deputy chief of staff Harold Ickes lied to the Senate about political favors he allegedly performed in exchange for Teamsters' support. Ickes was one of the chief architects of the 1996 presidential reelection campaign effort. Ickes allegedly testified to the Senate Governmental Affairs Committee that he was unaware that the Clinton administration did anything to assist the Teamsters with their strike against Diamond Walnut Company. The Teamsters union had been on strike for almost four years and was anxious to resolve the dispute in 1995, at the same time that Ickes was seeking the Teamsters' financial contributions. When asked whether the administration had taken any policy action on behalf of the Teamsters in that matter, he replied, "nothing that I know of." Again, internal documents contradicted Ickes. According to a Teamsters internal memo, Ickes asked U.S. trade representative Mickey Kantor to intervene with Diamond Walnut executives to encourage them to resolve their dispute with the Teamsters.[37] Congressman Peter Hoekstra, head of the House investigation against the Teamsters, said that Kantor had taken action to assist the Teamsters. "The information we developed strongly suggests that the attorney general must appoint an independent counsel," said Hoekstra.

Janet Reno requested a sixty-day extension of the initial investigation. The extension had to be approved by a three-judge panel, which immediately granted the extension, saying that Reno had "shown good cause."

On January 29, 1999, Reno announced that she had decided against appointing an independent counsel to investigate Ickes for allegedly lying to the Senate committee. Reno said, "There is no reasonable basis to believe that any additional investigation would discover additional evidence sufficient to prove that Ickes's testimony was knowingly and intentionally false. There is clear and convincing evidence that Ickes did not intend to lie."

President Clinton responded, "I have always had confidence that Harold Ickes acted lawfully and appropriately." Senator Fred Thompson commented, "The demise of the independent counsel law when it expires this year may be the most notable 'achievement' of her [Reno's] tenure as attorney general." Congressman Dan Burton said, "The attorney general is once again protecting the president and his friends. Janet Reno has defied the spirit and the letter of the independent counsel statute.... Her investigation has become a sham."[38]

Special Task Force chief investigator Charles La Bella, in his memorandum written the previous year, concluded that an independent counsel should have been appointed to investigate Ickes. "If Ickes used his official position to take official action or to cause official action to be taken in return for campaign contributions to the DNC, or if contributions were a reward for official action taken by Ickes or another official at his direction, a potential criminal violation exists. Apart from the underlying transaction, it seems clear that Ickes's sworn testimony is at odds with the substance of the internal Teamster memos. This suggests a potential perjury charge in connection with Ickes's Senate testimony which warrants investigation."

A New Clinton Investigation Begins

For the third time in two weeks, Janet Reno announced that she was going to begin a new ninety-day preliminary investigation—this time into the activities of President Clinton. The primary question was whether Clinton and his chief political advisors illegally controlled advertising expenditures for the Democratic National Committee, which was supposed to operate independently from the Clinton-Gore campaign effort. Federal law requires separation between the hard-money and soft-money efforts; otherwise the hard-money spending limitations would effectively be circumvented. Clinton had told FBI investigators that he had "no earthly idea" that the Democratic National Committee was automatically placing parts of contributions into accounts that were subject to strict limits. "It'd be stupid," said Clinton, for the Democratic National Committee to have engaged in a practice that would have put contributors in jeopardy of violating the law.[39]

On December 7, 1998, after the ninety-day preliminary investigation, Attorney General Reno announced that she had decided not to seek the appointment of an independent counsel to investigate whether Clinton misused Democratic Party funds to pay for the advertising blitz in his 1996 reelection campaign. Reno based her decision on the notion that Clinton's and Gore's attorneys had advised them that the advertising campaign was permissible and they thought they were following the law. Said Reno, "I find by clear and convincing evidence a lack of knowing and willful criminal intent required for criminal prosecution." To some extent,

Reno also sidestepped responsibility by saying that she wanted to defer to the Federal Election Commission on matters involving the enforcement of election laws. Senator Orrin Hatch said, "Janet Reno has sliced this broad scandal into narrower issues so that common threads, patterns and facts are not considered when weighing each decision whether to seek an independent counsel."[40]

Special Task Force chief Charles La Bella recommended that Janet Reno pursue the appointment of an independent counsel to investigate President Clinton on a number of campaign finance issues. La Bella said that Clinton's association with Charlie Trie warranted further investigation; he also said that Clinton was "implicated in a... conspiracy to violate soft money regulations," which "at a minimum... needs to be investigated fully." La Bella suggested that Clinton probably knew or had reason to know that foreign funds were being funneled into the DNC and the reelection effort.[41]

The Senate Governmental Affairs Committee also directly implicated President Clinton in the scandal. It detailed how Clinton assumed control of the DNC's finances and micromanaged its expenditures of money in order to "squeeze as much money out of the DNC as it could." Clinton used this money, according to the committee, to fund his advertising campaign; he illegally coordinated the ad campaign with the DNC; and he used White House aide Harold Ickes to control much of the DNC's activities. The committee concluded, "The nation's oldest political party simply became an arm of the White House with the primary mission of reelecting the President. The illegalities and improprieties discussed in this report stem from this simple fact. The President's attempt to slough responsibility for illegal and improper fundraising by the DNC in 1995-96 by pinning blame on 'the other campaign' rings hollow in the light of the facts uncovered by the Committee's investigation and outlined in this report."[42]

Justice Decides to Forego Big Fish

Without question, John Huang was the biggest of the big players (outside the administration) in the entire Democratic campaign finance network. But the Justice Department, after investigating him for two years, inexplicably indicated that it was not targeting Huang as a means to get at members of the Clinton administration. Rather, it was bargaining with him to testify against Maria Hsia (which he eventually did), who was not nearly as important a figure in the scandal as Huang himself. This was outrageously contrary to the Justice Department's professed strategy of working from the bottom up—to build cases against lower-level actors for the purpose of establishing cases against the major players.[43]

On May 25, 1999, the Justice Department announced that Huang had agreed to plead guilty to one felony charge of conspiring to violate campaign finance laws from 1992 through June 1994. As part of the agreement, he would not be charged with any illegal activity in connection with any of his fund-raising activities for the Democratic Party in the 1996 campaign. The Justice Department said that it would not seek any prison time for Huang because of his "substantial cooperation" with the investigation. This "substantial cooperation" apparently did not involve any incriminating information against President Clinton, Vice President Gore, or other high-ranking DNC officials.[44]

Significantly, in his testimony before the House Government Reform Committee, Huang averred that the Clinton campaign gave him explicit directions as to where to place the money, either to the DNC or to state party organizations. In a statement to the FBI, which was provided to the congressional committee, Huang stated that his illegal foreign fund-raising schemes predated the 1996 election and that he and James Riady had discussed various ways of having Lippo executives contribute to Democratic races.[45]

Huang later cooperated with the Justice Department in providing information that could be used to proceed against James Riady.

Chinese Espionage and the Cox Report

Following revelations of unauthorized transfers of satellite technology to China, a House committee, headed by Congressman Christopher Cox, began an investigation into the matter. On the last day of 1998, the committee unanimously approved its final report, finding that China had acquired more than just our satellite and missile technology. The committee issued a summary of the highlights but agreed not to release the full report until the White House had a chance to review it and comment upon it. After the Cox Committee submitted its report to the Clinton administration, the White House sat on it for some five months while saying it was reviewing it for security purposes. The bipartisan report concluded that for over twenty years China had been acquiring sensitive American military technology, including nuclear-weapons design. Alarmingly, according to the report, China had stolen much of the nuclear-weapons design technology from American nuclear laboratories. Witnesses before the committee testified that the Clinton administration, during its first term, had reduced background checks of various foreign visitors. The report found that Hughes and Loral had enhanced China's rocket launching and missile guidance capabilities and that supercomputer technology had also been transferred to China.

The committee did not investigate the connection between illegal Chinese campaign contributions and the relaxation of our nuclear security standards, but it did identify Liu Chao-ying—daughter of Liu Huaqing, who had been a senior official in the Chinese military—as one of many conduits for Chinese government contributions to the Democratic Party. The report said Liu and her father were involved in Beijing's effort to acquire military-related technology from the United States.[46] The Chinese military money that Liu delivered to the Democratic Party, said the report, "was an attempt to better her position in the United States to acquire computer, missile and satellite technologies."

The three-volume report concluded that China had stolen design secrets for all seven of the United States nuclear warheads. While the Clinton administration jumped on the report's conclusion that the Chinese espionage had been going on for twenty years, Republicans were quick to point out that previous Republican administrations had been unaware of it. The Clinton administration, by contrast, was aware and suppressed the information for fear of damaging its relationship with China. Elizabeth Dole said, "Previous administrations must share in the blame, but this Administration knew more and still chose not to take action."

The report also found that Hughes and Loral did in fact sometimes subordinate the national security of the United States to the "bottom line." While China displayed an "insatiable appetite" for U.S. military technology, the administration's laxity concerning exports and nuclear-laboratory security made the transfer of information possible. The committee found that there was an absence of procedures to detect and prevent the movement of sensitive information from secure computers to less secure computers at the nuclear labs. This problem enabled Wen Ho Lee to download some of our most classified nuclear secrets to a computer that was not secure.

Another revelation concerned a change in the testimony of national security advisor Sandy Berger. He originally testified that he had informed President Clinton of a security problem in

America's labs in early 1998. Berger later changed his story and said that he had first told Clinton in July 1997.[47] This was significant because Clinton had publicly denied (after July 1997) having been told of the problem.

Some of the report's other major findings were:

- the Chinese government has three thousand "front companies" in the United States, which China has used for espionage purposes;
- China stole nuclear secrets in the mid-1990s from U.S. nuclear laboratories, including thermonuclear weapons information, design secrets for our seven nuclear warheads—including the neutron bomb and the W-88—which is the most advanced and miniaturized warhead;
- China procured information on our reentry vehicles, which perform the function of shielding warheads as they return to earth;
- China acquired U.S. missile-guidance technology;
- in the late 1990s China obtained American research on electromagnetic-weapons technology concerning satellites.

If Chinese espionage had advanced during previous administrations, those administrations were unaware of it. By stark contrast, there is substantial evidence to suggest that the Clinton administration knew that Chinese espionage was ongoing and didn't act decisively to end it—savoring Chinese campaign contributions all the while.

Riady Indicted

On January 11, 2001, James Riady agreed to plead guilty to one felony charge of conspiring to defraud the United States government by unlawfully reimbursing campaign donors with foreign corporate funds. Pursuant to a plea agreement Riady will serve no jail time, but he and his companies, Lippo Group and LippoBank California, will pay a fine of $8.6 million. The agreement also will require Riady to continue to cooperate with federal authorities. [48]

Gore's Missing White House E-Mails

The House Government Reform Committee subpoenaed White House e-mails in connection with its campaign finance scandal investigation. Though the White House certified that all subpoenaed documents had been delivered to the committee, thousands of e-mails were missing, supposedly due to a computer glitch. The computer "glitch" was a problem with the automated record management system (ARMS), involving improper scanning, logging, and archiving of incoming, external e-mails to some five hundred White House employees, including top officials. During the committee hearings three Northrop Grumman contract employees, who were in charge of operating the White House e-mail system, made a startling claim. They said that White House officials Mark Lindsay and Laura Callahan told them if they disclosed the e-mail problem they would go to jail. The White House officials hotly denied the charge.

One of the Northrop Grumman employees, Robert Haas, filed a lawsuit against the government over the White House threats. In the lawsuit, filed by Judicial Watch, Haas alleged that he had been told that if he went public with the news about the missing e-mails, there would be a jail cell with his name on it. Another of the employees, Betty Lambuth, said that the White House tried to intimidate her in the same way. "We were not to talk to our spouses other than those of us who already knew about this particular project. They did tell me that if any of us did talk about this that my staff would be fired, would be arrested and would go to jail," said Lambuth. Northrop Grumman's program manager said that some of his staff felt so threatened by Callahan and Lindsay that they sought legal counsel to advise them in the matter.

The White House's motive to cover up the missing e-mails soon became apparent. Lambuth submitted an affidavit to the House committee attesting that many of the missing e-mails pertained to matters being investigated, including campaign finance, "Filegate," and the Lewinsky scandals. The Justice Department's Campaign Finance Task Force reported later that it had begun a criminal investigation into the missing e-mail situation. "As a result of these allegations, the [campaign finance] task force has begun an investigation into whether subpoenas issued to [the Executive Office of the President] by the task force were fully complied with, and whether persons were threatened with retaliation in order to prevent the existence of the affected e-mails from becoming known to the task force."[49]

House Government Reform Committee chairman Dan Burton released a written admission by the White House that all of Vice President Gore's e-mails from March 1998 through April 1999 had failed to be saved on back-up tapes. Despite the fact that Gore was briefed on this problem in April 1999 he neglected to notify White House counsel, the congressional committee, or the various independent counsels who had demanded the documents.[50] Later, in an affidavit filed in federal court in Washington, D.C., White House aide Howard Sparks said that Vice President Gore's top information expert told White House computer specialists in 1993 to "get lost" when they offered to make a tape back-up of Gore's e-mails for the purpose of preserving them for "potential legal proceedings." According to Sparks's affidavit, Gill said, "the Vice President's Office would take care of its own records."[51]

Yet Another Gore Investigation Begins (and Ends)—Gore's Iced Tea Defense

In June 2000 Congress released thousands of documents that it had obtained from the Justice Department involving the department's internal turmoil over whether an independent counsel should be sought to investigate Al Gore's questionable fund-raising activities. Word also leaked that, very recently, yet another Justice Department official had disputed Janet Reno's decision. Robert J. Conrad Jr., La Bella's successor as head of the Special Task Force, urged Reno to appoint a special counsel to investigate Gore.[52] Senator Arlen Specter, who had disclosed the leaked information, said that Senate subcommittee investigators had uncovered "very substantial evidence" showing that the Justice Department did not act on the recommendation. When asked about the new recommendation for an outside counsel, Janet Reno implied that she was considering it but said, "nothing should be rushed because too often when we rush to justice we don't get any."

Conrad based his recommendation to Reno largely on an official Justice Department interview he had conducted with Al Gore in April 2000, with two FBI agents present. After Senator Specter reported that Conrad had recommended a special counsel, Gore voluntarily released the transcript of the interview. Gore would later regret releasing that document. The transcript showed a different side of Gore. "I sure as hell did not have any conversations with anyone saying, 'This is a fundraising event,'" Gore told Robert Conrad and two FBI agents during the interview. In releasing the transcript Gore told reporters, "I think the truth is my friend in this." Yet, a Justice Department official purporting to have knowledge about the Conrad-Gore interview said that Gore was very combative, particularly concerning questions about the Buddhist Temple event. The anonymous source disputed Gore's assessment of his own veracity. "Essentially, it's one of these deals where X happened.... You say Y happened. Then, when you are being asked in detail about Y, you have to make statements that would make Y seem plausible. In saying things that are not particularly accurate in trying to make Y look plausible, you have other folks that your explanation deals with. And it doesn't mesh with what those people are saying."[53] In addition to his aggressive tone in the interview, Gore claimed memory failure at least eighty-five times.[54]

In the interview Gore strongly denied that he was well acquainted with convicted Democratic fund-raiser Maria Hsia. He insisted that he couldn't remember sitting next to her at the Buddhist Temple event. But, in fact, Hsia had helped Gore with campaign events for eight years. Gore once said that Hsia was a "great friend." And Gore had requested (and received) Hsia's help in writing his book *Earth in the Balance*. Gore's former chief of staff had written a letter of appreciation to Hsia for her assistance with the book. "The materials you got for Al's book on the environment were perfect. Thanks so much for taking the time to do it.... He would have been lost without your efforts, because the chapter on religion and the environment is integral to his work."[55]

Gore stubbornly clung to his story that he was unaware that the temple event was a fund-raiser. He said that he was paying a courtesy call to the temple. "I felt this visit was something they would be very pleased with because it showed honor to their community and to their place of worship." Gore's insistence on a mere casual awareness of the temple was belied by evidence that he had ties to it going back seven years.[56] Kenneth R. Timmerman, writing for the *Washington Times*, said, "so deep and so consistent are Mr. Gore's ties to the Fo Kuang Shan Buddhist order and to the convicted DNC fundraiser [Hsia] who first introduced him to the monks, that his denials are nothing short of breathtaking."

Timmerman explained that he happened on to Gore's relationship to the temple during an investigation for the *American
Spectator* on an entirely unrelated story. He said that in April 1988,
Maria Hsia, James Riady, and John Huang joined together to form
the Pacific Leadership Conference (PLC), which was to be used as
a vehicle for promoting the interests of Asian Americans, especially the Lippo Group. The PLC established ties to the temple
and became a significant fund-raiser for Democrats. The PLC
hosted an Asian tour for key Democratic senators. When one senator backed out, Hsia invited Gore to be a part of the tour. In her
letter recruiting Gore, Hsia wrote, "If you decide to join this trip,
I will persuade all my colleagues in the future to play a leadership
role in your future presidential race." During the tour, Gore visited the temple's headquarters in Taiwan with Hsia, James Riady,
John Huang, and others. Following the tour, Hsia kept her
promise and set up two large fund-raisers for Gore.[57]

Concerning another major issue under investigation—the
White House phone solicitations—Al Gore had vehemently
denied that he was aware that some of the money he was soliciting
from the White House phone calls would be used for hard-money
purposes. In his interview with Conrad he said that he must not
have been paying attention during a key Democratic National
Committee fund-raising meeting in November 1995 when this
subject was discussed. Gore testified that he could have missed the
discussion because he was drinking a great deal of iced tea and had
to make frequent visits to the restroom. Even Gore ally Robert
Litt, a Justice Department official who had reviewed the matter in
1998, didn't buy Gore's professed ignorance and thought an independent counsel should investigate it. In one of two 1998 memos
Litt wrote, "It was a question of whether there was clear and convincing evidence that Gore didn't intend to lie.... The statement

of a person without apparent reason to lie, corroborated by notes taken by an aide to the vice president, form a basis for concluding that the vice president did know what he claimed not to know—or certainly for investigating whether he may have…. It is not uncommon for us to bring a perjury case where the defendant's statements are contradicted by documents."

In one of the documents released by Congress, a Justice Department prosecutor, whose name had been scratched out, also weighed in on Gore's White House phone calls. "The evidence we now have… supports an argument that the vice president had to have known that hard money was a component of the Media Fund," he said.[58] The unnamed prosecutor also wrote that Harold Ickes, the White House aide who ran the meeting, always stopped for a break when either Clinton or Gore stepped out. "Not only is there no evidence that this occurred, but the agents' notes reflect that Ickes told them that when he conducted meetings, he would halt the proceedings if the president or vice president stepped out of the room; the meeting would resume when they returned," wrote the prosecutor. This same prosecutor added that former White House chief of staff Leon J. Panetta told the FBI that Gore had been "attentively listening" during the 1995 meeting. The prosecutor also revealed that a DNC official, Brad Marshall, similarly told the FBI that "his recollection was the same as Leon Panetta" about Gore paying attention at the meeting. The official disputed that Gore had to leave the room frequently for potty breaks. "Not only is there no evidence that this occurred—no witness recalls him leaving—but the agents' notes reflect that [former White House deputy chief of staff Harold] Ickes told them that when he conducted meetings—and he conducted the meeting on November 21—he would halt the proceedings if the president or vice president stepped out of the room. Rather than presume the vice president was not present, the presumption must be that he was."

In another memo, the Justice Department attorney wrote to his boss, Assistant Attorney General James K. Robinson—head of the criminal division—that the matter should be turned over to a grand jury. "A grand jury appearance under oath may well jog one's vague recollection as recounted in a voluntary interview." The released records also showed that two other Justice Department officials had recommended that Janet Reno appoint an independent counsel—FBI assistant director James DeSarno and FBI general counsel Larry Parkinson.[59]

The Conrad-Gore interview touched on an additional controversial question: whether Gore had broken the law by attending White House coffees that were allegedly disguised fund-raisers on federal property. During the period between November 1995 and August 1996, there were 103 White House coffees. The various guests contributed a total of $26.4 million, $7.7 million of which was paid within a month of the coffee party the particular donors attended. Although Charles La Bella had not recommended that an independent counsel investigate Gore on this matter, Robert Conrad asked him questions about it. Gore professed that he did not know whether he had served as host of twenty-three of those coffees and had attended eight more with Clinton present. He said he couldn't recall attending any coffees. "This was on the president's side of things," said Gore. "That's my memory and impression.... There may have been one that I attended briefly, perhaps because some of the invitees were known to me and wanted to say hello." Two days after the interview, Gore's attorney amended Gore's testimony by letter, saying that his client had misunderstood the question.[60]

While Reno was supposedly considering whether to appoint a special counsel for Gore, an additional embarrassing bit of evidence emerged. House Republicans obtained a video in which Gore made reference to "Riady" during one of the infamous White House coffees in December 1995. House Government Reform Committee chairman Dan Burton contended that the video clip showed Gore telling Arief Wiriadinata—who had illegally contributed $455,000 to the Democrats earlier that year—that they should make sure that Riady see the political ads developed by the Democratic Party (presumably with Riady's money). "We oughta, we oughta, we oughta show Mr. Riady the tapes, some of the ad tapes," Gore seemed to be saying on the video. Democrats sheepishly suggested that the audio wasn't clear and that Gore might have been saying "Dottie" or "Lottie" or "John Gotti." Justice Department officials refused to say whether they had seen the video or whether they planned on studying it.[61]

On August 23, 2000, Janet Reno defied her Special Task Force chief and for the third time rejected the idea of seeking an outside counsel (a special counsel) to investigate Vice President Gore, who was now in the thick of his presidential campaign. Gore's reaction was predictably political. His spokesman Chris Lehane said, "We are pleased with today's Justice Department announcement. But our focus is going to remain where it has always been—which is on using our prosperity to help America's families."

About a month after Reno's decision, some missing White House e-mails came to light casting even further doubt on Gore's (and Reno's) credibility. The just released e-mails, which had been reconstructed from backup tapes, showed that Gore knew the Buddhist Temple event was a fund-raiser—which meant that he had definitely lied to Robert Conrad and FBI investigators. (Lying to a federal agent during an investigation is a felony.) One of the e-mails from a Gore staffer dated three weeks before the temple event said, "Currently, we are committed in San Jose and [Los Angeles] for fundraising events." The message also included an official schedule for two fund-raisers for that day—the temple event and another in San Jose. Another of the recovered e-mails described an offer from a Taiwanese American businessman, George Chang, to raise $250,000 for the Democratic National Committee in exchange for a White House coffee and Clinton's commitment to give an interview to a Taiwanese reporter. (The offer to raise $250,000 apparently came through notorious Democratic fund-raiser John Huang.) The e-mail from a Gore staffer read, "Chang is trying to arrange a POTUS [President of the United States] coffee through the DNC, as well as a POTUS interview with a Taiwanese reporter.... In return for the DNC's efforts, Chang has promised to raise $250,000. John [Huang] feels there is a chance Chang has overpromised, but he plans to keep working with him."[62]

An earlier report by Carl Cameron of Fox News shed light on the Justice Department's consistently protective attitude toward Al Gore. Cameron reported that Lee Radek, chief of the Justice Department's Public Integrity Section, ordered federal prosecutor Steven Mansfield to stop his probe into Gore's Buddhist Temple fund-raiser. Radek, in a letter to Mansfield, said that the Justice Department should back off because it was a matter for an independent counsel to investigate. Yet, as is now abundantly clear, Janet Reno thwarted all efforts to seek an independent counsel to investigate Gore on the Buddhist Temple incident and all other matters, and, in fact, Radek was reportedly one of the most influential forces in persuading Reno not to seek one.[63] Two FBI investigators, one an assistant director of the FBI and the other a deputy director, said that Lee Radek told them in 1996 that he was under pressure due "to the fact the attorney general's job may hang in the balance" over how the Justice Department handled the campaign fund-raising scandal. Radek denied that he made such statements, but according to a memorandum by FBI director Louis Freeh, the FBI officials' stories corroborated each other on Radek's comments. The *Washington Times* reported on November 14, 2000, that the Justice Department had begun an investigation into accusations that Lee Radek misled Congress on whether he was "under a lot of pressure" to derail the department's campaign finance investigation. The inquiry, which was also supposed to review Reno's role in the campaign finance probe, was confirmed in a letter to Landmark Legal Foundation.[64]

Where's the Money?

Vice President Gore's 2000 presidential campaign was in high gear when reports surfaced that he was still benefiting from his and his party's misdeeds during the early 1990s. Gore's presidential campaign and other Democratic campaigns were helping themselves to $603,500 of illegal foreign contributions that had been raised primarily by fund-raisers John Huang and James Riady. The money was discovered by a Knight Ridder review of federal election records. The Democratic Party had already been forced to return $3.2 million, but this $603,500 remained with the Gore campaign, which was using it and declining to comment about it. It was clear that if the Democratic Party organizations were required to return the money, it would result in the loss of essential funds the Gore campaign was relying on—and had no intention of parting with. Though Democrats were speciously claiming the funds were legal, Huang had already told the FBI that the Lippo Group, Riady's foreign company, had reimbursed the contributions, making them clearly illegal.[65]

Beyond the $603,500, the Democratic Senatorial Campaign Committee retained an additional $43,500 in illegal foreign contributions. A spokesman for the committee said that the funds had been given to charities but could produce no records to verify the claim.

Republican National Committee chairman Jim Nicholson issued a strong statement condemning Al Gore for using illegal foreign campaign contributions while continuing to claim he was a champion of campaign finance reform. "Al Gore, Ed Rendell and Joe Andrew—tell the press and the public: Are you going to give up this illegal, foreign campaign cash? Or are you going to shamelessly spend it on yet another Democrat campaign—all the while claiming you are serious about campaign finance reform?"

But from Al Gore, there came no answer.

Chapter Ten

Bill Lann Lee: Quota King

The Clinton administration's approach to civil rights enforcement provided a glimpse into its willingness to subordinate the rule of law to its political aims. Its handling of the controversial appointment of Bill Lann Lee to head the Justice Department's Civil Rights Division in particular demonstrated its utter contempt for the integrity of the legislative and judicial branches of government.

The Civil Rights Division, which was created by the Civil Rights Act of 1957, is in charge of enforcing federal laws against discrimination, overseeing implementation of the Voting Rights Act, and pursuing cases to prevent the deprivation of constitutional rights. It litigates discrimination cases in employment, housing, education, and public accommodations. In November 1996, Deval L. Patrick, head of the division, announced he would be leaving the Justice Department for a position in private practice.

In June 1997, President Clinton nominated Bill Lann Lee, western regional counsel for the NAACP Legal Defense and

Educational Fund, Inc., to replace Patrick. Lee's nomination was subject to Senate confirmation. At the time of his nomination Lee was the darling of civil rights advocacy groups, having spent his entire legal career as a civil rights lawyer in the firm founded by the late Supreme Court justice Thurgood Marshall. Many viewed that firm, the "Legal Defense Fund," to be the most left-wing of all civil rights groups.

Conservative groups were very concerned about Lee's nomination because they feared he would not honor the Supreme Court's rulings against quotas. Specifically, in 1995 the Supreme Court in *Adarand v. Pena* held that race-based employment preferences are unconstitutional unless the government can show it has a compelling interest to enact such preferences, such preferences are narrowly tailored, and the preferences are of limited duration. Senate Judiciary Committee chairman Orrin Hatch indicated that his committee would thoroughly study Lee's record during the confirmation hearings.

Lee's advocacy record in certain high profile cases gave lawmakers ample reason for concern. One group of cases he handled in the 1980s, involving California supermarket chains, was of particular interest. Lee took on the supermarkets for imposing "structural barriers" that allegedly prevented women and minorities from advancing beyond entry-level positions. Referring to the cases, Lee said, "If an employer's work force is not reflective of the ethnic makeup of the total labor force available, then he has a potential vulnerability to a class action. He can change that situation by making sure his hiring practices more closely reflect the area's work-force population statistics." The supermarket case ended in a pretrial settlement in which the stores agreed to a system of numeric hiring and promotion goals for minority employees.[1]

Lee supported racial quotas whenever possible. For example, he maintained that the University of California was guilty of discrimination because its use of grades and standardized tests as admissions criteria resulted in fewer minority students being accepted into the school. Beyond Lee's ideological compatibility with the Clinton administration, he also sometimes spoke in Clintonese. In describing school busing, one of the pieties of liberal activists, Lee said, "The term 'forced busing' is a misnomer. School districts do not force children to ride a bus, but only to arrive on time at their assigned schools."

Lee shared Clinton's and Reno's philosophy that litigation should be used to trump Congress in making and amending law. As a civil rights prosecutor he was notorious for coercing companies to enter into pretrial settlements—known as consent decrees—to avoid the bankrupting expense of legally defending themselves. As Senator Hatch observed, "People don't realize that through consent decrees, you can enforce preferential policies because people have nowhere to go. They have to agree or find themselves in multi-million dollar attorney fee situations."

Conservatives were particularly exercised about the role Lee played in leading the Legal Defense Fund's challenge of California's Proposition 209. Prop 209 was a ballot issue overwhelmingly approved by California voters banning state affirmative action programs. The measure barred discrimination and preferences on the basis of race, sex, or ethnicity in state hiring, education, and contracting. Lee and his organization filed a friend-of-the-court brief urging the Ninth Circuit U.S. Court of Appeals to strike down the law on constitutional grounds. But the appeals court upheld the proposition as compatible with the state and federal constitutions.

Republican senators, such as Hatch, wanted assurances from the administration that if confirmed, Lee wouldn't marshal the formidable forces of the Justice Department to renew his attack on the California initiative because Lee believed that Proposition 209 violated the equal protection clause of the Fourteenth Amendment. "The Ninth Circuit Court of Appeals, arguably the most liberal of all the courts of appeals in this country, decisively rejected that argument," said Hatch, "saying, 'There is simply no doubt that Proposition 209 is constitutional. After all, the goal of the Fourteenth Amendment is a political system in which race no longer matters. The Fourteenth Amendment, lest we lost the forest for the trees, does not require what it barely permits.'"[2] Hatch added, "This is not an itty-bitty issue." Lee, himself, would be precluded from direct involvement in the case because of his previous participation in it.

It was not solely Lee's philosophy that concerned Republican congressmen. They anticipated that the zealous Lee would ignore his oath to uphold and enforce the law as established by Congress and interpreted by the courts. They believed he might be governed rather by his own opinion as to what the law should be. During the confirmation hearings, Republicans got the impression that Lee expressed a distorted view of existing law. He seemed to suggest that recent Supreme Court decisions that had restricted the permissible scope of affirmative action were instead supportive of it. Indeed, some argued that Lee's constitutional views were so "wrongheaded" that any senator voting to confirm Lee was violating his senatorial oath to support the Constitution.[3] This was a vote with more than symbolic consequences. As assistant attorney general for civil rights, Lee would be the nation's top law enforcement officer over an expansive area of law and would have some

250 lawyers at his command. The civil rights division had wide discretion both in deciding how to interpret judicial decisions and in drafting regulations and legislation. For these reasons, Senator Hatch ultimately decided to oppose Lee's nomination, saying that he believed Lee would use the Justice Department against states that prohibited race-based preferences. "Lee must be America's civil rights enforcer, not the civil rights ombudsman for the left," said Hatch. "To this day, he is an adamant defender of preferential policies that, by definition, favor some and disfavor others, based upon race and ethnicity."

In an unusual move (because the Senate has the sole authority to confirm such appointments) House Speaker Newt Gingrich came out against the confirmation. In a letter to Senate majority leader Trent Lott, Gingrich charged that Lee had tried to force a consent decree through the Los Angeles City Council that would have mandated "racial and gender preferences in the Los Angeles Police Department." This was an attempt, according to Gingrich, to thwart "the will of the people of California with regard to Proposition 209."[4]

Linda Chavez, head of the Center for Equal Opportunity, joined the chorus against Lee. "Lee does not believe in color-blind law," she said. "He believes in a legal system that is color coded." Other critics noted that Lee's views were far outside the legal mainstream. For example, in a case he brought against the Los Angeles Metropolitan Transit Authority he challenged as discriminatory a proposed bus fare increase that was earmarked to build and improve rail service because the majority of bus passengers were minorities, while the majority of train and trolley riders were white.

Republicans feared that Lee would push the civil rights division even further to the left than had Clinton's last appointee,

Deval Patrick, who forced private and public employers to enact race-based and sex-based hiring policies. Patrick had promised to defend all racially gerrymandered voting districts—before he had even investigated whether they were in violation of the Constitution. His view of his role was to expand the power of the federal government, not contract it. [5]

Clinton's first nominee to replace Patrick was Lani Guinier, who quickly became so controversial for her radical views on quotas—she became known as the "quota queen"—that Clinton had to withdraw her name before the confirmation hearing. Though Bill and Hillary Clinton were good friends with Guinier in law school, they abandoned her when her views became public. In a shameless attempt to distance himself from Guinier, Clinton said, "At the time of her nomination, I had not read her writings. In retrospect, I wish I had."

Clinton Plays the Race Card

The White House predictably painted Republicans who opposed Lee as racists. White House press secretary Mike McCurry said that Republicans might make Lee's nomination a matter of "race-based wedge politics." McCurry also took a shot at Hatch. "If Chairman Hatch believes that someone should follow the policies that he wishes to pronounce in the area of civil rights, which I suggest would amount to rolling back some of the progress we've made in civil rights, then Orrin Hatch should resign from the Senate, run for president, and he can name his own assistant attorney general for Civil Rights," said McCurry. An angry Clinton charged that by objecting to Lee's nomination, Republicans were interfering with the advancement of civil rights. "How can anybody in good conscience vote against him if they believe our civil rights laws ought to be enforced? That is the question we will be pressing to every senator without regard to party," said Clinton.[6] Clinton had said essentially the same thing when Republicans opposed Deval Patrick's nomination. [7]

Perhaps following Clinton's lead, Karen Narasaki, executive director of the National Asian Pacific American Legal Consortium, also intimated that Senator Hatch was a racist for opposing Lee. She pointed out that Hatch had recently voted to approve the nomination of Joel Klein to head the Justice Department's Antitrust Division, notwithstanding his policy differences with Klein. "Just a few months ago he said about a white male nominee, Joel Klein, 'I don't agree with all his views but he's qualified and he's the President's choice and he deserves the chance,'" said Narasaki. "Now when presented with Bill Lee it's a totally different standard."[8]

Some feminist leaders accused Republicans of opposing Lee because they wanted to keep women and minorities down. "The Republican Party is risking building the gender gap into a gender canyon," said Eleanor Smeal. "Make no mistake, this is another attempt to drive women and minorities back and slam the door on us, and we know what's going on." Senator Dianne Feinstein, the only woman on the Judiciary Committee, referred to her Republican colleagues as "white men" who were unwilling to grant the Asian American Lee a hearing.[9]

The Recess Appointment Angle

Congress adjourned for a ten-week recess in November 1997 before the Senate Judiciary Committee had acted on Lee's appointment. Actually, committee Democrats used parliamentary maneuvers to block a vote on the appointment when their head count told them he would be rejected. With Congress out of session, Clinton considered making Lee a "recess appointment." Officially, Lee's position would be temporary—he would be a placeholder—but Clinton could then rouse the civil rights lobby to pressure Congress into confirming Lee in his position. Article II, Section 2, of the Constitution empowers the president to fill vacancies in office "that may happen during the recess of the Senate." The appointee occupies the position until the close of the following congressional session. Previous presidents had used the recess appointment clause of the Constitution, but never in a situation where the Senate had already de facto rejected a nominee, as the Senate had with Bill Lann Lee. When used to circumvent the Senate, as opposed to filling the gap when the Senate is out of session, it is clearly an encroachment of the Senate's constitutional prerogative to "advise and consent" to such appointments.

Erskine Bowles, Clinton's chief of staff, defiantly promised that Lee would be the next assistant attorney general for civil rights. Said White House press secretary Mike McCurry, "In the course of the next week or so we're going to try to put public pressure on the Republicans to make them think about what they're doing and then we'll see where we are." At a Justice Department ceremony celebrating the fortieth anniversary of the civil rights division, Janet Reno said, "Others say [Lee] should be rejected because he shares the views of the President on affirmative action. I say no to that, and so does the President. Civil rights in America should not be about politics." Mr. Lee himself appeared on NBC's *Today* show and denied that he supported quotas.

On December 5, 1997, Democratic senator Robert Byrd wrote a letter to President Clinton telling him that it would be improper for him to use the recess appointment clause of the Constitution to appoint Lee. He pointed out that there was no emergency justifying such an appointment in that the Senate was scheduled to reconvene in just a few weeks. The appointment, said Byrd, "would smack of the desire to circumvent the regular nomination process."

Another Way to Circumvent the Senate

Apparently not wanting to ruffle Senator Byrd's feathers, Clinton, on December 16, decided to use a different procedural avenue to install Lee over the opposition of the Senate. Instead of using the recess appointment clause, he named Lee acting deputy attorney general for Civil Rights—a position not requiring Senate confirmation—and then graduated him immediately to acting head of the division. Clinton's move was just barely less objectionable to Senate Republicans than a recess appointment would have been. Clinton said he was confident the Senate would change its mind and confirm Lee once it observed him in office. He said he looked forward to eliminating the word "acting" from his title. Clinton said, "I have done my best to work with the United States Senate in an entirely constitutional way. But we had to get somebody into the Civil Rights Division."

By law, acting appointees can serve only 120 days. But the governing statute contains no enforcement provision. So Lee could, in fact, serve until the end of Clinton's term without ever being confirmed by the Senate. Clint Bolick, litigation director for the Institute for Justice, described acting appointments and recess appointments as two sides of the same coin. "Either way, the Administration has abrogated the Senate's advise and consent role," he said. "Bill Lann Lee will carry the taint of illegitimacy throughout his tenure because he did not receive Senate confirmation."[10]

Following Clinton's appointment of Lee, Senators Byrd and Hatch sent separate letters of protest to Attorney General Reno.

They cited the federal Vacancies Act, which provides that such temporary "vacancy" appointments shall be limited to 120 days, after the Senate has rejected a nomination.[11] The precise purpose of the 1868 Vacancies Act was to prevent thwarting the Senate's constitutional role in executive branch appointments.

The law authorized that if an executive officer resigned, his "first assistant" could act in his place for 120 days. If the president nominated a permanent replacement, the first assistant could remain as acting executive until the nomination was confirmed or until 120 days after it was rejected. The problem with Lee's appointment was that Lee could hardly qualify as a "first assistant," since he was not even serving in the Justice Department at the time of his appointment.[12] Janet Reno argued that a separate federal law permitted the administration to make an appointment without reference to the Vacancies Act.

The law Reno invoked, however, has nothing to do with the appointment of officers to fill vacant positions. Rather, it is a statute authorizing the attorney general to delegate her powers to subordinates in the department. There are many such statutes on the books applying to different government departments, which allow most department heads to delegate their authority to their employees for the purpose of efficiency. If these efficiency statutes were permitted to authorize vacancy appointments, they would virtually emasculate the Senate's constitutional role in approving important appointees.[13]

Senator Byrd pointed this out to Reno. And as columnist George Will observed, when Congress amended the Vacancies Act in 1988, "the Senate Governmental Affairs Committee's report reaffirmed the supremacy of the act as 'the exclusive authority' for filling offices subject to Senate confirmation."[14]

The Congressional Research Service affirmed that Lee's appointment was subject to the Vacancies Act and not to the statute Reno was attempting to use. In a memorandum, the agency said that the White House had violated the act in naming Lee to fill the position. Its reasoning was that the act had been invoked when Clinton appointed Acting Assistant Attorney General Isabelle Pinzler to fill the slot when Deval Patrick had resigned. The agency concluded that "the sole lawful option immediately available" to Clinton was to make Lee a "recess appointment" before Congress reconvened on January 27.[15]

Because Clinton and Reno failed to yield, Senator Byrd co-sponsored a bipartisan bill with Senator Fred Thompson of Tennessee to amend the Vacancies Act so that it was absolutely clear who could serve as an "acting" officer. The bill also specified that the interim official would have no legal authority to carry out the duties of the head of the department.[16]

After Lee had served as acting head of the civil rights division for over a year, Clinton renominated him to serve as official head of the division. White House press secretary Joe Lockhart said that Lee had "done an excellent job on a wide variety of issues over the last year" and deserved to be confirmed. The Senate Judiciary Committee declined to act on this nomination because Senator Hatch took the position that Lee had been rejected once, and there was no need to go through the process again, especially since Clinton had ignored and defied the Senate's action.

Senate's Opposition Vindicated

During Lee's illegal tenure the Justice Department was involved in the case of *Sonntag v. McConnell*. William Sonntag was a federal employee who filed a reverse discrimination case against the government for denying him a promotion on the basis of his race and sex. U.S. attorney for Maryland Lynne Battaglia, in defending the government, sidestepped the issue of whether racial and sexual preferences were legal and chose to defend solely on the "facts." The court rejected her contention that there was in fact no discrimination, calling it "frivolous, if not disingenuous." According to the court, the government had discriminated against Sonntag because he was a white male. The court said the government was obliged to defend or deny the applicability of such race- and sex-based preferences.

Battaglia refused. She said she had been directed "in no uncertain terms" by her "masters" not to argue the law. The court condemned such "a suspiciously unyielding opposition" and demanded that Battaglia reappear to argue the law within two weeks. The government missed two such deadlines before it hurriedly settled the case with Sonntag. The brief that the government finally presented to the court contained only "eight double-spaced pages of perfunctory text." The court lambasted the U.S. attorney, saying, "the integrity of the judicial process has been compromised by considerations that apparently forced upon the United States Attorney a choice between allegiance to politics and service to the court." Battaglia "evidenced almost a contemptuousness toward the court."[17] By instructing Battaglia not to argue the law and to settle the case, Lee may very well have been trying to avoid constitutional scrutiny of his racially and sexually biased hiring policies that could be used against him in future Senate confirmation hearings.[18]

The Sonntag case was not the only one in which Lee revealed his passion for unconstitutional preferences. Roger Clegg, general counsel for the Center for Equal Opportunity and a deputy in the Civil Rights Division between 1987 and 1991, in an op-ed piece in the *Wall Street Journal*, detailed twenty-three instances of Lee's aggressive promotion of preferences during his first year in office.[19] For example, in testimony before the House Judiciary Subcommittee on the Constitution, Lee defended federal racial preferences as necessary "to have a country we can all be proud of" and said they shouldn't end "anytime soon." And Lee filed a brief supporting an EPA regulation requiring contractors, when hiring subcontractors, to "assure that small, minority, and women's businesses are used when possible as sources of supplies, construction and services." Lee also filed an appellate brief arguing in favor of a Virginia school district's use of racial and ethnic preferences in admissions to ensure diversity in its student body.[20]

In addition, Lee took over from his predecessor an action that had been filed against the city of Torrance, California. The Justice Department was trying to force the city to adopt racial preferences in its hiring practices. The federal judge (a Carter appointee) held that the case was "frivolous, unreasonable and without foundation." As a result, the Civil Rights Division was ordered to pay $1.8 million in legal fees to the city.[21] The Ninth U.S. Circuit Court of Appeals affirmed the trial judge's decision. Torrance mayor Dee Hardison said, "The city stood up to the Justice Department... because it believed it had acted lawfully in choosing the very best police officers and firefighters to protect its citizens."

Apparently learning nothing from his experience with Torrance, Lee filed a suit in February 1998 against the city of Garland, Texas, claiming that it had failed to recruit enough minorities into its police and fire departments. He alleged that the city's hiring application tests had a "disparate impact" on blacks and Hispanics. The city contended that its examinations were fair and were the type widely used by police departments throughout the state. One of Lee's deputies was quoted in the local paper as saying, "This is the worst possible way to select applicants." An African-American fireman in Garland disagreed. "I don't see how they can say they have bad hiring practices by looking at the test. All the questions in the test are fire-related," he said.[22]

Lee's division also started a disturbing practice of attempting to force cities into acquiescing to federal monitoring of their police forces. In 1998, Lee charged the Pittsburgh Police Department with violating civil rights, based on a federal lawsuit in which sixty plaintiffs alleged separate incidents of abuse by the city's police officers. Lee reportedly filed the case without conducting an independent investigation of the charges. Chuck Bosetti, a Pittsburgh police officer, said, "They never interviewed a single officer about the allegations brought against them." Among the Justice Department's list of grievances were findings from a 1996 Pittsburgh City controller's performance audit of the police bureau. But that audit concluded that there was no "systemic, racially motivated police misconduct." Eventually the division strong-armed the city into accepting a consent decree rather than spending hundreds of thousands of dollars in legal fees. The decree, however, would prove even more costly than the legal fees would have. It mandates federal oversight with an alarming degree of big-brother controls, such as giving the federal government full access to all staff records, including databases, files, and quarterly statistical summaries, and authority to review discipline and remedial training. The decree further requires the city's officers to take cultural diversity training, in which officers learn how to "relate to persons from different racial, ethnic, and religious groups, and persons of the opposite sex." Compliance with the decree has cost Pittsburgh more than $5 million. The decree required the creation of a $495,992 early warning system to identify potentially troubled police officers. Get this: if an officer stops a minority or female suspect, regardless of the reason, he is "red-flagged" into the database, and subject to possible disciplinary action.[23]

The civil rights division is trying the same thing in Columbus, Ohio. It has filed a lawsuit alleging a pattern and practice of civil rights violations by the city's police officers. It is seeking to have at least three outside monitors appointed to oversee training, staff assignments, and internal-affairs investigations. The federal magistrate assigned to make findings and recommendations in the case, though agreeing that individual police officers were guilty of civil rights violations, did not recommend that the city itself be found liable. For the Justice Department to prevail in the case, said the magistrate, it would have to prove that the city and its high-ranking officials condoned these violations. The magistrate's ruling prompted a group of fourteen congressmen, led by Democrat John Conyers, to request permission to file a friend-of-the-court brief on behalf of the Justice Department.[24]

One Justice official admitted that these cities were just the beginning. Also being investigated were Buffalo; Los Angeles; New Orleans; Charleston, West Virginia; Riverside, California; East Pointe, Michigan; Orange County, Florida; Prince George's County, Maryland; Scottsdale, Arizona; South Bend, Indiana; and Springfield, Massachusetts.[25] Lee later launched an investigation into New York's police department following the police shootings of Amadou Diallo and Patrick Dorismond.

In addition, Lee filed a lawsuit against the city of Lawrence, Massachusetts, under the Voting Rights Act. He was seeking to force the city to hire more Hispanic workers for the polls and to alter its school districts and school boards to ensure that more

290 _____ ABSOLUTE POWER

school districts contain a majority of Hispanics. As a result of a settlement of a portion of the case with the Justice Department,
Lawrence will install bilingual workers in polling places and will
print voter information in Spanish. The settlement, according to
the Justice Department, sought to establish a long-term program
to ensure that all voters in the city come to the polls armed with
the same information and equal opportunity. Anita Hodgkiss, the
Justice Department's deputy director for civil rights, said, "We are
very excited and encouraged by the agreement and by what the
city is planning to do. What this will do is give Hispanic citizens a
chance to have a voice in the democratic process and make that
process as accessible to them as it is to English-speaking citizens."
Lawrence officials estimate that between 50 percent and 60 percent of the city's 70,000 residents are Hispanic.[26] Despite the settlement, the Justice Department continued to pressure the city to
elect its city councilors from districts, rather than from a citywide
slate, in order to increase Hispanic representation.

United Charter School of East Baton Rouge, Louisiana, was
yet another victim of Lee's social engineering designs. Because of
failing schools brought on by years of government-ordered deseg-
regation, mandatory busing, and other "progressive" educational
remedies, Louisiana enacted a charter school law, which provided
for the establishment of public schools that would be free from
state supervision. United Charter, with 650 students from kindergarten through eighth grade, was one of the new schools. But Lee's
civil rights lawyers prevented the school from opening. The
reason: the school might be too successful and attract white children from surrounding areas, which could upset the school's racial
balance. Residents scoffed that there were so few whites in the area
that such concern was misplaced.[27] While the school promised

new educational opportunity, one Justice Department official remarked, "What the parents want isn't important to me. I'm interested in the law."

Clinton Rubs Congress's Nose in It Again

In early August 2000, with less than six months left in his second term, President Clinton finally used the recess appointment clause of the Constitution to appoint Bill Lann Lee to serve as head of the Civil Rights Division of the Justice Department. This would allow Lee to serve out Clinton's term and through the end of the next Senate session in 2001 unless the next president removed him. Senator Hatch stated that Clinton's recess appointment of Lee in the thick of the presidential race was "further evidence of what we have come to know is true: The Clinton-Gore White House is intent on dividing our people rather than uniting us for the common good."

The White House again chose to depict the Republicans as opponents of civil rights. Referring to the GOP convention in Philadelphia, White House press secretary Joe Lockhart said that the Senate Republicans' refusal to confirm Lee stood "in sharp contrast to the theatrical performance in Philadelphia designed to obscure" a lack of "commitment to civil rights enforcement."[28] Other White House aides admitted that Lee's recess appointment was in part a rebuke to the Republican Party's effort to establish an image of racial inclusiveness. "It's one thing to put on a show of diversity," said White House spokesman Elliot Diringer. "It's another thing to support vigorous civil rights enforcement, and that's what we are doing here."[29] Democratic senator Patrick Leahy also used the appointment as an opportunity to twist the knife into Republicans. "The kinder, gentler Republican mood is either a myth, or maybe that memo never made it to the Republican Senate," said Leahy.

The entire sordid episode of Bill Clinton's appointment of Bill Lann Lee illustrates his administration's contemptuous disregard for the rule of law and the Constitution. Lee's conduct bore out Senate Republicans' fears of confirming him. As Clinton's quota king, Lee ensured that the power of the federal government would be used to enforce raced-based preferences over merit and that the federal government's power grows ever stronger to dictate outcomes in education, jobs, and other activities in every community in America.

Chapter Eleven

Treating with Terrorists

P uerto Rico is a Spanish-speaking Caribbean island of 3.8 million people that has been ruled by the United States since 1898. Its people are U.S. citizens who serve in the military and receive billions in federal funds but cannot vote in presidential elections and have no voting members in Congress. Most Puerto Ricans oppose independence from the United States, having rejected it in two recent referenda. In 1993 only 4.4 percent of Puerto Rican voters cast ballots to break away. In 1998, less than 3 percent voted for independence. An ever popular move for statehood, on the other hand, garnered 46 percent of the vote in 1998.[1]

Nevertheless, some Puerto Ricans support independence to the point of violence. Law enforcement officials say that between 1974 and 1983 the "Armed Forces of National Liberation"—a Puerto Rican terrorist group that goes by the initials FALN— bombed more than 130 American military, business, and political "targets." Another Puerto Rican terrorist group that operates mostly in Puerto Rico is the Popular Boricua Army, known as the Macheteros, "the machete wielders."

Many of the Puerto Rican terrorist bombings occurred in New York City and Chicago. The most devastating incident was in 1975 at the historic Fraunces Tavern in lower Manhattan where four people were killed and more than sixty were injured. Another high-profile series of bombings occurred in the Wall Street area in early March 1982. At the time the FALN took credit for the bombings. Many of the members made the FBI's most wanted listed for bombing corporate buildings, department stores, and restaurants.[2]

During the 1980s twelve FALN members and four of the Macheteros were convicted of crimes in federal court. The charges included armed robbery, conspiracy to commit armed robbery, weapons violations, conspiracy to overthrow the United States government, and prison escapes. But on August 11, 1999, President Clinton offered clemency deals for these sixteen terrorists. He agreed to release eleven of them from prison, reduce the prison sentences of two others, and lower the fines of three who had already been released from prison.

The immediate question was: Did the White House commute the sentences to win Puerto Rican votes for Hillary Clinton's senatorial campaign? Before this, the Clinton administration had granted clemency in only three of the more than three thousand cases that had been brought before it. The White House denied that politics played a role and claimed the president acted on the strong recommendation of departing chief White House counsel Charles F. C. Ruff. The president defended his action on the grounds that the parole candidates had not been accused of violent acts. Many human rights figures, including South African archbishop Desmond Tutu, Coretta Scott King, John Cardinal O'Connor, and former president Jimmy Carter, urged Clinton to release the terrorists because their prison sentences had been disproportionately severe, anywhere from thirty-five to ninety years. Most had already served nineteen years. Clinton and White House press secretary Joe Lockhart advanced the argument that, in Lockhart's words, "They had already served sentences that exceeded what they'd be sentenced for now under the minimum sentencing guidelines which all parties agree are tougher than they were 20 or 30 years ago." In fact, that was not true. Senator Orrin Hatch of Utah later showed the sentences would actually have been *greater* under current federal sentencing guidelines.[3]

FALN victims and their families, including police officers scarred by the FALN, strongly criticized the pardons. Joseph Connor, whose thirty-three-year-old banker-father died in the 1975 Fraunces Tavern bombing, said, "It makes me sick. It's a betrayal. Is my father's life worth less than his [Clinton's] wife's election?"[4] New York police officer Rocco Pascarella lost part of his leg from an FALN bombing outside his Manhattan police headquarters on New Year's Eve in 1982. His colleague Richard Pastorella lost five fingers and was blinded, and Officer Anthony Stent lost an eye.[5] Pastorella said, "How can I tell you what the psychological effect was to my family, to my children, to my wife? Certainly, it took me fully two years to physically recover. But the emotional injuries remain. You wake up with nightmares at night and cold sweats. It never leaves. It never goes away."[6] Police Commissioner Howard Safir was even more forceful in his criticism of Clinton. "This type of action will encourage terrorism worldwide. We should never make deals with terrorists."

Though the FALN claimed responsibility for the bombings, no one had been convicted of the crimes. The suspected architect of the Fraunces Tavern bombing had escaped from a prison ward in 1979 and fled from the United States to Cuba. In 1993, he told the

Cleveland Plain Dealer that the FALN bombing was in response to an attack by the CIA on Puerto Rican nationalists. "It may sound heartless to say it that way, but it is hard to fight a war without bystanders getting injured."[7]

Thwarting Justice

Ordinarily, a pardon is granted only after a prisoner applies for clemency and expresses remorse. But Clinton offered clemency without its being requested; the FALN prisoners refused to send letters of contrition even though the Justice Department had strongly urged them to do so. Instead they issued a statement saying "innocent victims were on all sides." The White House and Justice Department played proactive roles in the process. While the administration claimed dignitaries were pressuring it, in at least one case it was the other way around. The White House actually approached former president Carter and recruited him to recommend clemency.[8] Also, notes obtained by the House Government Reform Committee during its investigation of the matter reveal that White House aides planned to identify "liberal supporters in key media outlets" in an effort to drum up more support for clemency.[9] And one deputy attorney general directed the pardon attorney to call certain congressional offices to "see where we stood on getting" a statement addressing the repentance of the prisoners.[10]

Clinton made the clemency offer conditional on the prisoners renouncing the use of violence and consenting to ordinary requirements of parole. The prisoners did not immediately agree to the conditions or accept the offer. Their Chicago-based attorney, Jan Susler, objected that "There is really no reason for any conditions. If they are released and violate the law, there's a process to address it." Susler even rejected the requirement that the prisoners, if freed, not consort with felons—a common condition of parole or probation—saying, "These men and women are not every convicted felon. They are not criminals. They are political people who intend to become involved in the open, legal, political non-violent process to shape the future of the country."[11]

Two of the sixteen refused to renounce violence. When the remaining fourteen did finally accept the deal, Susler said it was because of their fervent desire to see Puerto Rico a sovereign nation. "They felt they could do more by being out on the street and integrating into society," she said. "They are like political beings.... They are like fish out of water. They want to jump back in the water and swim."[12]

Shortly after Clinton's offer became public, reports leaked that federal law-enforcement agencies were opposed to it. The FBI, the Bureau of Prisons, and United States attorneys in Illinois and Connecticut all "flatly opposed" the deal.[13] The FBI pointed out that it was improper to grant leniency to militants who claimed responsibility for terrorist acts, especially considering that the United States had declared war on terrorism. More troublesome was the opinion of Bureau of Prison officials, based on their monitoring of prison visits, phone calls, and letters to FALN members, that the prisoners would resume their criminal behavior if they were released.[14] One inmate was secretly tape-recorded making statements that were hardly repentant. In a conversation just after the clemency offer had been made, he was recorded saying that he need not ask for forgiveness. "My conscience is at peace with itself. You see, it's a question of rights, of the violations that have been committed against our people for the past 100 years."[15]

The Justice Department had included the agencies' objections in its final report to the White House but parted from its usual practice by offering the president no recommendation on whether to grant clemency, giving him a number of options instead. This was a de facto rejection of the expert advice of the FBI, the Bureau of Prisons, and the U.S. attorneys.

According to the House Government Reform Committee, the Justice Department in considering such cases examines "disparity or undue severity of sentence, critical illness or old age, and meritorious service rendered to the government by the petitioner." Also important are the type of offense and whether the petitioner has accepted responsibility and shown remorse. The committee found that the FALN and Macheteros clemency candidates failed to meet any of the criteria.[16]

Another factor making the Justice Department's action even more suspicious was that around the same time, Deputy Attorney General Eric Holder released the department's Five-Year Interagency Counterterrorism and Technology Crime Plan. The plan was issued under Janet Reno's specific authority and concluded that the release of FALN members would heighten the risk of domestic terrorism. Also, during subsequent Senate Judiciary Committee hearings, it was discovered that in 1996 the Justice Department specifically recommended against the release of FALN prisoners, changing its mind only after Hillary Rodham Clinton became a senatorial candidate in New York.

The Hillary Trap

Hillary Clinton said that although she supported clemency if the prisoners first renounced violence, she had "no involvement whatsoever" in the decision.[17] But a few days later Hillary reversed herself and called upon her husband "to immediately withdraw" his clemency offer. Senator Phil Gramm was among those who put two and two together and called the clemency decision a political ploy that had been "badly miscalculated."[18]

While Bill and Hillary Clinton were trading public statements denying any influence on the other's decision, the president and first lady were spending the weekend together at Camp David, and ostensibly did not discuss politics.[19]

This wasn't the first time Mrs. Clinton had publicly distanced herself from President Clinton in her New York Senate race. Earlier she had joined New York politicians and labor leaders in criticizing the president's planned reductions in Medicare reimbursements to hospitals. She had also taken a position on Jerusalem contrary to the State Department's official stance when she announced that Jerusalem should be the "eternal and indivisible capital of Israel."[20]

The first couple's feigned disagreement reached new heights of absurdity when ABC News revealed that two days before Mrs. Clinton publicly demanded that her husband rescind the clemency offer, the White House already knew it had been accepted.[21] When pressed about her denial that she had discussed clemency with her husband, Hillary said, "There's one thing I'm not going to talk about and that's my private conversations with the president."

Hillary's denials of conversations with Bill belie what has always been said of their relationship. In 1996, the *Washington Post* reported that, "At the end of the day, she and her husband talk. They talk, according to White House officials, about virtually everything. White House and campaign personnel, public policy, the coming campaign. The Clintons are so accustomed to talking about politics, one aide said, 'they can go from talking about Chelsea's math home-work one moment to welfare policy the next.'"[22]

Flip-Flop Politics

Jose E. Serrano, the Hispanic New York congressman from the South Bronx, began as a strong supporter of Mrs. Clinton's cam-paign. But he roundly condemned her withdrawal of support for clemency: "By the same arrogance and inability to understand issues and people that allowed them to advise her to make that blunder, they now are beginning to downplay my role in a senatorial elec-tion. I'm not one who says, 'I'm very powerful, I control votes,' but you shouldn't try to test that, because you might be shocked at what you find." Serrano said that before her reversal, 99.9 percent of the people in the Bronx didn't have a problem with her but afterwards they were evenly divided.[23]

When Hillary came under fire from Serrano and other Hispanic spokesmen for changing her position, she changed it again. She told a group of Hispanic, Asian, and black women in Manhattan that she might have been too hasty in opposing the release. "I have a number of Hispanic advisors and... I have to admit that the consultation process was not what it should have been and that will never happen again. I have reached out to and have been talking with many people in the Hispanic community who have been very helpful to me and I look forward to contin-uing to work with them, and hearing from them, and having their advice and counsel as we move forward."[24]

Investigation

The president's decision and reports of agency dissent prompted committees in both houses of Congress to make inquiries.

The House committee, chaired by Dan Burton of Indiana, issued subpoenas to the White House for its records concerning the clemency decision, and even Democrats came out against Clinton. New York senator Daniel Patrick Moynihan and Vermont senator Patrick Leahy, for example, both opposed clemency, which should only be granted, Leahy said, to those who show "an extraordinary sense of remorse." New York congressman Vito Fossell remarked, "It is a tragic day that terrorists may very soon again be allowed to walk America's streets. I call on the President to unconditionally reject this offer of clemency. I don't want to see one more innocent American killed by this group." Thirty-five congressmen co-sponsored a resolution condemning Clinton's decision as sending "an unmistakable message to terrorists that the United States does not punish terrorists in the most severe manner possible under the law, making terrorism more likely and endangering every American." The House resolution passed with overwhelming bipartisan support, 311-41. The Senate followed suit with a nearly unanimous (95-2) bipartisan resolution condemning Clinton's clemency offer. Senator Phil Gramm of Texas remarked, "When you pardon terrorists, you lower the costs of committing terrorist acts."

Clinton defended his position to reporters on the White House lawn following the House resolution. "None of them were convicted of doing bodily harm to anyone. And they had all served sentences that were considerably longer than they would serve under the sentencing guidelines, which control federal sentencing now. I did not believe they should be held in incarceration in effect by guilt by association." Clinton responded as if his decision were merely routine, completely divorced from politics. "I got the memo from Ruff. I didn't know it was coming. It came with all the other papers I get every day and every week, and I dealt with it the way

I deal with everything."[25] Clinton's national security advisor, Sandy Berger, supported Clinton's contention that the prisoners were nonviolent. Berger said on national television that "they're not individuals who personally were involved in violence."

During congressional hearings Republican congressmen pointed out that there is no distinction in the law between accessories to violent crimes and those who actually pull the trigger (or detonate the bombs). Chairman Burton remarked, "The only reason some of them didn't commit murders or bombings is because they were arrested before they got a chance to." Moreover, law enforcement authorities were convinced that eight of the prisoners who received clemency were in the process of attempting to kidnap millionaire Henry Crown when they were arrested in Evanston, Indiana, in April 1980.[26] In addition, according to the House committee, "the seditious conspiracy counts in the indictments of fourteen of the individuals included the construction and planting of explosive and incendiary devices [bombs] at 28 locations in Illinois between the period of June 14, 1975, through November 24, 1979. Thus, many of those granted clemency actually were convicted of conspiring to place bombs."[27] The committee also noted that in 1987 the Second Circuit Court of Appeals said, "The [federal] district judge also found that [one of the FALN prisoners] had organized and taken part in the attack in Puerto Rico on a United States Navy bus taking sailors to a radar station, on December 3, 1979, in which two sailors were killed and nine were wounded."[28] Finally, the committee revealed that there was videotape footage of some of the prisoners making bombs and that one of them had planned two prison escapes by violent means, including the use of fragmentation grenades, gunfire, and plans to murder a gun dealer.[29]

The Politics of Clintonian Privilege

Clinton denied on several occasions that political considerations had anything to do with his decision. However, even beyond the obvious political motive and the unusual nature in which the White House handled this clemency, there is direct evidence that politics played a role. The House committee found that one of the key White House staff members during the clemency process wrote (presumably with political considerations in mind) that the release of the sixteen terrorists would "have a positive impact among strategic Puerto Rican communities in the U.S." The committee also found that White House personnel believed that pardoning the prisoners would politically benefit the president and vice president. An important presidential advisor on the FALN matter, Jeffrey Farrow, in an e-mail obtained by the committee, wrote, "We should think about a meeting soon with Reps. Gutierrez, Velazquez, and Serrano on the Puerto Rico independence crimes prisoners issue. They have requested one with the POTUS [President] but the options include the VP and John as well. The issue should be resolved soon—the petitions have been before us for a long time. The VP's Puerto Rican position would be helped: The issue is Gutierrez's top priority as well as of high constituent importance to Serrano and Velazquez."[30]

It's also telling that President Clinton asserted executive privilege and refused to release to Dan Burton's committee internal White House documents concerning his clemency decision. The White House did, however, volunteer to deliver documents that supported clemency. Burton said that Clinton's invocation of executive privilege was tantamount to telling Congress and the American people that it was his decision and none of their business. In a letter to Congress seeking to justify his decision Clinton employed familiar semantic shenanigans, declaring that the grants of clemency were not pardons but reductions in prison sentences, allowing the prisoners to qualify for parole. During the committee hearings an assistant attorney general testified that Clinton was justified in using the privilege to withhold documents "because the pardon power is an exclusive constitutional prerogative of the president."

FBI assistant director Neil Gallagher—though barred from disclosing particulars—told the House committee that the FALN members still represented a threat to the United States. Gallagher cited a "disturbing" string of bombing incidents in the 1990s linked to the FALN. A draft letter from FBI director Louis Freeh said the release of the prisoners would likely "return committed, experienced, sophisticated and hardened terrorists to the clandestine movement" for Puerto Rican independence, terrorists whose violent acts resulted in "no fewer than nine fatalities, hundreds of injuries, millions of dollars in property damage, and armed attacks on U.S. government facilities." The statement made clear that Clinton had not consulted with Freeh before announcing his clemency offer on August 11, 1999.[31] Freeh apparently never signed the statement, which was in the form of a letter to Congressman Henry Hyde, because the Justice Department refused to approve it. The Justice Department also denied the FBI permission to submit to Congress a written statement of the criminal history and current terrorist capability of the FALN and Macheteros.[32]

Victims of the bombings complained to the committee that they had not been notified of the prisoners' imminent release, as federal law required. Vice President Al Gore, who was a self-proclaimed champion of victims' rights, even to the point of advocating a constitutional amendment to guarantee those rights—was conspicuously silent on the matter.

Unquestionably, the Constitution provides that the president shall have power to grant reprieves and pardons for federal offenses, except in cases of impeachment. The Supreme Court has made clear just how expansive this presidential prerogative is. It is equal to that of English kings and extends to all offenses without modification or regulation by Congress.

Without disputing the president's *right* to pardon anyone, what possible *reason* other than politics did he have in the case of the FALN and Macheteros? These are terrorists who, according to federal law-enforcement experts, still represent a threat to citizens of the United States. For a man who claimed to feel our pain, Clinton did a masterful job of putting American citizens at risk of more pain, dismemberment, and death, and completely disregarded the pain of the victims' families.

Given the unanimous opposition of law-enforcement officials, the marked absence of contrition by the prisoners, and the extreme rarity with which the president had previously handed out pardons, it is a logical conclusion that Clinton and Reno abused their offices and betrayed justice to promote Hillary Clinton's and Al Gore's political ambitions. For that worthy goal, freeing a few anti-American terrorists seemed a small price to pay—at least to the Clintons.

Chapter Twelve

Elian

On Sunday, November 22, 1999, in Cardenas, a city east of Havana on Cuba's north coast, fourteen Cubans crammed into a flimsy seventeen-foot aluminum motorboat and left for the United States. Among the fourteen passengers were five-year-old Elian Gonzalez, his mother Elizabeth, and his stepfather. Elizabeth had been separated for several years from Elian's biological father, Juan Miguel Gonzalez, a Cuban national park employee.

Elizabeth and Elian's route was well traveled. Every year more than a thousand Cubans flee Castro's communist dictatorship, navigating the perilous Florida Straits to gain freedom in America.

Just two days after mother, son, and stepfather set sail, their small boat capsized under the relentless assault of rough weather. Seven of the fourteen people drowned. The other seven split into two groups, each sharing one of the two inner tubes that were on the boat. Even though they were in view of the Florida coast, four of the remaining seven wouldn't make it, drowning at sea.

Near dawn on Thursday off Key Biscayne, fishermen found two of the three survivors, a thirty-three-year-old man and a twenty-three-year-old woman. Not long after, two men on an early morning dolphin expedition saw an inner tube bobbing in the ocean off Fort Lauderdale. Donato Dalrymple told his cousin Sam Ciancio he saw a person in the inner tube. Ciancio thought it was a doll that had been tied to the tube as "a sick joke." Donato persisted, saying he was sure he had seen a hand moving.

Ciancio dived into the water and when he approached the inner tube found a little boy shaking with cold. He swam with the boy back to the boat and lifted him up to Donato. Donato asked the boy, "Do you speak English?" No answer.

"Habla español?"

"Si."

Ciancio went to the boat's phone to call for help. The emotional Donato—a former Christian missionary—kissed the boy's face, his forehead, his cheeks, and his chin and held him tightly. Exhausted, the little boy then fell asleep. "I've traveled around the world as a missionary, but I have never felt like this. What a gift to find this kid today. I would like to see his face again," Donato said.[1] After returning to shore Dalrymple and Ciancio took the boy, Elian Gonzalez, to a hospital near Fort Lauderdale where he was found to be in stable condition and was treated for exposure and dehydration. Doctors were amazed that Elian had survived after going without water for two days.

Shifting Political Responses

While Elian was in the hospital, his great-uncle Lazaro Gonzalez, of Miami, contacted the Immigration and Naturalization Service (INS). Lazaro told INS officials that before Elian was discovered at sea, his father Juan Miguel had telephoned him and asked him to take care of Elian if he made it to the United States. When the boy was released from the hospital on November 26, 1999, the INS paroled Elian into Lazaro's custody. Elated, Lazaro's daughter (and Elian's second cousin) Marisleysis Gonzalez, twenty-one years old, exclaimed, "God wanted him here for freedom. And he's here and he will get it."

The next day Juan Miguel asked for Elian's return to Cuba, but the Clinton administration's position at the time was that the issue of Elian's custody should be determined by a Florida family court. The INS announced that it would contact the Florida Department of Children and Families to discuss Elian's future. "We are involved because of the humanitarian interest for Elian Gonzalez," said INS spokesman Dan Kane. "We are concerned about his health and welfare."[2]

On December 1, 1999, the INS issued its first public statement on Elian:

> Although INS has no role in the family custody decision process, we have discussed this case with State of Florida officials who have confirmed that the issue of legal custody must be decided by its state court. Elian will remain in the U.S. until the issues surrounding his custody are resolved. If Elian's family is unable to resolve the question of his custody, it is our understanding that the involved parties will have to file in Florida family court. Either Elian's father in Cuba or his U.S.-based family members may initiate proceedings.

Meanwhile, Cuban president Fidel Castro entered the fray. He demanded that Elian be returned to Cuba and organized anti-U.S. demonstrations. At first the Clinton administration was firm in its resolve to allow the case to be decided by the Florida courts. "We're not intimidated by Fidel Castro. He obviously exercises considerable intimidation over his own people, but not over the government of the United States," said State Department spokesman James Foley.[3] Foley said the administration would "be guided by the interests of the child."

Castro continued to apply pressure, asserting that Elian had been kidnapped by U.S. officials and his Cuban relatives in Miami. On December 5, 1999, he imposed a seventy-two-hour deadline for the United States to return the child. A furious Castro threatened to unleash "a battle of public opinion that will move heaven and earth."[4]

The Flip-Flop

Shortly after the deadline expired the Clinton administration did an about face. Folding under Castro's pressure and threats, the State Department, which customarily has no role in custody or immigration matters,[5] reversed course, saying, "We are committed to working with the family of Elian Gonzalez, including the father, and all relevant officials to achieve an appropriate resolution to this case." The department added that U.S. immigration regulations "recognize the right of a parent to assert parental interests in an immigration proceeding."[6]

Later, Richard Nuccio, a former Clinton aide, said that the reason the administration changed course is because Castro threatened to send more refugees to the United States than it could handle, as happened with the 1980 Mariel boatlift.[7] The State Department admitted that the prospect of a renewed Cuban exodus was never far from the minds of U.S. policymakers.[8] The Cuban refugee problem had been one of Clinton's biggest nightmares as governor of Arkansas, and he certainly didn't want to experience anything like it again. In May 1980, President Carter had decided to resettle nearly twenty thousand Cuban refugees at Fort Chaffee, Arkansas. Local residents became very nervous when riots broke out among the prisoners. Later, a thousand of the refugees escaped and charged down the highway. As they approached the outskirts of a small town, state troopers, National Guardsmen, and deputies finally stopped them. Clinton's 1980 gubernatorial opponent Frank White capitalized on the incident with a vivid political ad depicting the escape. After that, Clinton was, temporarily, political toast. He became the first Arkansas governor to lose a reelection bid since 1954.[9] The idea that Cuban refugees spelled trouble was burned deep into Clinton's mind.

The Miami Cuban exile community saw Clinton's capitulation to Castro as a betrayal. "They are obviously bending to Castro's pressure. Clinton is a coward," said Jose Basulto, leader of the Brothers to the Rescue anti-Castro movement in Miami. Juan Miguel Gonzalez boasted, "When our comandante talks, they tremble."

On December 10, 1999, Lazaro Gonzalez filed an application for asylum on behalf of Elian with the INS, alleging that Elian had a well-founded fear of persecution if he were returned to Cuba. In the meantime, U.S. officials were trying to contact Juan Miguel Gonzalez to inform him of the procedure to reclaim his son. On December 13, while Elian was visiting Disney World with his Miami relatives, Juan Miguel met with INS representatives in Cardenas, Cuba, and established his paternity of Elian to their satisfaction. At that meeting Juan Miguel argued that six-year-old Elian could not speak for himself about such matters as asylum. He reiterated his demand that Elian be returned to him in Cuba and assured INS officials that his desire for Elian's return was genuine and not being coerced by the Cuban government.

Elian's Miami relatives, Lazaro and Marisleysis Gonzalez, met with INS officials in Miami on December 20. They tried to convince the INS that Juan Miguel was being pressured by Castro to demand Elian's return. In an effort to demonstrate the totalitarian conditions in Cuba, the Miami family provided the officials copies of congressional testimony from Orestes Lorenzo, the Cuban pilot who escaped Cuba in a MiG jet in 1991. His testimony revealed that as a young boy he was forced to repeat revolutionary slogans and was taught how to assemble and disassemble a Cuban rifle.

Whose Best Interests?

The INS had scheduled an "inspection" interview with Elian for December 23 but abruptly cancelled it the day before—asserting a need for more information—and rescheduled it for January 21. U.S. diplomats in Havana then asked the Cuban government to permit Juan Miguel to attend Elian's January 21 hearing.

INS officials met with Juan Miguel again on December 31 to ensure that he was expressing his own wishes, not Castro's. The INS concluded that he was. Elian's lawyers later complained that they were not given advance notice of that meeting and an opportunity to attend.

Without even interviewing Elian Gonzalez as its guidelines suggested, the INS in a nationally televised news conference on January 5 announced that he belonged with his father. The INS ruled that Juan Miguel was a fit parent who alone had the authority to speak for Elian. It rejected Elian's asylum applications as legally void and set January 14 as the target date for Elian's return to Cuba. The decision triggered angry protests in downtown

Miami where hundreds of protesters spilled onto the streets, and Spencer Eig, one of the lawyers employed by Elian's Miami relatives, announced that the family would appeal the decision to Attorney General Janet Reno.

On January 7, there was legal action on three other fronts: Congressman Dan Burton subpoenaed Elian to testify before the House Government Reform Committee on February 10; Lazaro Gonzalez petitioned a Florida family court in Miami for temporary custody of Elian; and Bill Clinton rejected a request by Florida governor Jeb Bush that the president use his executive authority to reverse the INS decision.

The Miami relatives scored an unexpected victory on January 10 when Miami-Dade County circuit judge Rosa Rodriguez granted Lazaro temporary custody of Elian until March 6 when the court would hear the case. In her ruling the judge found that the Miami relatives had shown that Elian would face imminent and irreparable harm if he were returned to Cuba, including the loss of due process rights and harm to his physical and mental health and emotional well-being. In a surprise move the judge also ordered Elian's father to appear at the hearing in March and warned that his failure to appear could result in a decision adverse to his interests.

Janet Reno, however, immediately repudiated the state court ruling and upheld the INS's decision rejecting Elian's asylum petition, saying that the state court had no jurisdiction over the asylum issue. But she did lift the INS repatriation deadline of January 14 in order to give Elian's Miami relatives time to challenge the INS decision in federal court. Yet the signs were still not good for Elian's staying in the United States because the Justice Department announced that Lazaro's second asylum petition—filed after the Dade County Circuit Court had rejuvenated his hopes—would again be rejected by the INS.

On January 19, lawyers on behalf of Elian filed an action in federal district court to compel the INS to reconsider Elian's asylum application and sought an injunction to prevent the INS from returning Elian to Cuba.

Judicial Battles and the Public Relations War

The U.S. National Council of Churches now decided to inject itself into the conflict. The liberal organization persuaded Elian's two grandmothers to come from Cuba to New York to lobby for Elian's return. They arrived in Manhattan on January 21. Raquel Rodriguez, mother of Elian's deceased mother, Elizabeth, said that her daughter would have wanted Elian to return to Cuba. "I knew her. I was her mother. I knew how she thought and what she believed in."

The two adult survivors of the boat that had carried Elian and Elizabeth told a different story. They described how Elizabeth denied herself drinking water so that Elian might have a chance to live. She constantly cried out in prayer, they said, that Elian would survive and reach freedom in the United States.[10] In Miami, Elian's cousin Marisleysis said she didn't doubt the grandmothers' love for Elian, but they were "spouting the words of Fidel Castro."

The next day the grandmothers traveled to Washington and met with Janet Reno, tearfully asking permission to take Elian to Cuba. Reno promised to resolve the custody battle as soon as possible. The INS then issued an order requiring Elian's Miami relatives to allow his grandmothers to see him at what it considered a "neutral" site—the Miami Beach home of Barry University president Jeanne O'Laughlin, a longtime personal friend of Janet Reno who favored returning Elian to Cuba.

After the meeting, Sister O'Laughlin changed her mind. She saw "fear" in Elian's grandmothers—fear of the Castro regime—and thought it morally wrong to return Elian to Cuba. O'Laughlin was so upset that she decided to go to Capitol Hill at her own expense to lobby Reno to allow Elian to stay in the United States. INS officials immediately declared that the sister's opinion would not affect their stance. Reno met with Sister O'Laughlin but was unmoved. "I continue to believe based on all the information made available to me, including the information that Sister Jeanne shared with me, that the person who speaks for this child is his one surviving parent, his father."

Three weeks later Sister O'Laughlin gave more details about her change of heart—details she had kept secret so as not to endanger other relatives of Elian in Cuba. "This is more about the little boy," she said, "than anyone else, and I have to do whatever I can do to help him." She said she had learned that one of Elian's grandmothers wanted to defect to the United States; that Elian's father, Juan Miguel, had been physically abusive to Elian's mother; and that Juan Miguel and his family knew about Elizabeth's plan to escape with Elian to Miami ten days before they left—and supported the decision.

Sister O'Laughlin said she was so devastated by these revelations that she wept and prayed most of the night. Major Steve Robbins of the Miami Beach Police Department, who had been in the house during O'Laughlin's meeting with the grandmothers, verified that O'Laughlin's demeanor completely changed after she talked to them. "She was happy and relaxed when she went up, but when she came down after talking to them, she looked terribly distressed." Later there was some confusion over how Sister O'Laughlin acquired this disturbing information. She denied having told the

Miami Herald that she learned it directly from the grandmothers. In an affidavit she submitted to the federal district court she explained her reasons and partially divulged her sources.

In her affidavit O'Laughlin said Cuban officials tightly controlled the meeting: they demanded to see plans of the home, complained about lack of security,[11] and obviously didn't want the meeting to happen. O'Laughlin said the president of the National Council of Churches confessed to her that Castro was dictating the negotiations. The most disturbing thing, said O'Laughlin, was that the Cuban officials insisted that the family members not see one another. "Although the American family asked to see and talk to the grandmothers, the grandmothers I believe were under strict instruction not to see or speak to anyone other than Elian. What I found to be particularly poignant was that Doris, the sister of Raquel, asked if she could give her sister condolences for the loss of her daughter or simply embrace her. The answer to both requests was cold rejection. This seemed unnatural and reinforced my belief that the grandmothers could not act under their own free will."

O'Laughlin concluded that if the Cuban government were exerting this kind of control over the grandmothers, it was obviously doing the same to Juan Miguel. She added that she noticed how Elian reacted with joy when he was reunited with his cousin, Marisleysis, with whom he appeared to have a strong mother-child bond. Finally, she said that her sources were "INS officials, American family members, and persons present at [her] home prior to the grandmothers' meeting." Sister O'Laughlin offered this sobering opinion: "I also believe that Elian will not remain with his father but will become a ward of the state if he is returned to Cuba."

Other affidavits from various first cousins of Juan Miguel Gonzalez filed in federal court lent further support to the notion that he was under coercion from the Cuban government. These relatives swore that Juan Miguel had repeatedly told them in the past that he wanted to live in the United States. One said that Juan Miguel said in front of his mother and friends that sometime in the future he would come, "even if it had to be in a tub." The affidavits also supported Elian's claim that he would face persecution if he returned to Cuba.

In a Senate Judiciary Committee hearing on March 1, Elian's relatives and others testified about the conditions in Cuba. One powerful witness was Alina Fernandez, Fidel Castro's daughter who had left Cuba in 1993 using a disguise and fake passport. She told the senators that Americans who championed Juan Gonzalez's parental rights didn't understand life in Cuba and were playing right into Castro's hands. "In Cuba, the terms 'parental rights' or 'freedom of expression' are meaningless," she said. Cuban musician Juan-Carlos Formell, who fled Cuba in 1993, told lawmakers, "What I would like you to know about Cuba is that the very air we breathe is polluted with the smell of fear; it is a fear so strong that it makes the soul cringe. The issue here is whether Elian will be able to have the same right of personal autonomy that you take for granted here, or whether he will have to adapt his life to a dictatorship."

On March 9 a hearing was held in federal district court in Miami to determine whether the INS had properly denied Elian's asylum application. Marisleysis Gonzalez, who had been hospitalized for stress, could not attend the hearing. Judge K. Michael Moore recessed the proceedings without announcing his decision.

Juan Miguel, who had previously been without legal counsel, hired President Clinton's high-powered impeachment attorney and Yale Law School classmate, Gregory Craig, to represent him in the various lawsuits. A Clinton spokesman denied administration involvement. After appearing to be sympathetic to the legal position of Elian's Miami relatives during the hearing on March 9, Judge Moore ruled against them on March 21. He ruled that Reno and the INS had acted within their discretion in holding that only Elian's father could speak for him in immigration matters. Elian's Miami relatives appealed to the Eleventh U.S. Circuit Court of Appeals, asking the court to forbid Elian's repatriation to Cuba until after their appeal was decided.

A few days later, an increasingly confident Justice Department issued the Miami relatives an ultimatum. Reno threatened to revoke Lazaro's temporary custody of Elian unless the family agreed to an expedited appellate process and to surrender Elian if they lost the appeal. Reno set a deadline for Lazaro to respond. The government extended the deadline as INS officials and Lazaro negotiated.

Castro, meanwhile, announced that Juan Miguel was ready to travel to the United States—but only if Elian would return with him. The House of Representatives responded by passing a resolution encouraging the Department of Justice not to return Elian before the conclusion of the legal process.

Juan Miguel Gonzalez arrived in the United States on April 6 with his new wife and their six-month-old son. Justice Department officials promised to deliver Elian as soon as they could obtain him from the Miami relatives. Instead of going to Miami where Elian was located, Juan Miguel and his family were lodged in Bethesda, Maryland, at the home of Cuba's chief U.S. diplomat. The Miami relatives offered to meet with Juan Miguel at the home of Sister O'Laughlin or "any other neutral place in South Florida." Juan Miguel declined.

On April 12 Janet Reno met with the Miami relatives and ordered them to surrender Elian by delivering him to a nearby airport (Opa-Locka) by 2 P.M. the next day. Lazaro refused, but his spokesman, Armando Gutierrez, said Lazaro would not obstruct justice and would surrender Elian to federal marshals if they came to his house. Lazaro himself had earlier said, however, that he would "not turn over the child—anywhere. They will have to pry Elian out of my arms." Reno said that she fully intended to enforce the order in a fair and prompt way.

The next day, decisive legal action occurred in both the federal and state courts. Lazaro's lawyers obtained an emergency temporary stay from the Eleventh Circuit Court of Appeals, enjoining Juan Miguel from taking Elian back to Cuba pending the outcome of the appeal and giving the government one day to respond. This order had no effect on Reno's directive that the child be delivered to Juan Miguel so long as Elian remained in the United States. The state court, however, dismissed Lazaro's lawsuit seeking temporary custody of Elian during the pendency of the asylum action in federal court. Judge Jennifer Bailey ruled that federal authority preempted her jurisdiction in the matter.

On April 14 Reno had the INS formally revoke Lazaro's temporary custody of Elian and asked the federal district court to order that he be returned to his father. In its revocation letter to Lazaro the INS threatened him with civil and criminal penalties for failing to comply with its orders to surrender Elian. The letter also said that Juan Miguel would agree to keep Elian in the United States pending the appeal.

On April 19 the Eleventh Circuit Court issued a major ruling: the full three-judge panel granted an injunction barring Elian's removal from the country pending the outcome of the asylum appeal. Before granting the injunction the court had to satisfy itself that irreparable harm would likely occur to Elian unless the injunction were granted. The court determined that such harm would result if Elian were removed to Cuba because it would place him outside the jurisdiction of the court and would render moot the issues before the court.

As a condition to entering the order, the court also had to be convinced that Elian had a substantial case on the underlying asylum claim. Most of the court's sixteen-page decision, then, involved a discussion of the merits of Elian's claim. That claim would turn on whether the INS, in refusing even to consider six-year-old Elian's asylum application, was thwarting the clear intent of Congress in the statute on federal asylum that said that "any alien," with specified exceptions, could apply for asylum. School-age children, the court pointed out, were not among those statutory exceptions.

"To some people," said the court, "the idea that a six-year-old child may file for asylum in the United States, contrary to the express wishes of his parents, may seem a strange or even foolish policy. But this Court does not make immigration policy, and we cannot review the wisdom of statutes duly enacted by Congress. If Congress intended—as evidenced by the plain meaning of section 1158—that a school-age child (such as Plaintiff) be able to file personally an application for asylum, this Court and the INS are bound to honor the policy-decision made by Congress."

The court also noted that regulations and guidelines adopted by the INS added further strength to Elian's claim that he was entitled to apply for asylum. It reviewed in some detail various regulations promulgated by the agency, which expressly provide that minors may apply for asylum, sometimes even against the express wishes of their parents. The court cited INS guidelines that included suggestions about how to interview minors about their asylum applications. The guidelines went so far as to say, "Asylum Officers should not assume that a child cannot have an asylum claim independent of the parents." The guidelines also required INS asylum officers "to gather as much objective evidence as possible to evaluate the child's claim." The guidelines even mandated that when there was a conflict between the child's wishes and those of the parents, the officer would have to decide whether the minor's fear of persecution (upon being returned to his native country) was well founded, giving the minor "a liberal application of" the benefit of the doubt.

Finally, the guidelines established three age-based developmental stages of children (0-5, 6-12, 13-18 years old) and provided guidance for asylum officers in dealing with each category. The guidelines had an example of a statement from a six-year-old child and showed how to assess such statements.[12]

After discussing the statute and setting out the pertinent INS guidelines in painstaking detail, the court pointed out that the INS had never even attempted to interview Elian before making its decision. It appeared to have completely ignored its own guidelines in summarily rejecting Elian's asylum application without bothering to ascertain all the relevant facts.

In granting the injunction preventing Elian's removal from the United States pending its decision on Elian's asylum appeal, the court did warn that "no one should feel confident in predicting the eventual result in this case."

In a parting footnote the court said that it would not decide who should have custody of Elian pending a decision on the merits, only that Elian should not be removed.

Elian's Miami relatives continued to express their willingness to allow Elian to meet with his father, but Juan Miguel's attorney,

Greg Craig, said that such a meeting would not occur unless Elian were first turned over to his client. Lazaro's attorney, Kendall Coffey, said that the families should get together without lawyers or anyone from the government present to resolve this matter. Reno let it be known that she was considering forcible removal of Elian from the Miami relatives. Experts warned about the impact of such a raid on the psychology of a small boy. One federal agent said, "This will be a traumatic extraction for the child. The child will consider it a kidnapping."[13]

But President Clinton put the official weight of the presidency on the side of repatriating Elian to Castro's Cuba, going so far as to contradict the Eleventh Circuit Court by saying that the law required that Elian be returned to his father immediately. Clinton denied that he was pressuring Janet Reno.

The Raid

Shortly after 5 A.M. on April 22—Easter weekend—more than twenty federal agents, firing off rounds of pepper spray and tear gas, swarmed the home of Lazaro Gonzalez. They rammed through the chain fence and front door and seized Elian at gunpoint from his rescuer Donato Dalrymple. The little boy was screaming and crying as he was taken from the house by a female INS agent and swept away to the airport in a white van.

Elian's attorneys were shocked. They had been negotiating with the government all night—right up to the very minute of the raid. The family, they said, was about to reach a deal by fax when the raid went down. Kendall Coffey said, "We're angry and disgusted. We were in communication with the mediator handling negotiations and discussion with the government when they knocked the door down."

Controversy swelled around the raid. Miami mayor Joe Carollo declared it a "dark day in the history of the United States," and it was hard to disagree as graphic pictures showed a horrified and sobbing Elian staring down the barrel of a federal agent's rifle. There were also allegations that the helmeted, flak-jacketed, and armed agents came charging in spewing obscenities. The facts of the picture, the allegations of obscenities, even the commonsensical criticism that the government had overreacted were denounced as lies by Reno and the Clinton administration.

Elian's frantic Miami relatives flew to Washington, D.C., to visit with Elian but were turned away at the gate to Andrews Air Force Base, supposedly at the direction of Juan Miguel. That afternoon photographs of Elian's smiling reunion with his father were given to the media. Janet Reno insisted in a post-raid press conference that she had done everything in her power to resolve the matter peaceably and that the raid had been a last resort. President Clinton reiterated his argument that the law was being upheld. Despite the federal court's express refusal to act on the custody issue, Clinton said that "there was no alternative but to enforce the decisions of the INS and the federal court, that Juan Miguel Gonzalez should have custody of his son."

Florida governor Jeb Bush and both U.S. senators from Florida condemned the federal raid. Republican Connie Mack said he was outraged and Democrat Bob Graham, describing the raid as a gross and excessive use of force, said that April 22 would be "another day that will live in infamy." Graham, who had been a staunch supporter of the administration in other areas, said that Clinton had reneged on two assurances made during a private meeting at the White House that no action would be taken to seize Elian at night. He said that he told Clinton about the "tremendous anxiety" in the Miami community and the Gonzalez family about a nighttime raid and that people were going without sleep, which was affecting Elian. Graham said that when he requested of Clinton that nothing take place at night, Clinton responded, "We can do that." Furious over the betrayal, Graham said that his friendship with Clinton "may be in the past tense now."

Following the raid, several allies of Clinton and Reno roundly criticized them. One former Justice Department official,[14] ordinarily supportive of the administration and Janet Reno, said that Reno's tenure in office would be known by "the bookends of Waco and Little Havana."[15] Even Harvard professors Lawrence Tribe and Alan Dershowitz condemned the raid, saying the Miami relatives' Fourth Amendment rights had been violated.

Dershowitz, one of the Clinton administration's fiercest allies, especially against impeachment, said that the INS had no right to conduct the raid and that it took the law into its own hands. He said the government's appropriate remedy would have been to procure a court order holding the family in contempt for not delivering Elian. He properly recognized, however, that the reason Reno didn't try to obtain a court order was that the Miami family "was not breaking the law."

Tribe, in a *New York Times* piece, questioned where Reno derived the legal authority to invade the Miami home. Though Tribe said he believed Elian should be returned to his father, "the government's actions appear to have violated a basic principle of our society, a principle whose preservation lies at the core of ordered liberty under the rule of law."[16] Tribe likened the federal agents' forcible entry into the home to a noncustodial parent breaking into the custodial parent's home to seize a child. He dismissed the INS's claim that its raid was supported by a warrant, saying that the warrant it obtained was a search warrant, "not a warrant to seize the child." Search warrants, he pointed out, were for the seizure of evidence, not people, and "it is a semantic sleight of hand to compare his forcible removal to the seizure of evidence." Tribe's closing paragraph will stand as an enduring indictment of the Clinton-Reno Justice Department from the unlikeliest of sources: "Ms. Reno's decision to take the law as well as the child into her own hands seems worse than a political blunder. Even if well intended, her decision strikes at the heart of constitutional government and shakes the safeguards of liberty."

As it turns out the warrant was obtained by an affidavit filed by INS agent Mary Rodriguez. The INS did not present the warrant to Judge Michael Moore, the federal district judge handling the case, but waited until after 7 P.M. on Good Friday when the only judge available was a federal magistrate unfamiliar with the case.[17] The affidavit and supporting memoranda contained a number of inaccurate statements, including that Elian was being concealed and unlawfully restrained at Lazaro's home and that Elian was an illegal alien. As Professor Tribe noted, "no one suspected that Elian was in the United States illegally." Later, other immigration experts disputed Tribe's assertion, saying that once the INS revoked Lazaro's parole over Elian, Elian became an illegal alien, or at least an "unadmitted alien."[18] Paragraph 12 of the affidavit contained the flagrantly false statement that "Once the INS revoked Elian's parole, his remaining in the United States is a violation of law." The Eleventh Circuit Court had, in fact, just entered an order a few days earlier precisely to the contrary.

Why Force?

If there was no court order entitling Juan Miguel to custody— and there was not—and if there was no urgency requiring Elian's immediate removal from his Miami relatives—and there was not—something other than the child's best interests must have motivated Clinton and Reno to remove him at gunpoint in the dead of night. Indeed, Senator Graham remarked that "one of the mysteries is what is motivating the administration to act in such a perverse way."

What would Clinton's agents have done if they had been met with resistance? Would they have used those weapons? Would they have killed people?

On April 25, Cuban Americans called a general strike in Miami to protest the raid. Thousands of employees participated in the strike, including three active players on the Florida Marlins baseball team. Miami-Dade County mayor Alex Penelas said the strike signified the deep anger and pain of the exile community. "People are responding to a very violent and unjust action with a peaceful expression of their emotions."[19]

Distressed that the raid took place during the Easter weekend, a group of more than forty Hispanic Catholic priests from South Florida sent a protest letter to President Clinton. "Democratic governments always have respected religious holy days. You chose to conduct a nighttime raid in the midst of one of the most sacred of Christian seasons, trampling on the religious sensitivity of our community and the entire nation." Many Americans were especially upset that Clinton showed no sensitivity to Elian's Catholic family or the pro-Elian Catholic Cubans—American citizens—of Miami, given that he called a moratorium on his wag-the-dog bombing of Iraq at the onset of Ramadan, the Islamic period of religious fasting.

On April 27, the Eleventh Circuit Court rejected a request by the Miami relatives to visit Elian, saying they would only be entitled to reports from Elian's psychiatrist and social worker. But the

court also ordered that Elian not travel outside the jurisdiction of
the court, specifically mentioning areas with "diplomatic immunity," which would include the Cuban Embassy.

That same day, twelve federal prosecutors and thirteen staff
members from the Miami U.S. attorney's office, most of whom
were Cuban-American, "dressed in black to tell the Cuban-
American community that not everyone is in agreement with the
actions taken." A few days later, while protests over the raid were
continuing in Miami, an unapologetic INS held a Rescue Reunion
picnic in Broward County during which several agents involved in
the raid posed for photographs.

The Department of Justice issued an internal report justifying
the INS raid. According to the report the INS raiders pointed
their guns at no one, used no profanity, no physical force, and no
tear gas. The key "debriefing results" contained in the report
were: "No one on the team threatened to shoot anyone during the
operation. Team members made no threats to use force against
anyone in the home. Marisleysis Gonzalez was not touched in any
way during the operation. No force was required to remove Elian
Gonzalez from Donato Dalrymple's arms. No team member
struck anyone with a weapon during the operation. The fire selec-
tor lever on the MP-5 depicted in photographs is positively in the
safe position."

The report went on to conclude: "The news footage of the
operation clearly shows that the team members acted with discipline and restraint under extraordinary circumstances." The report
doesn't mention that the "extraordinary circumstances" were created entirely by the raid itself. After all, nonmilitarized agents could
have simply knocked on the door and asked for the boy, an alternative that seems not to have appealed to Janet Reno or the other

Waco veterans of the Clinton administration. Far from being the last option, force seemed to be the first option.

Shortly after the Justice Department's report was made public an NBC cameraman who was inside the house during the raid called the report "a pack of lies." "To read the report, you would think this was the most perfect, uneventful mission they ever carried out," said Tony Zumbado, the forty-five-year-old cameraman. Contrary to the report, Zumbado said, "The agents were physically and verbally abusive; they said every bad word in the book and kept me from doing my job." They knocked him to the floor and kicked him in the lower back. They warned him not to move or they would shoot.

Zumbado said that he hadn't planned to speak out because he understood that it was a military-style raid that presupposed roughing people up verbally and physically. He was offended, however, by the sanitized version of the agents' behavior in the report. He denied that he had any ax to grind, saying that he believed that Elian should have been with his father. "But when I read how the agents exonerated themselves of any wrongdoing, my faith in this administration was shaken." Kendall Coffey, the Miami family's lead attorney, said he was "astounded" at the report's claim that no pepper spray or tear gas was used. He said that he felt the fumes himself.[20] Marisleysis said that during the raid the agents yelled and told them, "Give us the f—ing kid! Give us the f—ing kid!" and threatened to shoot. Zumbado backs up her claim.[21]

Aftermath

On June 1 the Eleventh Circuit Court ruled that the INS was within its lawful discretion in denying Elian's asylum application.[22] The court emphasized that under our constitutional system it is not the prerogative of the court to make policy. The executive branch—and thereby the INS and the Justice Department—is given wide latitude under the asylum statute,[23] and the court's judicial review is limited. As it had in its ruling on April 19, the court considered the merits of Elian's asylum application under the statute. The important legal question in this case, it said, "is not whether [Elian] *may* apply for asylum; that a six-year-old is eligible to apply for asylum is clear. The ultimate inquiry, instead, is whether a six-year-old *has* applied for asylum within the meaning of the statute when he, or a non-parental relative on his behalf, signs and submits a purported application against the express wishes of the child's parent."

In other words, the statute is clear that "any alien"—including a six-year-old—may apply for asylum, but it doesn't say how he may apply. Since the statute is silent on the question the INS acted within its authority in fashioning a policy to fill in the gaps—a policy requiring that a six-year-old must apply for asylum through one of his parents, even when the sole surviving parent is not in the United States. One logical implication of this not taken up by the court is that it must be assumed that Elian's mother would have applied for asylum on Elian's behalf had she survived, and the presumption must also be that she would have opposed Elian's repatriation to Cuba. Elizabeth Gonzalez gave her life to free Elian from communism. Elian's great-uncle Lazaro, in applying for asylum for the boy, was merely executing Elizabeth Gonzalez's obvious will.

Lawyers for the Miami relatives argued that the INS's position was not a policy at all but was adopted solely to enhance its position in this litigation. The court rejected that argument, saying that the policy "was not created by INS lawyers during litigation, but instead was developed in the course of administrative proceedings before litigation commenced." In a footnote to its decision the court specified that the INS and the attorney general had promulgated this policy in a series of documents dated from January 3, 2000, forward. But the court did not explain why it permitted the agency to change its guidelines in the middle of the proceeding.

When Elian applied for asylum the INS had no policy to cover his particular situation, though it did have guidelines on asylum applications by minors—guidelines, the court noted, that were not in harmony with the policy the INS ultimately adopted, though the guidelines themselves were not legally binding. The guidelines emphasized protecting the right—independent of a parent's wishes—of a minor in an asylum case. The INS crafted a policy effectively to deny a specific six-year-old those rights. The court acknowledged that this policy decision by the INS "was within the outside border of reasonable choices." It "neither approves nor disapproves the INS's decision to reject the asylum applications filed on Plaintiff's behalf, but the INS decision did not contradict 8 U.S.C. Sec. 1158."

The court added, however, that "We are not untroubled by the degree of obedience that the INS policy appears to give to the wishes of parents, especially parents who are outside this country's jurisdiction."

"Some reasonable people might say," the court went on, "that a child in the United States inherently has a substantial conflict of interest with a parent residing in a totalitarian state when that parent—even when he is not coerced—demands that the child leave this country to return to a country with little respect for human rights and basic freedoms."

On June 23 the Eleventh Circuit Court denied an application for rehearing,[24] and on June 28 the Supreme Court declined to hear the matter. The legal battle was over. Elian returned with his father to Cuba.

The Bottom Line

The Clinton-Reno claim that throughout the Elian saga they were merely upholding the law is patently untrue because, as the court showed, there was no definitive precedent controlling Elian's case. The INS's initial position, in fact, was that a state family court should decide Elian's fate. It was the INS itself that had given Lazaro custody of Elian.

Indeed, the court noted that if the INS had adopted a policy that allowed Elian to apply for asylum on his own, it would have upheld it as reasonable. The court stated that it did "not mean to suggest that the course taken by the INS is the only permissible approach."

Because the INS completely ignored its own guidelines when considering Elian's case, never conducted a personal interview with Elian, and changed its policy so dramatically once Castro threatened another Mariel boat lift, there seems little doubt that its actions were designed solely to suit the political needs of the Clinton administration. The bottom line is that Bill Clinton and Janet Reno ensured that Elian Gonzalez never had his day in court. He never had an asylum hearing or a family court hearing to determine his best interests.

The administration's uninterrupted pattern of deceit, betrayal, brute force, and politicized justice in this case are indefensible. In the Clinton-Reno Justice Department the wishes of Fidel Castro— and perhaps the American electorate, which was largely unsympathetic to Elian Gonzalez's asylum plea—carried more weight than the wishes of the young boy, his dead mother, or Elian's relatives in Miami—American citizens—who wanted to raise the boy in freedom. Instead, justice was designed for President Clinton's poll numbers and delivered via the barrel of a gun.

Afterword

Fewer than six hundred votes, cast in a single state, are all that stood in the way of a Clinton-Reno–style Justice Department lasting for at least another four years. There's no need to relive the tawdry spectacle of Al Gore suing to win the presidency. But what might have escaped many readers' notice was that near the end of the Florida imbroglio, the Justice Department reportedly dispatched the illegally appointed Bill Lann Lee to investigate alleged civil rights abuses in the Florida election. While the Justice Department probably had no authority to bring any legal action that could have changed the results, it could have wielded its considerable power to try to undermine the election's legitimacy. There is certainly nothing wrong with the Justice Department investigating actual civil rights abuses, but it crosses the line when it allows itself to be used as an agent to serve the administration's political ends.

Shortly after assuming office, Clinton assigned two men, Bernard Nussbaum and Peter Edelman, to conduct a top-down review of the department. The result was a book-length, scathing indictment of Justice under the previous twelve years of Reagan and Bush. "The attorney general shapes the image of Justice by communicating the core values and ideas that all Americans expect from the government's lawyers," read the report. "The Department now faces a crisis of credibility and integrity. Its performance over the past twelve years has diminished the trust and respect the Department once enjoyed among the Bar, the legal academy and political leaders.... [The Department] is perceived as politicized when it speaks on matters of central importance.... The Department has lost its reputation as an even-handed tribune for those needing judicial and other legal protection." While those words were unfairly applied to Republican administrations by the Clinton team, they couldn't be more appropriate for the Clinton-Gore-Reno Justice Department.

Article II, Section 1, of the United States Constitution makes the president the nation's chief executive officer. Article II, Section 3, provides that the president "shall take care that the laws be faithfully executed." The Department of Justice is the primary government agency charged with the implementation of the president's constitutional duty to execute the laws faithfully. As the Department of Justice is entrusted with the duty of impartially enforcing the law, it is important that to the maximum extent possible it stay above politics. When justice is administered unfairly, when those in power are treated as being above the law, the system disintegrates.

Sadly, however, this has been the legacy of the Clinton-Gore-Reno Justice Department. As we've seen, this was a Justice Department that, among other things:

- assisted the Clinton administration in framing permanent, loyal, and exemplary White House employees in the travel office so that those "slots" could go to Bill and Hillary Clinton's cronies;
- sat idle as the Clinton-Gore campaign machine inhaled illegal foreign contributions and relaxed our national security—refusing to allow an independent counsel to investigate this "mother of all scandals" notwithstanding the unambiguous opinion of four high-ranking Justice officials that it do so;
- subverted the very independent counsel whose appointment it had recommended;
- was complicit by its inaction in the White House's egregious violation of whistle-blower Linda Tripp's privacy rights;
- allowed itself to be used as a campaign tool for the candidacies of Hillary Clinton and Al Gore, by compromising its objectivity in evaluating the pardon requests for terrorist groups;
- directed its Immigration and Naturalization Services to change its immigration policy in midstream to accommodate the shifting political concerns of the Clinton administration regarding the asylum claim of Elian Gonzalez;
- trampled on the Fourth Amendment rights of Elian's Miami relatives in bringing the Elian matter to a disgracefully violent close.

These offenses are so stark, so stunning, and, most of all, have gone so unpunished, that it leaves you breathless. The lesson of the Clinton-Gore administration is that you can politicize justice, use the executive branch of government to punish political enemies, abuse executive power for personal and political ends—and get away with it. All it requires is brazenness, stubbornness, a loyal staff of yes-men, dagger-men, and smear artists, and an absent conscience. It's a recipe that other politicians are sure to follow. Unless, that is, the new administration—and Congress, which has oversight authority—takes drastic steps to restore the integrity of the Justice Department. There are, of course, many good and true lawyers in the department, and much reform will come almost automatically with the appointment of a new attorney general.

But these last eight years should serve as a warning. The Clinton-Gore administration's politicization of the Justice Department has no parallel in our nation's history, and this dangerous period, which made federal law enforcement a political calculation, must never be repeated. It is up to George W. Bush's administration to set a different course, the right course—one where law trumps politics and justice is administered equally. That's what America deserves. As involved citizens, that's what we should expect.

Notes

Introduction

1. Theodore Olson, "The Most Political Justice Department Ever: A Survey," *American Spectator*, September 2000, 24.

One: Waco

1. Mark 13: 32-33.
2. James D. Tabor and Eugene V. Gallagher, *Why Waco? Cults and the Battle for Religious Freedom in America* (Berkeley: University of California Press, 1995), 48. Dick Reavis, *The Ashes of Waco: An Investigation* (New York: Simon and Schuster, 1995), 53.
3. Tabor and Gallagher, *Why Waco? Cults and the Battle for Religious Freedom in America*, 35.
4. Reavis, *The Ashes of Waco: An Investigation*, 62.
5. Tabor and Gallagher, *Why Waco? Cults and the Battle for Religious Freedom in America*, 39. John 15:5.
6. David B. Kopel and Paul H. Blackman, *No More Wacos* (Amherst, N.Y.: Prometheus Books, 1997), 26.
7. Warren W. Wiersbe, *Wiersbe's Expository Outlines on the New Testament* (Colorado Springs, CO: Victor Books, 1992), 809.
8. Charles C. Ryrie, *Revelation* (Chicago: Moody Press, 1996), 48.
9. Tabor and Gallagher, *Why Waco? Cults and the Battle for Religious Freedom in America*, 54.
10. Ibid., 55.

11. Ibid., 54.
12. David Thibodeau and Leon Whiteson, *A Place Called Waco: A Survivor's Story* (New York: Public Affairs, 1999), 108.
13. Ibid., 111.
14. Tabor and Gallagher, *Why Waco? Cults and the Battle for Religious Freedom in America*, 68.
15. Ibid., 81.
16. Thibodeau and Whiteson, *A Place Called Waco: A Survivor's Story*, 114.
17. Tabor and Gallagher, *Why Waco? Cults and the Battle for Religious Freedom in America*, 56.
18. Thibodeau and Whiteson, *A Place Called Waco: A Survivor's Story*, 116.
19. Ibid., 117.
20. Ibid., 120.
21. Ibid., 121.
22. Reavis, *The Ashes of Waco: An Investigation*, 33.
23. Ibid., 34.
24. Ibid., 33-34.
25. Kopel and Blackman, *No More Wacos*, 55.
26. Ibid., 56.
27. Tabor and Gallagher, *Why Waco? Cults and the Battle for Religious Freedom in America*, 101.
28. Reavis, *The Ashes of Waco: An Investigation*, 37.
29. U.S. Department of the Treasury, *Report of the Department of the Treasury on the Bureau of Alcohol, Tobacco, and Firearms, Investigation of Vernon Wayne Howell also known as David Koresh* (Washington, D.C., 1993), 37. Hereinafter, *Treasury Report*.
30. U.S. House of Representatives, Committee on Government Reform and Oversight in conjunction with the Committee on the Judiciary, *Investigation into the Activities of Federal Law Enforcement Agencies Toward the Branch Davidians*, Report 104-179, 104th Cong., 2nd sess. (Washington, D.C., 1996), 14. Hereinafter, *Committee Report*.
31. Kopel and Blackman, *No More Wacos*, 53.
32. Ibid., 53.
33. Ibid., 58.
34. Ibid.
35. Marc Breault and Martin King, *Inside the Cult* (New York: Signet, 1993), 299-300.

36. Kopel and Blackman, *No More Wacos*, 64.
37. Reavis, *The Ashes of Waco: An Investigation*, 38.
38. Ibid., 32.
39. *Committee Report*, 14.
40. Ibid.
41. *Treasury Report*, 85.
42. Ibid., 89.
43. Ibid.
44. Ibid., 91.
45. U.S. House Committee on the Judiciary, and House Committee on Government Reform and Oversight, *Investigation into the Activities of Federal Law Enforcement Agencies Toward the Branch Davidians* (Part 1): *Hearings Before the Subcommittee on Crime and Subcommittee on National Security, International Affairs, and Criminal Justice*, 104th Cong., 1st sess. 163 (1995), 177. Hereinafter, *Hearings*, Part 1.
46. Ibid.
47. *Treasury Report*, 91.
48. *Hearings*, Part 1, 788.
49. *Committee Report*, 21.
50. Ibid.
51. Ibid., 22.
52. Reavis, *The Ashes of Waco: An Investigation*, 183.
53. Ibid., 123.
54. Kopel and Blackman, *No More Wacos*, 88.
55. Ibid., 103.
56. *Committee Report*, 29.
57. Kopel and Blackman, *No More Wacos*, 105.
58. Reavis, *The Ashes of Waco: An Investigation*, 140.
59. Kopel and Blackman, *No More Wacos*, 104.
60. Reavis, *The Ashes of Waco: An Investigation*, 140-141.
61. *Committee Report*, 25.
62. Kopel and Blackman, *No More Wacos*, 229.
63. James Bovard, "Clues to Collapsing a Cover-up on Waco?" *Washington Times*, August 16, 1995.
64. Kopel and Blackman, *No More Wacos*, 229.
65. Ibid., 235.
66. Alan A. Stone, "Sifting Waco's Ashes," *Boston Review*, October/November 1997.
67. Tabor and Gallagher, *Why Waco? Cults and the Battle for Religious Freedom in America*, 103.

68. Ibid., 104.
69. Ibid., 73.
70. Ibid., 104.
71. Nancy T. Ammerman, "Waco, Federal Law Enforcement, and Scholars of Religion," in *Armageddon in Waco: Critical Perspectives on the Branch Davidian Conflict*, ed. Stuart A. Wright (Chicago: University of Chicago Press, 1995), 282.
72. Ibid., 283-284.
73. Kopel and Blackman, *No More Wacos*, 137.
74. Ibid., 136.
75. Ibid., 134.
76. Ibid., 138.
77. *Committee Report*, 64.
78. Kopel and Blackman, *No More Wacos*, 147.
79. Reavis, *The Ashes of Waco: An Investigation*, 256.
80. Thibodeau and Whiteson, *A Place Called Waco: A Survivor's Story*, 246.
81. Ibid., 248.
82. *Committee Report*, 65.
83. Lee Hancock, "Koresh Vowed Not to Give In," *Dallas Morning News*, April 21, 1993.
84. Kopel and Blackman, *No More Wacos*, 133.
85. *Danforth Report*.
86. Thibodeau and Whiteson, *A Place Called Waco: A Survivor's Story*, 247.
87. Kopel and Blackman, *No More Wacos*, 161.
88. Ibid., 162.
89. Ibid.
90. Reavis, *The Ashes of Waco: An Investigation*, 277.
91. Edward Timperlake and William C. Triplett II, *Year of the Rat* (Washington, D.C.: Regnery Publishing, 1998), 13-14.
92. James Bovard, "Waco Must Get a Hearing," *Wall Street Journal*, May 15, 1995.

Two: Tobacco Wars

1. News Services, "U.S. Urged to Escalate Tobacco War," *Washington Post*, January 12, 1994.
2. Ibid.
3. John Schwartz, "Tobacco Executive Defends Testimony; As

Industry Is Attacked on Hill, Justice Dept. Considers Probe," *Washington Post*, June 24, 1994.

4. John Schwartz, "Lawmaker Asks Reno to Take Up Tobacco Probe," *Washington Post*, December 14, 1994.

5. James V. Hansen, "Their Drug, Your Kids," *Washington Post*, July 28, 1995.

6. John Schwartz, "Firm's Claim on Nicotine Contradicted; 3 Ex-Workers Swear Philip Morris Adjusted Levels in Cigarettes," *Washington Post*, March 19, 1996.

7. Ibid.

8. John Schwartz," Judge Rules That FDA Can Regulate Tobacco," *Washington Post*, April 26, 1997.

9. Charles W. Hall, "U.S. Probing Firm That Studied Secondhand Smoke," *Washington Post*, February 16, 1996.

10. John Schwartz, "Probe of Secondhand Smoke Data Ends," *Washington Post*, December 12, 1996.

11. John Schwartz, "Minnesota Anti-tobacco Suit Clears a Major Legal Hurdle; Court Allows Health Care Insurer to Stay in Case," *Washington Post*, July 26, 1996.

12. Pierre Thomas and John Schwartz, "Government Intensifies Tobacco Company Probe; Papers Culled for Signs of False Statements," *Washington Post*, May 3, 1997.

13. John Schwartz and Ceci Connolly, "Nicotine Conspiracy Alleged; U.S. Brings First Charge In Tobacco Firms Probe," *Washington Post*, January 8, 1998.

14. Alissa J. Rubin and Myron Levin, "Federal Suit Over Tobacco's Impact On Medicare Weighed," *Washington Post*, August 16, 1998.

15. Walter Jones Jr., "Should the Federal Government Sue Tobacco Companies for Medicare and Medicaid Payments? Tobacco Farmers Must Be Supported," *Roll Call*, September 28, 1998.

16. Ross MacKenzie, "With Better Logic, Maybe the Government Should Sue Itself," *Richmond Times Dispatch*, October 3, 1999.

17. Editorial, "A Duplicitous Deal With Big Tobacco," *San Antonio Express-News*, October 18, 1999.

18. Ross MacKenzie, "With Better Logic, Maybe the Government Should Sue Itself," *Richmond Times Dispatch*, October 3, 1999.

19. Sandra Sobieraj, "Justice to Sue Over Medicare, Medicaid Spent on Smoking Illnesses," *Associated Press State & Local Wire*, January 19, 1999.

20. Editorial, "Smoking Suit Dishonesty," *Press Journal*, February 8, 1999.

21. Matthew Rees, "Tobacco Railroad," *Weekly Standard*, August 16, 1999.
22. Alissa J. Rubin and Myron Levin, "Federal Suit Over Tobacco's Impact on Medicare Weighed," *Washington Post*, August 16, 1998.
23. Staff Reports, "FDA Loses Tobacco Powers: Firms Still Smoking Over Lawsuits," *Medical Industry Today*, August 18, 1998.
24. Matthew Rees, "Tobacco Railroad," *Weekly Standard*, August 16, 1999.
25. Robert Pear, "White House Considering Suit Against Big Tobacco," *New York Times News Service*, August 17, 1998.
26. Kevin Sack, "Gore's Brother-in-Law Plays Crucial Campaign Role," *New York Times*, October 14, 2000.
27. Matthew Rees, "Tobacco Railroad," *Weekly Standard*, August 16, 1999.
28. James Morrow, "The Butt of All Lawsuits," *U.S. News & World Report*, February 1, 1999.
29. Samuel Goldreich, "Tobacco Suit May Seek $500 Billion," *Washington Times*, January 21, 1999.
30. Mark Helm, "Justice Department Considers Strategy for Suing Tobacco Industry," *Times Union*, January 22, 1999.
31. "Leading U.S. Tobacco Companies Respond to President Clinton's State of the Union Address," *PR Newswire*, January 20, 1999.
32. Louise D. Palmer, "Tobacco Firms Aghast at U.S. Legal Plan: Analysts See Massive Liability in Suits," *Boston Globe*, January 21, 1999.
33. Mark Helm, "Justice Department Considers Strategy for Suing Tobacco Industry," *Times Union*, January 22, 1999.
34. David S. Cloud, "Congress May Have to Play Key Role in Justice Department's Tobacco Suit," *Wall Street Journal*, January 27 1999.
35. Saundra Torry, "Lawyer Who Led Minnesota Case Will Advise U.S. on Tobacco Suit," *Washington Post*, April 7, 1999.
36. "The Feds, Tobacco and Fairness," *Tampa Tribune*, September 8, 1999.
37. Victor E. Schwartz and Mark A. Behrens, "Equal Justice Denied If Congress Assists DOJ Quest to Sue Unpopular Defendants," *Legal Backgrounder*, May 14, 1999.
38. Marc Lacey, "U.S. Sues Tobacco Firms for Fraud; The Lawsuit Seeks Billions of Dollars, Tapping into the Industry's Ill-Gotten Gains," *Portland Press Herald*, September 23, 1999.
39. Brit Hume, "The Government Versus Big Tobacco," *Fox News Network*, September 22, 1999.

40. "DOJ Follows Smoke Trail Blazed by State Against Big Tobacco," *State Health Monitor*, October 1, 1999.
41. Victor E. Schwartz and Mark A. Behrens, "Equal Justice Denied if Congress Assists DOJ Quest to Sue Unpopular Defendants," *Legal Backgrounder*, May 14, 1999.
42. Ibid.
43. Laurie Asseo, "Tobacco Companies Seek Dismissal of Federal Lawsuit," *Associated Press*, June 2, 2000.
44. Nancy Zuckerbrod, "Lawmakers, Reno at Odds Over Funding for Tobacco Suit," *Associated Press*, March 30, 2000.
45. Ibid.
46. Steven A. Holmes, "House Reverses Itself on a Suit Over Smoking," *New York Times*, June 21, 2000.
47. Eric Peters, "Greed Not Just a TV Show," *Washington Times*, April 30, 2000.

Three: A Genuine Conspiracy

1. Toni Locy, "For White House Travel Office, a Two-Year Trip of Trouble," *Washington Post*, February 27, 1995.
2. David Brock, "The Travelgate Cover-up," *American Spectator*, June 1994.
3. Ibid.
4. Ibid.
5. Susan Schmidt and Toni Locy, "Papers Detail Clinton Friend's Contract Push," *Washington Post*, October 25, 1995.
6. Deposition of Harry Thomason, House Committee on Government Reform and Oversight, *Investigation of the White House Travel Office and Related Matters*, May 17, 1996.
7. Toni Locy, "Ex-Travel Office Workers Condemn Administration 'Lies'; In Testimony Before Hill Panel, Seven Fired in 1993 Accuse White House of Abusing Power," *Washington Post*, January 25, 1996.
8. Susan Schmidt, "FBI Agent Says Aides Inquired on Travel Staff; White House Firings Followed, Probers Told," *Washington Post*, June 26, 1996.
9. Richard L. Berke, "White House Ousts Its Travel Staff," *New York Times*, May 20, 1993.
10. Ann Devroy, "Clinton Friends Cited in Travel Staff Purge; Report Says First Lady Monitored Actions," *Washington Post*, July 3, 1993.
11. Ann Devroy, "Volunteer Travel Aide Got $1,400; White House Calls Fee a 'Mistake,'" *Washington Post*, June 2, 1993.

12. Ann Devroy, "Travel Office Flap Cited as Evidence of Need for White House Staff Changes," *Washington Post*, May 27, 1993.
13. Ann Devroy, "Clinton Apologizes for 'Glitches' in White House Handling of Events; President's Explanation of Missteps Doesn't Precisely Match the Facts," *Washington Post*, May 28, 1993.
14. Al Kamen, "Penultimate in Seniority, First in Laughs," *Washington Post*, February 2, 1996.
15. John F. Harris, "Angry Clinton Revokes Fees Pledge in Travel Case," *Washington Post*, August 2, 1996.
16. Stephen Barr and R. H. Melton, "Senate Votes to Reimburse Fired Travel Office Chief," *Washington Post*, September 13, 1996.
17. Ellen Edwards, "Networks Balk at White House Bill," *Washington Post*, October 20, 1993.
18. Joann Byrd, "A Whole Lot of Baggage," *Washington Post*, June 6, 1993.
19. Susan Schmidt and Toni Locy, "Papers Detail Clinton Friend's Contract Push," *Washington Post*, October 25, 1995.
20. Annie Groer and Ann Gerhart, "The Harry & Markie Sell-a-Plan Plan," *Washington Post*, October 30, 1995.
21. Susan Schmidt and Toni Locy, "Papers Detail Clinton Friend's Contract Push," *Washington Post*, October 25, 1995.
22. Mary McGrory, "Great Foster's Ghost," *Washington Post*, October 29, 1995.
23. Toni Locy, "Travel Office Trial Enlivened By Outburst," *Washington Post*, November 2, 1995.
24. Toni Locy, "FBI Agent Says Travel Office Unsecured on Day of Firings; Ex-Director's Defense Suggests White House Moved Files," *Washington Post*, November 4, 1995.
25. Ibid.
26. Toni Locy, "Jury Gets Differing Pictures of Travel Office Defendant; On 1st Day, Embezzlement Trial Avoids Politics," *Washington Post*, October 31, 1995.
27. Toni Locy, "Ex-Travel Office Director Cites Networks' Pressure; Dale Says White House Media Griped About Costs," *Washington Post*, November 9, 1995.
28. Toni Locy, "Government Presses Travel Office Case; Ex-Director's Family Budget at the Heart of Prosecution Evidence," *Washington Post*, November 5, 1995.
29. Toni Locy, "Journalists Defend Former Travel Office Director," *Washington Post*, November 7, 1995.

30. Toni Locy, "Ex-White House Travel Chief Testifies He Didn't Steal Funds; Dale Acknowledges Deposits to His Account," *Washington Post*, November 8, 1995.

31. Toni Locy," Fraud Expert Doubts Motive in Travel Case," *Washington Post*, November 14, 1995.

32. Toni Locy, "Travel Office Case Given to U.S. Jury; Handling of Costs to Media at Issue," *Washington Post*, November 16, 1995.

33. Toni Locy, "Fired Travel Office Director Acquitted of Embezzlement; Dale Charged After Ouster from White House," *Washington Post*, November 17, 1995.

34. Editorial, "The Acquittal of Billy Dale," *Washington Post*, November 20, 1995.

35. Toni Locy, "Fired Travel Office Director Acquitted of Embezzlement; Dale Charged After Ouster from White House," *Washington Post*, November 17, 1995.

36. Toni Locy, "Acquitted Aide Blames Clinton for Difficulties; Fired Travel Office Director Says, I'm Bitter... 'It Hurt,'" *Washington Post*, November 18, 1995.

37. Bill Clinton denied even knowing about the firings, much less ordering them, even though it was common knowledge at the White House that he was briefed on the firings two days before they occurred. His public disavowals "sent a chilling message to all those individuals who were aware of President Clinton's prior knowledge of the firings, in effect creating a conspiracy of silence." Susan Schmidt, "'Vast Cover-up' Alleged in Travel Office Affair; Panel's GOP Report Assails Clintons," *Washington Post*, September 14, 1996.

38. Susan Schmidt and Toni Locy, "Travel Office Memo Draws Probers' Ire: Ex-Aide Contradicts Hillary Clinton on Firings," *Washington Post*, January 5, 1996.

39. Ibid.

40. Ibid.

41. Susan Schmidt and Toni Locy, "Ex-Aide Tells of Pressure for Travel Office Firings," *Washington Post*, January 18, 1996.

42. Susan Schmidt, "McLarty Recalls 'Pressure to Act' on Travel Office from First Lady," *Washington Post*, August 6, 1996.

43. Editorial, "The Hillary Clinton Questions," *Washington Post*, January 8, 1996.

44. John F. Harris and Ann Devroy, "Her Way Versus the Washington Way; Ambition and Suspicion in First Year Are Redounding on Hillary Rodham Clinton," *Washington Post*, February 9, 1996.

45. Ibid.
46. Ibid.
47. Bill Dale and Steven C. Tabackman, "Stop Lying About My Record; Travelgate Scapegoat Tells His Side of the Story," *Washington Post*, January 21, 1996.
48. Toni Locy, "Ex-Travel Office Workers Condemn Administration 'Lies'; In Testimony Before Hill Panel, Seven Fired in 1993 Accuse White House of Abusing Power," *Washington Post*, January 25, 1996.
49. George Lardner Jr., "Chairman Wants Starr to Review Testimony; Inconsistencies on Travel Office, FBI Files Cited," *Washington Post*, October 16, 1996.

Four: Investigating the Investigator

1. Ceci Connolly, "Old Friends Rushed to the Rescue," *Washington Post*, October 3, 1993.
2. Philip Weiss, "The Secret Sex Addict Speech Morris Offered Clinton," *New York Observer*, February 1, 1999.
3. Ceci Connolly, "Old Friends Rushed to the Rescue," *Washington Post*, October 3, 1993.
4. John F. Harris and Peter Baker, "White House Shoves Back at Clinton Attackers; Lieutenants Adopt More Combative Approach to Starr, Jones and Campaign Fund Cases," *Washington Post*, June 8, 1997.
5. Terry Lemons, "Starr Leaks Called Smear of Clintons; Letter Accuses Counsel of Using 'Code Words,'" *Washington Post*, June 4, 1997.
6. Transcript, "James Carville Discusses Possible Motives for the Allegations Against President Clinton," *Meet the Press*, January 25, 1998.
7. Thomas M. DeFrank and Thomas Galvin, "Hillary Clinton Is Firmly in Charge of White House Damage Control; First Lady Mapped Out Battle Plan to Defend Husband," *New York Daily News*, February 1, 1998.
8. Ibid.
9. Richard Morrin and Claudia Deane, "President's Popularity Hits New Highs," *Washington Post*, February 1, 1998.
10. Dan Balz, "Clinton Advisors Agree to Attack Starr," *Washington Post*, February 7, 1998.
11. Dan Balz, "The Story So Far: Week Six; Tables Turn as Starr Faces Questions," *Washington Post*, March 1, 1998.

12. John Solomon, "Clinton Camp Attacks Starr Over News Leaks," *Associated Press*, February 6, 1998.
13. Ibid.
14. John F. Harris, "Defending Starr, Republicans Call Leaks Complaints a Ruse," *Washington Post*, February 9, 1998.
15. Ibid.
16. Charles R. Babcock and Ruth Marcus, "Clinton Camp Battles Starr on Two Fronts," *Washington Post*, February 11, 1998.
17. Ken Ringle, "Lenzner: Private Eye or Public Enemy," *Washington Post*, March 2, 1998.
18. Ibid.
19. Peter Baker and Susan Schmidt, "Starr Searches for Source of Staff Criticism," *Washington Post*, February 24, 1998.
20. Ibid.
21. Peter Baker and Toni Locy, "Prosecutor Decries 'Avalanche of Lies,'" *Washington Post*, February 26, 1998.
22. Dan Balz, "The Story So Far: Week Six; Tables Turn as Starr Faces Questions," *Washington Post*, March 1, 1998.
23. Susan Schmidt and Toni Locy, "Starr Examines Ex-Intern's Career, Takes Aim at Critics," *Washington Post*, February 25, 1998.
24. Howard Kurtz, "Starr Is Urged to Curtail Inquiry," *Washington Post*, March 2, 1998.
25. Howard Kurtz, "Prosecutor Lobs a Grenade," *Washington Post*, February 25, 1998.
26. Peter Baker and Toni Locy, "Prosecutor Decries 'Avalanche of Lies,'" *Washington Post*, February 26, 1998.
27. Ruth Marcus, "Privacy Takes Beating in Lewinsky, Jones Cases," *Washington Post*, February 22, 1998.
28. Walter Pincus and George Lardner Jr., "ABA Chief Criticizes 'Prosecutorial Zeal,'" *Washington Post*, February 20, 1998.
29. Terry Frieden, "Judges Hear Ethics Complaints Against Starr," *CNN*, March 5, 1998.
30. Letter to Janet Reno from John Conyers Jr., John D. Dingell, and Joseph Moakley, March 4, 1998.
31. Richard A. Serrano, "Starr Hid Perjury as GM Lawyer, Complaint Says," *Los Angeles Times*, March 5, 1998.
32. Toni Locy, "Lewinsky's First Attorney Tries to Block Subpoena," *Washington Post*, March 5, 1998.
33. John Mintz, "Anti-Clinton Billionaire Goes Before Grand Jury," *Washington Post*, September 29, 1998.

34. Roberto Suro and Susan Schmidt, "Justice Department Urges Starr to Probe Conservative Critics," *Washington Post*, April 10, 1998.
35. Susan Schmidt and Robert Suro, "Clinton Lawyer Renews Assault on Prosecutor," *Washington Post*, April 14, 1998.
36. Ibid.
37. Jonathan Broder, "Fallout from Content Bombshell," *Salon*, June 16, 1998.
38. Adam Clymer, "Starr Admits to Leaks, Denies Acting Illegally," *New York Times*, June 14, 1998.
39. Ibid.
40. Jonathan Broder, "Fallout from Content Bombshell," *Salon*, June 16, 1998.
41. Wolf Blitzer, Eileen O'Connor and Kathleen Koch, "Judge Meets with Lawyers over Alleged Starr Leaks," *CNN*, June 15, 1998.
42. Peter Baker, "Judge Orders Probe of Starr Team over Leaks," *Washington Post*, August 8, 1998.
43. Ibid.
44. Howard Kurtz, "McHale Assails Attack on His Military Record," *Washington Post*, August 27, 1998.
45. John F. Harris, "As Outcry Grows, Aides Prepare Fight," *Washington Post*, September 4, 1998.
46. Dan Balz, "Clinton Lawyers Hit Back," *Washington Post*, September 13, 1998.
47. Robert Suro, "Potential Starr Conflicts Weren't Discussed," *Washington Post*, October 17, 1998.
48. Peter Baker and Susan Schmidt, "Starr Defends Clinton Probe against Attacks; Partisanship Marks Daylong Appearance," *Washington Post*, November 20, 1998.
49. Susan Schmidt and Michael Weisskopf, *Truth at Any Cost* (New York: HarperCollins, 2000), 18.
50. Ibid.
51. Susan Schmidt, "Starr Denies Misconduct in New Letter," *Washington Post*, December 13, 1998.
52. Lynn Sweet, "Dems Grill Starr on Ties to Jones Case," *Chicago Sun-Times*, November 20, 1998.
53. Peter Baker and Susan Schmidt, "Starr Defends Probe against Attacks," *Washington Post*, November 20, 1998.
54. For a good history of impeachment in English and American common law, see Ann Coulter's *High Crimes and Misdemeanors* (Washington, D.C.: Regnery Publishing, 1998).

55 Kevin Merida, "Hill Doesn't Rise to Flynt's Bait," *Washington Post*, October 7, 1998.

56. Howard Kurtz, "Larry Flynt, Investigative Pornographer," *Washington Post*, December 19, 1998.

57. Ibid.

58. Howard Kurtz, "Larry Flynt and the Barers of Bad News," *Washington Post*, December 20, 1998.

59. Howard Kurtz, "White House Angry about GOP Charge," *Washington Post*, December 18, 1998.

60. David Johnston and Don Vann Natta Jr., "Reno to Investigate Starr Team's Conduct, Officials Say," *New York Times*, February 10, 1999.

61. Ibid.

62. Transcript, CNBC, *Rivera Live*, October 16, 1998.

63. Peter Baker and Juliet Eilperin, "Inquiry May Turn Tables on Starr, Jones Lawyers," *Washington Post*, October 15, 1998.

64. Schmidt and Weisskopf, *Truth at Any Cost*, 264-266.

65. Robert Suro, "U.S. Advised Starr of Probe Last Month," *Washington Post*, February 11, 1999.

66. David Johnston and Don Vann Natta Jr., "Reno to Investigate Starr Team's Conduct, Officials Say," *New York Times*, February 10, 1999.

67. Robert Suro, "Reno Seeks Pact With Starr on Probe," *Washington Post*, February 20, 1999.

68. "Former Starr Aide Not Guilty in News Leak Case," *Reuters*, October 6, 2000.

69. Robert Suro, "Justice Department Argues Right to Probe Starr," *Washington Post*, March 9, 1999.

70. Leef Smith and Patricia Davis, "Willey Depicts Steele as Opportunist," *Washington Post*, May 6, 1999.

71. "Steele Jury Foreman Urges New Trial," *Associated Press*, May 23, 1999.

72. Thomas Scheffey, "Catch a Falling Starr?" *Law News Network*, February 22, 2000.

73. Scrapbook, "Lowering the Bar," *Weekly Standard*, June 5, 2000.

74. Linda Satter, "Judge Rejects Bid to Investigate Starr Misconduct Allegations in Clinton Prosecution Unfounded, He Says," *Arkansas Democrat-Gazette*, May 19, 2000.

75. Editorial, "Legal Ethics and Spin," *Washington Post*, May 24, 2000.

76. Robert G. Kaiser, "Clinton Critics Cleared of Tampering Charges," *Washington Post*, July 29, 1999.

77. Bill Miller, "Starr Leaks Not Illegal, Appeals Court Rules," *Washington Post*, September 14, 1999.

78. Editorial, "Leaks and the Law," *New York Times*, September 16, 1999.
79. Robert Suro, "Justice Investigation of Starr Approved," *Washington Post*, March 19, 1999.
80. Robert Suro, "Investigation of Starr on Hold," *Washington Post*, June 6, 1999.
81. Byron York, "Ken Starr in Limbo, Status of Supposed Leaks Investigation Remains Unanswered," *New York Press*, February 15, 2000.
82. Robert Suro, "Starr Blames His Accusers, Expresses Some Regret," *Washington Post*, April 15, 1999.

Five: "A Substantive, Savvy, and Experienced Professional"

1. Jeff Leen and Gene Weingarten, "Linda's Tripp," *Washington Post*, March 15, 1998.
2. Ibid.
3. Ibid.
4. Ibid.
5. Ibid.
6. Ibid.
7. Ibid.
8. Ibid.
9. "Excerpts: After Subpoenas, Tripp and Lewinsky Discuss Options," *Washington Post*, January 25, 1998.
10. Paul W. Valentine, "Maryland Jury to Probe Tripp's Taping," *Washington Post*, July 8, 1998.
11. Paul W. Valentine, "Md. Official Takes over Taping Probe," *Washington Post*, February 12, 1998.
12. Paul W. Valentine, "Maryland Jury to Probe Tripp's Taping," *Washington Post*, July 8, 1998.
13. Mary McGrory, "Hurricane Linda," *Washington Post*, February 26, 1998.
14. Marc Fisher, "Tripp's Tapes: Listening in on a Betrayal," *Washington Post*, November 18, 1998.
15. Jeff Leen, "Calls About Tripp Lead to Subpoena: White House Drug Policy Spokesman Questioned Over Contacts With Local Democrats," *Washington Post*, January 31, 1998.
16. Jeff Leen, "Tripp Friend Says Arrest Followed Prank," *Washington Post*, March 17, 1998.

17. Elaine Sciolino, "Testing of a President: The Pentagon; Linda Tripp's Security Form Draws Inquiry," *Washington Post*, March 14, 1998.
18. Thomas Galvin, "Starr's Panel Turns Wary of Questionable Witness," *New York Daily News*, March 18, 1998.
19. Greg Pierce, "Inside Politics," *Washington Times*, March 19, 1998.
20. Editorial, "Fire Kenneth Bacon," *Washington Times*, April 11, 2000.
21. Jerry Seper and Bill Sammon, "Ickes Denies Setup of Tripp; Grand Jury Probes Leak of Her Records," *Washington Times*, June 11, 1998.
22. Bill Miller, "Pentagon Official Sorry About Tripp Disclosure," *Washington Post*, May 22, 1998.
23. Brian Blomquist, "Starr Plots His Next Move on Lewinsky," *New York Post*, May 1, 1998.
24. Bill Miller, "Pentagon Official Sorry About Tripp Disclosure," *Washington Post*, May 22, 1998.
25. Howard Kurtz, "The Starr Report's Resourceful Reporters," *Washington Post*, October 12, 1998.
26. Tucker Carlson, "Linda Tripp's Pentagon Papers," *Weekly Standard*, March 30, 1998.
27. Jay Nordlinger, "Smoking Bacon," *Weekly Standard*, June 1, 1998.
28. Bill Sammon and Paul Bedard, "Pentagon's Bacon 'Sorry' About Tripp Leak, Says He Acted on His Own," *Washington Times*, May 22, 1998.
29. Bill Sammon, "Tripp Leak Violated Policy at Pentagon; 'Unwarranted' Privacy Invasions Banned," *Washington Times*, June 8, 1998.
30. Jay Nordlinger, "Saving Clinton's Bacon," *Weekly Standard*, October 19, 1998.
31. Editorial, "Skirting the Truth," *Investor's Business Daily*, June 8, 1998.
32. Bill Miller, "Tripp Files Suit, Alleging a Plot to Smear Her," *International Herald Tribune*, September 29, 1999.
33. Jerry Seper, "Justice Ignored Findings of Probe in Tripp File Case; Inspector General Says Law Was Broken," *Washington Times*, April 7, 2000.
34. "Bacon's Fate Now in Cohen's Hands," *White House Bulletin*, April 7, 2000.

Six: Presidential Privilege

1. Letter to John E. Moss, Chairman, Foreign Operations and Government Information Subcommittee of the Committee on Government Operations, March 31, 1965.
2. Ibid.
3. Ibid.
4. *United States v. Nixon*, 418 U.S. 683 (1974).
5. *United States v. Nixon*, Footnote 19.
6. Ruth Marcus, "Executive Privilege: An Old, Uphill Struggle," *Washington Post*, February 20, 1998.
7. Referral to the U.S. House of Representatives pursuant to Title 28, United States Code, Sec. 595 (c) Submitted by the Office of Independent Counsel, September 9, 1998, Grounds, Section XI. Hereinafter, *Starr Report*.
8. *In re Bruce R. Lindsey* (Grand Jury Testimony), No. 98ms0095, (U.S.D.C. May 26, 1998).
9. Editorial. "Law in the Clinton Era; the Abuse of Privilege, Again," *New York Times*, March 24, 1998.
10. *Starr Report*, Grounds, Section XI.
11. Susan Schmidt and Ruth Marcus, "Executive Privilege Claim is Revived," *Washington Post*, August 6, 1998.
12. *In re Bruce R. Lindsey* (Grand Jury Testimony), No. 98-3060, (D.C.C. July 27, 1998).
13. John F. Harris, "Clinton Finds There's No Escape; In Africa, President Sidesteps Executive Privilege Questions," *Washington Post*, March 25, 1998.
14. *Starr Report*, Grounds, Section XI.
15. Ibid.
16. Ibid., Footnote 494.
17. Susan Schmidt and Peter Baker, "Clinton Refused to Order Agents to Talk," *Washington Post*, May 20, 1998.
18. Ibid.
19. Robert Suro, "Justice Department to Fight Starr on Secret Service Testimony," *Washington Post*, April 15, 1998.
20. George Lardner Jr. and Bill Miller, "Starr Cites Danger in Secret Service Silence," *Washington Post*, May 15, 1998.
21. Ibid.
22. Peter Baker, "Secret Service Agents Told to Testify," *Washington Post*, May 23, 1998.

23. Peter Baker and Susan Schmidt, "Starr Disputes Assassination Predictions," *Washington Post*, June 20, 1998.
24. *Starr Report*, Grounds, Section XI.

Seven: The Mother of All Scandals

1. George Stephanopoulos, "The View from Inside," *Newsweek*, March 10, 1997.
2. Bob Woodward, "Gore Was 'Solicitor-in-Chief,'" *Washington Post*, March 2, 1997.
3. Charles G. La Bella, Interim Report for Janet Reno, Attorney General, July 16, 1998.
4. The Senate Committee on Governmental Affairs, *Final Report of the Investigation of Illegal or Improper Activities in Connection with 1996 Federal Election Campaigns, Summary of Findings*, 18-19.
5. Ibid., 2-3.
6. Ibid., 14-15.
7. Alan Miller, "Democrats Return Illegal Contribution; Politics: South Korean Subsidiary's $250,000 Donation Violated Ban on Money from Foreign Nationals," *Los Angeles Times*, September 21, 1996.
8. Ibid.
9. "Campaign Finance Key Players: The Riady Family," *Washington Post*, March 4, 1998.
10. Byron York, "Roots of a Scandal," *American Spectator*, October 1998.
11. Brian Duffy, "A Fundraiser's Rise and Fall," *Washington Post*, May 13, 1997.
12. Editorial, "Heed the Senate Hearings," *St. Petersburg Times*, July 20, 1997.
13. Brian Duffy, "A Fundraiser's Rise and Fall," *Washington Post*, May 13, 1997.
14. Ibid.
15. Ibid.
16. Byron York, "Roots of a Scandal," *American Spectator*, October 1998.
17. Brian Duffy, "A Fundraiser's Rise and Fall," *Washington Post*, May 13, 1997.
18. Senate Governmental Affairs Committee Report, *Summary of Findings*, 5.
19. Donald Lambro, "Bridge across a Chasm of Corruption," *Washington Times*, November 4, 1996.
20. Brian Duffy, "A Fundraiser's Rise and Fall," *Washington Post*, May 13, 1997.

21. Ibid.
22. Ibid.
23. Donald Lambro, "Furor Grows Over DNC Finances; Democrats Seek to Stave off Inquiries Until after Election," *Washington Times*, October 30, 1996.
24. Brian Duffy, "A Fundraiser's Rise and Fall," *Washington Post*, May 13, 1997.
25. Ibid.
26. Jeffrey Silva, "GOP Vows to Investigate Clinton's Link to Vietnam Trade Status," *Crain Communications, Radio Comm. Report*, December 9, 1996.
27. "Washington Wire Reports, Contributions Might Be Illegal; Indonesian Donations Troublesome for Demos," *Times-Picayune*, October 18, 1996.
28. Alan Miller, "The Democrats Are Accused of Embracing International Donors and Possibly Accepting Illegal Contributions," *Guardian* (London), October 15, 1996.
29. Ibid.
30. Editorial, "The Huang Affair," *Sacramento Bee*, November 1, 1996.
31. Ruth Marcus and R.H. Melton, "DNC Donor Controversy Widens As Republicans Step Up Criticism," *Washington Post*, October 18, 1996.
32. Michael Isikoff and Mark Hosenball, "The Man in the Middle," *Newsweek*, July 21, 1997.
33. Ruth Marcus and R. H. Melton, "GOP Steps Up Attack On Democrats' Funds," *Fort Lauderdale Sun-Sentinel*, October 18, 1996.
34. Ruth Marcus and R. H. Melton, "DNC Donor Controversy Widens as Republicans Step Up Criticism," *Washington Post*, October 18, 1996.
35. Stephen Labaton, "Democrats Suspend Fund Raiser; Official Has Ties to Foreign Family," *Fort Lauderdale Sun-Sentinel*, October 19, 1996.
36. Editorial, "The Buddhists and the Democrats," *Washington Times*, October 20, 1996.
37. Alan Miller, "Democrats Return $325,000 Gift from Gandhi Relative," *Los Angeles Times*, November 7, 1996.
38. Ibid.
39. Transcript, "Haley Barbour, Chairman Republican National Committee, Discusses Democratic National Committee Refusal of Pre-Election FEC Report," 1996 Presidential Campaign Press Materials, October 29, 1996.

40. Peter Baker and John F. Harris, "Clinton's Call for Finance Reform Gets Mixed Reviews," *Austin American-Statesman*, November 2, 1996.

41. "Dodd: End Foreign Gifts," *Commercial Appeal* (Memphis), November 4, 1996.

42. Editorial, "Fundraising and Cost-cutting at the DNC," *Washington Times*, November 10, 1996

43. Ibid.

44. Donald Lambro, "Furor Grows over DNC Finances; Democrats Seek to Stave off Inquiries until after Election," *Washington Times*, October 30, 1996.

45. "Dateline: Washington, Democrats Defend Contribution from Iraqi Group," *Associated Press*, November 5, 1996.

46. Martin Walker, "The Pitfalls: Clinton Short of a Big Idea as Skeletons Continue to Rattle," *Guardian* (London), November 6, 1996.

47. "Statement by Former CIA Director on Clinton Ties to Loutchansky," *U.S. Newswire*, November 3, 1996.

48. Terry Frieden, "Convicted Cocaine Smuggler Posed With Mrs. Clinton, Gore," http://www.cnn.com/ALLPOLITICS, October 23, 1997.

49. David Jackson, "DNC Leader Takes Blame for Fund Woes; New Procedure Unveiled to Flag Illegal Donations," *Dallas Morning News*, November 13, 1996.

50. Editorial, "Democrats' Finance Irregularities Warrant Higher Level of Concern," *Omaha World Herald*, November 18, 1996.

51. Ruth Marcus and Lena H. Sun, "Democrats Return $253,000 More; Campaign Contributions Were Made by Thai Living in U.S.," *International Herald Tribune*, November 22, 1996.

52. "Contributions to Democratic Party Office Not Reported in 1992," *Bulletin's Frontrunner*, December 3, 1996.

53. James Rowley, "Justice Department Opposes Dem. Immunity," *Associated Press*, October 15, 1997.

54. Jerry Solomon, "Congressman, House, Holds White House, Security and Foreign Policy 'For Sale,'" *Congressional Press Releases*, December 20, 1996.

55. Patrick Brogan, "Democrats 'Accepted Funding' from China," *Herald* (Glasgow), February 14, 1997.

56. Brian Duffy and Bob Woodward, "FBI Warned 6 on Hill about China Money," *Washington Post*, March 9, 1997.

57. Brian Duffy and Bob Woodward, "Chinese Embassy Role in Contributions Probed," *Washington Post*, February 13, 1997.
58. David Hess and R. A. Zaldivar, "Campaign Finance: Can the Loopholes Be Closed and the Abuses Stopped?" *Record*, January 19, 1997.
59. Ibid.
60. Robert Shogan, "Panel Wants More Money to Police Campaign Funding," *Los Angeles Times*, February 11, 1997.
61. Michael Kranish, "GOP Angry with Clinton's Funds Charge: White House Offers No Details," *Boston Globe*, January 23, 1997.
62. Gretchen Coo, "U.S. Campaign Finance Flap Tars Many but Ensnares Only Foreigners," *Agence France Presse*, February 18, 1997.
63. Narayan D. Keshavan, "DNC Moves to Accept Legal Alien Funds," *News-India Times*, May 9, 1997.
64. John King, "DNC Audit Finds More Suspect Contributions; White House Official: Democrats to Return Additional $1 Million," *Chicago Tribune*, February 22, 1997.

Eight: The Mother of All Scandals Moves to Congress

1. James W. Brosnan, "Limits Put on Campaign Fund-Raising Investigation; 'Soft Money' Won't Be Checked," *Commercial Appeal* (Memphis), March 7, 1997.
2. Senate Governmental Affairs Committee Report, *Summary of Findings*, 3-4.
3. Eric Schmitt, "GOP Campaign Funds Also to Be Probed," *State Journal-Register*, April 10, 1997.
4. Marc Lacey, "GOP Ally Targeted Foreign Donors, Memos Indicate," *Los Angeles Times*, May 10, 1997.
5. Susan Schmidt, John F. Harris, "Ickes' Papers Offer Insight into Clinton Fund-Raising; President Frequently Reviewed Details of Campaign Money Efforts, Files Indicate," *Washington Post*, April 3, 1997.
6. Bob Woodward, "Gore Was 'Solicitor-in-Chief,'" *Washington Post*, March 2, 1997.
7. John F. Harris, "Gore: Calls Broke No Law," *Washington Post*, March 4, 1997.
8. Robert Suro, "Reno Formally Rejects Independent Counsel," *Washington Post*, April 15, 1997.

9. "Thompson Committee to Hear from Buddhist Nuns; Lott Indicates Senate in No Hurry to Pass Finance Reform Legislation," *White House Bulletin*, September 2, 1997.

10. "Barbour Defends Loan to National Policy Forum," *Bulletin's Frontrunner*, April 29, 1997.

11. Edward Walsh, "GOP's Barbour Comes Out Firing, Denounces 'Outright False Claims,'" *Washington Post*, July 25, 1997.

12. Guy Gugliotta, "Barbour Meets the Committee Head-On; Former GOP Chairman Comes Well-Prepared to Stand His Ground," *Washington Post*, July 25, 1997.

13. Connie Cass, "Republicans Return $102,400 in Foreign Donations," *AP Worldstream*, May 8, 1997.

14. Donald Lambro, "RNC Returns Illegal Donation; Democrats Seek to Redirect Probe," *Washington Times*, May 9, 1997.

15. James W. Brosnan, "Democrats Reject Immunity in Fund Probe; Miffed Thompson Warns of Cover-up," *Commercial Appeal* (Memphis), June 13, 1997.

16. James W. Brosnan, "Heat Spurs the Smell of Cover-up," *Commercial Appeal* (Memphis), June 15, 1997.

17. James W. Brosnan, "Democrats Reject Immunity in Fund Probe; Miffed Thompson Warns of Cover-up," *Commercial Appeal* (Memphis), June 13, 1997.

18. James W. Brosnan, "Heat Spurs the Smell of Cover-up," *Commercial Appeal* (Memphis), June 15, 1997.

19. Edward Walsh and Guy Gugliotta, "Chinese Plan to Buy U.S. Influence Alleged," *Washington Post*, July 9, 1997.

20. Judi Hasson and Judy Keen, "Glenn Cites 'Bipartisan Abuses,'" *USA Today*, July 9, 1987.

21. Edward Walsh and Guy Gugliotta, "Chinese Plan to Buy U.S. Influence Alleged," *Washington Post*, July 9, 1997.

22. Lawrence M. O'Rourke, "Fund-Raising Spotlight Lands on Sacramentan," *Sacramento Bee*, July 10, 1997.

23. Bennett Roth, "DNC Denies Huang Solicitation; 'I Would Have Personally Walked Him to the Elevator,' Official Says," *Houston Chronicle*, July 11, 1997.

24. "Direct Link: Lippo to Huang to DNC, *The Hotline*, July 16, 1997.

25. Amy Bayer, "Demos Campaign Finance Troubles Linked to 1992 Illegal Foreign Contributions," *Copley News Service*, July 15, 1997.

26. Greg McDonald, "Evidence Points to Illegal Donation to Democrats," *Houston Chronicle*, July 16, 1997.

27. Ibid.
28. Editorial, "The Proved and the Unproved," *New York Times*, July 13, 1997.
29. Glenn F. Bunting, "Finance Hearing to Focus on Contributions from Trie," *Los Angeles Times*, July 28, 1997.
30. "Two Women Tell of Money Switch," *United Press International*, July 29, 1997.
31. John F. Harris, "Documents Detail Gore's Calls for DNC," *Washington Post*, August 27, 1997.
32. Bob Woodward, "Gore Donors' Funds Used as 'Hard Money,'" *Washington Post*, September 3, 1997.
33. Ibid.
34. Robert Suro and Lena H. Sun, "Justice Department to Probe Gore Fund Calls," *Washington Post*, September 4, 1997.
35. Peter Baker, "White House Seeks to Protect Gore in Temple Inquiry," *Washington Post*, September 3, 1997.
36. Ibid.
37. Lena H. Sun and John Mintz, "Nuns Tell of Panic About Fundraiser," *Washington Post*, September 5, 1997.
38. Ruth Marcus, "GOP Hits Gore on Temple Fundraiser," *Washington Post*, February 10, 1998.
39. Edward Walsh, "Ex-NSC Aide Describes Pressure to Help Donor," *Washington Post*, September 18, 1997.
40. Senate Governmental Affairs Committee Report, *Teamsters*, 3-4.
41. Ibid., 9.
42. Ibid., 11-12.
43. Steven Greenhouse, "3 Top Teamster Aides Plead Guilty; Probe of Union Chief Found Fund-Raising Link to Democrats," *International Herald Tribune*, September 20, 1997.

Nine: The Mother of All Scandals and the Justice Department

1. Robert Suro, "Reno Moves to Expand Fund-Raising Inquiry," *Washington Post*, September 17, 1997.
2. Robert Suro and John F. Harris, "Reno is Now Probing Clinton's Fund-Raising," *Washington Post*, September 21, 1997.
3. Susan Schmidt and Roberto Suro, "Basic Conflict Impeded Justice Probe of Fund-Raising," *Washington Post*, October 3, 1997.

4. Ibid.
5. Ibid.
6. Robert Suro, "Reno Decides Against Independent Counsel to Probe Clinton, Gore," *Washington Post*, December 3, 1997.
7. Robert Suro, "Trie Enters Plea of Not Guilty," *Washington Post*, February 6, 1998.
8. Robert Novak, "Fund-raising Probe Stonewalled," *Chicago Sun-Times*, June 10, 1999.
9. Robert Suro, "Clinton Fundraiser to Plead Guilty," *Washington Post*, May 22, 1999.
10. Robert Suro, "Fundraiser Makes Plea of Not Guilty," *Washington Post*, February 20, 1998.
11. Bill Miller, "Campaign Probe Dealt Setback," *Washington Post*, September 11, 1998.
12. Bill Miller, "Hsia is Convicted of Illegal Donations; Gore Ally Aided '96 Fund-Raising," *Washington Post*, March 3, 2000.
13. Robert Suro, "Chung Makes Deal With Prosecutors," *Washington Post*, March 6, 1998.
14. Robert Suro and Bob Woodward, "Chung Ties Funds to DNC," *Washington Post*, May 16, 1998.
15. Robert Suro, "Chung Alleges DNC Sought Illegal Funds," *Washington Post*, June 20, 1998.
16. Ibid.
17. Robert Suro, "Not Chinese Agent, Chung Says," *Washington Post*, May 12, 1999.
18. Morton Kondracke, "GOP Should Launch New Probe of Reno's Wrist-Slaps on China," *Roll Call*, August 2, 1999.
19 Jeff Gerth and Raymond Bonner, "Companies Are Investigated for Aid to China on Rockets," *New York Times*, April 4, 1998.
20. Juliet Eilperin, "GOP Leaders Demand Satellite Export Data," *Washington Post*, May 12, 1998.
21. Jeff Gerth and John M. Broder, "Papers Show White House Staff Favored a China Satellite Permit," *New York Times*, May 23, 1998.
22. Jeff Gerth and Raymond Bonner, "Companies Are Investigated for Aid to China on Rockets," *New York Times*, April 4, 1998.
23. Jeff Gerth and John M. Broder, "The White House Dismissed Warnings on China Satellite Deal," *New York Times*, June 1, 1998.
24. Jeff Gerth and Raymond Bonner, "Companies Are Investigated for Aid to China on Rockets," *New York Times*, April 4, 1998.

25. Juliet Eilperin, "GOP Leaders Demand Satellite Export Data," *Washington Post*, May 12, 1998.

26. Jeff Gerth, "Congress Investigating Sales of Satellite Technology to China," *New York Times*, April 16, 1998.

27. Jeff Gerth and David E. Sanger, "How Chinese Won Rights to Launch Satellites for U.S.," *New York Times*, May 17, 1998.

28. Jeff Gerth, "Reports Show Chinese Military Used American-Made Satellites," *New York Times*, June 13, 1998.

29. Eric Schmitt and Jeff Gerth, "White House Memos to President Reveal Strategy to Shift Purview Over Satellite Sales," *New York Times*, July 18, 1998.

30. Jeff Gerth, "Satellite Company Faulted Over Rocket Aid to China," *New York Times*, December 9, 1998.

31. William C. Rempel and Alan Miller, "Internal Justice Memo Excuses Loral from Funds Probe," *Los Angeles Times*, May 23, 2000.

32. Reed Irvine, "The Course of Corruption," *Chattanooga Times*, June 11, 2000.

33. Bill Miller and Michael Grunwald, "Thai Women Indicted in Fund-Raising Probe," *Washington Post*, July 14, 1998.

34. Editorial, "The Prosecutor Who Spoke Up," *New York Times*, August 4, 1998.

35. Robert Suro and Michael Grunwald, "Reno Orders 90-Day Investigation of Gore," *Washington Post*, August 27, 1998.

36. Robert Suro, "Reno Rejects Probe of Gore on Lying," *Washington Post*, November 25, 1998.

37. Robert Suro, "Preliminary Probe Ordered in Ickes Case," *Washington Post*, September 2, 1998.

38. Michael J. Sniffen, "Ickes Probe Rejected," *Associated Press*, January 29, 1999.

39. "Justice's Clinton, Gore Inquiry Criticized," *USA Today*, December 16, 1999.

40. Robert Suro, "Reno Won't Seek Probe By Counsel On '96 Ads; Reno Decides Against Independent Counsel Probe of 1996 Clinton Ads," *Washington Post*, December 8, 1998.

41. La Bella Memo, 46-51.

42. Senate Governmental Affairs Committee Report, *White House and DNC*, 40.

43. Robert Suro, "Prosecutors' Approach to Huang Signals Shift in Probe," *Washington Post*, October 2, 1998.

44. Edward Walsh and Robert Suro, "Clinton Fundraiser Huang to Offer Guilty Plea," *Washington Post*, May 26, 1999.

45. Chris Mondics, "Democrats Kept $603,500 in Campaign Contributions," *Knight Ridder*, September 22, 2000.

46. Jeff Gerth and Eric Schmitt, "House Panel Says Chinese Obtained U.S. Arms Secrets," *New York Times*, December 31, 1998.

47. Jeff Gerth and James Risen, "Nuclear Secrets: The Overview; Spying Charges Against Beijing Are Spelled Out by House Panel," *New York Times*, May 26, 1999.

48. Bryan Sierra and Associated Press, "Riady to Plead Guilty to Illegally Funding Clinton's Campaign," *Fox News*, January 11, 2001.

49. Amy Paulson, "White House Officials Acknowledge E-mail Glitch Secrecy, Say No Threats Were Made; Justice Department Opens Criminal Investigation," *CNN*, March 23, 2000.

50. Dan Burton, "White House Admits Over One Year of Vice President's E-Mails Were Not Saved," House Committee on Government Reform, June 8, 2000.

51. George Lardner Jr., "Offer to Back Up Gore Records Rebuffed, Aide Says," *Washington Post*, June 21, 2000.

52. The Independent Counsel Act had expired in 1999.

53. Toni Locy, "The Buddhist Business: Gore Is Quizzed About a Controversial Fundraiser," *U.S. News & World Report*, July 3, 2000.

54. Paul Sperry, "Gore's Memory Fails Him 85 Times," http://worldnetdaily.com, June 27, 2000.

55. Paul Sperry, "Hsia Helped Gore Write 'Earth' Book," http://worldnetdaily.com, June 27, 2000.

56. Kenneth R. Timmerman, "Tracking Gore's Temple Woes," *Washington Times*, June 30, 2000.

57. Ibid.

58. Kenneth T. Walsh and Marianne Lavelle, "The Iced-tea Defense," *U.S. News & World Report*, June 19, 2000.

59. Jerry Seper, "Memos Suggest Gore 'May Have Lied' in Funds Testimony," *Washington Times*, June 8, 2000.

60. Don Van Natta Jr. and David Johnston, "The Tale of Two Gores: A Primer on the Fundraising Inquiry," *New York Times*, July 5, 2000.

61. John Whitesides, "Justice Department Won't Discuss Gore Video," *Reuters*, July 21, 2000.

62. "Staff Memos to Gore Describe Temple Event as a Fundraiser," *Wall Street Journal*, September 24, 2000.

63. Morton Kondracke, "GOP Should Launch New Probe of Reno's Wrist-Slaps on China," *Roll Call*, August 2, 1999.

64. Jerry Seper, "Justice Probes Whether Congress Was Misled," *Washington Times*, November 14, 2000.

65. "Democrats Still Have Tainted Cash," *St. Petersburg Times*, September 22, 2000.

Ten: Bill Lann Lee: Quota King

1. Robert Suro, "Civil Rights Nominee Has Made Allies of Adversaries; Solution-Oriented Lee Faces Scrutiny in Senate," *Washington Post*, August 20, 1997.

2. "Excerpts from Comments on Nominee," *New York Times*, November 7, 1997.

3. Roger Clegg, "Senators Are Right to Doubt Justice Nominee," *New York Times*, December 12, 1997.

4. Steven A. Holmes, "Senator Deals Serious Setback to Clinton Choice for Rights Job," *New York Times*, November 5, 1997.

5. Clinton Bolick, "Law Enforcement or Ideological Activism," Institute for Justice Press Release, Fall 1997.

6. Robert Suro, "Justice Nominee's Confirmation in Jeopardy; GOP Making Issue of Stand on Affirmative Action by Civil Rights Lawyer," *Washington Post*, November 5, 1997.

7. Clinton Bolick, "Law Enforcement or Ideological Activism," Institute for Justice Press Release, Fall 1997.

8. Steven A. Holmes, "Senator Deals Serious Setback to Clinton Choice for Rights Job," *New York Times*, November 5, 1997.

9. Robert Suro, "Lee Nomination Fails as Panel Divides on Affirmative Action," *Washington Post*, November 14, 1997.

10. John M. Broder, "Clinton, Softening Slap at Senate, Names 'Acting' Civil Rights Chief," *New York Times*, December 16, 1997.

11. Helen Dewar, "Senators Question How Long Lee Can Stay in Rights Post," *Washington Post*, December 20, 1997.

12. Matthew M. Hoffman, "The Art of 'Acting,'" *Washington Post*, January 1, 1998.

13. James C. Ho and Steven J. Duffield, "The Lawless Tenure of Bill Lann Lee," *Washington Times*, September 3, 1998.

14. George F. Will, "Time to Evict Bill Lann Lee," *Washington Post*, March 26, 1998.

15. "Clinton Justice Appointment Was Violation, Agency Says," *New York Times*, January 18, 1998.

16. "Clinton Again Seeks Rights Enforcer's Confirmation," *Washington Post*, March 6, 1999.
17. James C. Ho, "A Year of Bill Lann Lee," *Washington Times*, December 24, 1998.
18. Ibid.
19. Roger Clegg, "Lee Loves Quotas, Just as the Senate Feared," *Wall Street Journal*, December 14, 1998.
20. Ibid.
21. "Lee's Way," *National Review Online*, February 16, 1999.
22. Ibid.
23. Michael Catanzaro, "Bill Lann Lee's Big Victory," *American Spectator*, June 2000.
24. Robert Ruth, "U.S. Lawmakers File Comments on Civil-Rights Suit," *Columbus Dispatch*, September 7, 2000.
25. Michael Catanzaro, "Bill Lann Lee's Big Victory," *American Spectator*, June, 2000.
26. Ed Hayward, "Lawrence Agrees to Assist Hispanic Voters at Polls," *Boston Herald*, September 10, 1999.
27. Editorial, "Charter Hypocrites," *Wall Street Journal*, October 20, 1999.
28. Al Kamen, "No Advise, No Consent, No Ask," *Washington Post*, August 4, 2000.
29. Christopher Marquis, "Clinton Sidesteps Senate to Fill Civil Rights Enforcement Job," *New York Times*, August 4, 2000.

Eleven: **Treating with Terrorists**

1. Mark LeBien, "Puerto Rican Nationalists Facing Freedom," *Chicago Tribune*, September 10, 1999.
2. Deborah Ramirez, "Puerto Ricans Gain Support in Freeing Radicals; Nobel Winners, Church Leaders Help Jailed FALN Nationalists," *Chicago Tribune*, August 10, 1997.
3. David A. Vise and Lorraine Adams, "Hatch Faults Justice Department as Clemency Report is Released," *Washington Post*, October 21, 1999.
4. "Lawmakers Want Answers," http://abcnews.com, September 1, 1999.
5. Michael Cooper, "Police Victims of Bombing Fight Clemency," *New York Times*, August 24, 1999.
6. Ibid.
7. Neil MacFarquhar, "Clemency Opens Old Scars for Sons of Bombing Victim," *New York Times*, August 23, 1999.

8. U.S. House of Representatives Committee on Government Reform, *The FALN and Macheteros, Executive Summary*, 3.

9. Ibid.

10. Ibid.

11. J. Jennings Moss, "FALN Prisoners OK Clemency Deal," http://abcnews.com, September 7, 1999.

12. Julie Deardorff, "12 Jailed FALN Members Take U.S. Clemency Deal," *Chicago Tribune*, September 8, 1999.

13. David Johnston, "Federal Agencies Opposed Leniency for 16 Militants," *New York Times*, August 27, 1999.

14. U.S. House of Representatives, Committee on Government Reform, *Clemency for Terrorists, Final Report*, 52.

15. Tamara Lytle, "Reno Called FALN 'an Ongoing Threat,'" *Chicago Tribune*, October 21, 1999.

16. House Committee on Government Reform, *Clemency for Terrorists*, 52.

17. James Dao, "G.O.P. Wants Clinton to Explain Clemency for Puerto Rican Nationalists," *New York Times*, September 2, 1999.

18. Katharine Q. Seeyle, "Political Memo; The First Lady's Minuet on Clemency," *New York Times*, September 6, 1999.

19. Adam Nagourney, "First Lady Urges President to Withdraw Clemency Offer for Terrorist Group," *Post and Courier*, September 5, 1999.

20. Jennifer Harper, "Backpedaling Generates a Backlash; Hillary's Reversal on FALN Angers Some Hispanics," *Washington Times*, September 7, 1999.

21. J. Jennings Moss, "FALN Prisoners OK Clemency Deal," http://abcnews.com, September 7, 1999.

22. John F. Harris and Ann Devroy, "Her Way Versus the Washington Way; Ambition and Suspicion in First Year Are Redounding on Hillary Rodham Clinton," *Washington Post*, February 9, 1996

23. Tim Weiner, "Puerto Rico an Issue of the Heart for a Clinton Loyalist," *New York Times*, September 13, 1999.

24. "Hasty Comment?" http://abcnews.com, September 11, 1999.

25. Katharine Q. Seelye, "Clinton Says Clemency Plan Was Unrelated to First Lady," *New York Times*, September 10, 1999.

26. Mike Dorning, "FBI Warned Clinton Clemency Was Risky," *Chicago Tribune*, September 22, 1999.

27. House Committee on Government Reform, *What Did We Learn at the FALN Hearing? Post Hearing Update*, 2.

28. House Committee on Government Reform, *Clemency for Terrorists*, 2.
29. Ibid., 6.
30. Findings of the Committee on Government Reform, Rep. Dan Burton, Chairman, 1.
31. Katharine Q. Seelye, "F.B.I. Director Was Opposed To Freeing Puerto Ricans," *New York Times*, September 22, 1999.
32. House Committee on Government Reform, *Clemency for Terrorists*, 65.

Twelve: Elian

1. Lisa Arthur, Bruce Taylor Seeman, and Elain De Valle, "5-year-old Found on Inner Tube, 2 Other Cuban Rafters Survive but 11 Feared Dead at Sea," *Miami Herald*, November 26, 1999.
2. Jay Weaver, "Elian's Fate Unclear," *Miami Herald*, December 1, 1999.
3. Juan O. Tamayo and Christopher Marquis, "U.S. Rebuffs Castro on His Demand for Return of 6-year-old Rafter," *Miami Herald*, December 7, 1999.
4. Ibid.
5. "Elian's Best Interests?" *National Review Online*, April 24, 2000.
6. Carol Rosenberg and Elaine De Valle, "Boy May Be Sent Back," *Miami Herald*, December 8, 1999.
7. Morton Kondracke, "Reno's Used Force to Aid Clinton, Not Elian," *Roll Call*, April 24, 2000.
8. Juan O. Tamayo and Christopher Marquis, "U.S. Rebuffs Castro on His Demand for Return of 6-year-old Rafter," *Miami Herald*, December 7, 1999.
9. Roger Morris, *Partners in Power: The Clintons and Their America* (Washington D.C.: Regnery Publishing, 1996), 241-247.
10. Lincoln Diaz-Balart, "Congress, Protect Elian; U.S. Can't Bow to Castro's Ultimatum," *Washington Times*, January 21, 2000.
11. Affidavit of Sister Jeanne O'Laughlin, February 24, 1999.
12. *Gonzalez v. Reno*, No. 00-11424-D, 2000 WL 381901 (11th Cir 2000).
13. Manny Garcia, "Tactics Experts: Removal Would Be 'Nightmare,'" *Miami Herald*, April 22, 1999.
14. Eric Lichtblau, "Past Tragedy a Factor in Reno's Caution," *Los Angeles Times*, April 14, 2000.
15. Frank Davies, "Reno Has 'No Regrets' Over Raid to Seize Child," *Miami Herald*, April 25, 2000.

16. Lawrence Tribe, "Justice Taken Too Far," *New York Times*, April 25, 2000.
17. Andrew P. Napolitano, "Reno's Raid Was Based on a Tissue of Lies," *Wall Street Journal*, April 26, 2000.
18. Andres Viglucci, "Experts Dispute Warrant to Seize Elian from Home," *Miami Herald*, April 29, 2000.
19. Alfonso Chardy, "Businesses Set for Shutdown," *Miami Herald*, April 25, 2000.
20. Luisa Yanez, "NBC Cameraman Disputes INS on Raid," *Fort Lauderdale Sun-Sentinel*, June 9, 2000.
21. Ibid.
22. *Gonzalez v. Reno*, 212 F3d 1338 (11th Cir 2000).
23. 8 U.S.C. Sec. 1158(a)(1).
24. *Gonzalez v. Reno*, 215 F3d 1243, (11th Cir 2000).

Acknowledgments

I want to thank my friend Greg Mueller of Creative Response Concepts for introducing me to Regnery Publishing and for supporting this project. Regnery was great in every respect. I especially want to acknowledge the editorial staff. My editor, Harry Crocker, was outstanding to work with. He was extraordinarily patient, diligent, and responsive. A real pro, he made excellent suggestions throughout which helped me tighten and refine the final product. During the final weeks of proofreading, Kimberly Pierce, Brian Robertson, and Emily Dateno were particularly helpful in making last-minute corrections.

I would also like to thank two bestselling Regnery authors, Ann Coulter and Barbara Olson, whose practical advice as fellow lawyers and writers was invaluable. Mark Levin, a legal and constitutional scholar of the first order, and a good friend, is one of the best at separating the extraneous from the germane. I only hope that some of it has rubbed off. He helped reignite my passion for constitutional law and for writing. My friend Sean Hannity was also extremely supportive and encouraging.

Finally, I want to thank my brother Rush. He has been a true inspiration to me. At the risk of fraternal pride I will say that I think he almost single-handedly resurrected talk radio and with it the mainstreaming of conservative political thought. Beyond his God-given talents, he has worked very hard to perfect his craft and strives every day to stay on the cutting edge. People who think it is easy to entertain and educate for three hours a day before an audience of twenty million have never tried it, or anything remotely resembling it. And Rush will continue to contribute to their misunderstanding by forever making it look easy.

Index

Adams, Arlin, 134–35
Adams, John, x
Adarand v. Pena, 276
Aguilera, Davy, 15
Air Advantage, 70
Airline of Americas, 72
Albright, Madeleine, 191
Aldrich, Gary, 140
American Bar Association, 105
American Cancer Society, 40
American Express Travel, 71
American Heart Association, 40
American Lung Association, 40
American Spectator, 109–10, 136, 267
Americk, Peter, 28–29
Ammerman, Nancy, 27
Andrew, Joe, 273
APAC. *See* Asia Pacific Advisory
  Council
Arkansas Project, 109
Armed Forces of National
  Liberation (FALN), 293–96
Arnold, Philip, 26
Aronson, Mary, 52
Ashcroft, John, xiii, 99–100

Asia Pacific Advisory Council
  (APAC), 194–95

Bacon, Ken: Tripp's right to pri-
  vacy and, 145–54
Bailey, Jennifer, 319
Bakaly, Charles, 128
Ballesteros, Roland, 23
Bam Chang International, 194
Bank of China, 217
Barbour, Haley, 187–88, 189, 211
Barr, Bob, 123
Barr, William P., 164
Barrett, David, xii–xiii
Basulto, Jose, 311
Bates, Joseph, 3
Battaglia, Lynne, 286
Begala, Paul, 97, 100, 103
Bell, Griffin B., 164
Bennett, Jackie, 115, 166; Tripp
  tapes and, 117–19
Bennett, Robert, 95, 97, 141
Berger, Sandy, 219, 261–62
Bernath, Clifford: Tripp's right to
  privacy and, 146–54

Betrayal (Gertz), 245
Bilbray, Brian, 122
Bittman, Bob, 166
Blackman, Paul, 22–23, 25–26
Bloodworth-Thomason, Linda, 76–77
Blue Cross and Blue Shield of Minnesota, 45
Blumenthal, Sidney: executive privilege and, 159; Starr's staff and, 102, 103; subpoena of, 103–4
Bolick, Clint, 283
Bork, Robert, 161
Bosetti, Chuck, 288
Bowles, Erskine, 282
Boxer, Barbara, 252–53
Brady rule, 24
Branch Davidians: drugs and, 21–22; FBI tactics against, 27–29; investigation of, 12–14; Koresh and, 4, 6–7, 29–30; religious beliefs of, 27; SDA and, 2; Seven Seals and, 9–10; split in, 7; Waco fires and, 32–33; Waco property and, 8; Waco raid and, 21, 22, 27
Brasseaux, Barney, 70
breast implants, 63
Breault, Marc, 11, 12, 15
Breaux, John, 176
Breuer, Lanny, 97, 162
Brill's Content, 110
Brill, Steven, 110
Brothers to the Rescue anti-Castro movement, 311
Brown, Ron, 194, 206, 245
Brown and Williamson Tobacco Corporation, 46
Bureau of Alcohol, Tobacco, and Firearms (ATF): Branch Davidian investigation by, 12–14; Koresh's treatment of children and, 11–12; sexual harassment allegations against, 16; Waco investigations and, 33; Waco raid and, 1, 8, 16–26; warrants obtained by, 14–16
Bureau of Prisons, 297, 298
Burton, Dan, 123, 126; campaign finance investigation and, 204, 205, 237; campaign finance scandals and, 239; Clinton's clemency offers and, 301, 302; Elian and, 313; Independent Counsel Act and, 256; missing e-mails and, 264
Bush, George, 69, 158, 164
Bush, Jeb, 313, 323
Byrd, Robert, 282–84, 285

Caires, Greg, 148
California, 277–78
Callahan, Laura, 263, 264
Cameron, Carl, 237, 271
Cammarata, Joseph, 140
campaign finance scandals: Buddhist Temple fund-raiser and, 183; Chung and, 239–41; Clinton and, 169–74, 205–6, 220, 239, 257–58; DNC and, 170, 171, 189–95, 200; FBI and, 197; Federal Election Commission and, 189, 198, 211; Gore and, 170, 181, 189, 205–8, 239, 253–55, 265–72; Hillary Clinton and, 170, 192; Hsia and, 184, 224, 237–39; Huang and, 176–80, 216, 218–20; Ickes and, 205–6; illegal foreign contributions and, 173–74, 179–88, 191–92, 200–201, 216; investigation of, 203–5; Justice Department and, 169, 175–76, 188, 193, 195,

208–10, 234–37, 241, 248–52;
La Bella and, xii, 169–70;
Lippo Group and, 174–76, 218;
Lums and, 194–95; Morris and,
170; Red Chinese and, 218–20;
reform and, 192–93, 198–200;
Reno and, xii, 193, 208–10,
230–32; Riadys and, 174–75,
262-63; RNC and, 210–12;
Thompson and, 211; Trie and,
236–37; White House access
and, 169–71
Campaign Finance Task Force, 169
Campane, Jerry, 221
Campbell, William, 42
Carey, Ron, 227–30
Carney, Betta, 66
Carollo, Joe, 323
Carter, Jimmy, 39–40, 121, 158,
294, 311
Carter, John, 225–26
Carville, James, 94, 96, 103
Castro, Fidel, 307, 309, 311, 318
Cavanaugh, James, 19
Central Intelligence Agency (CIA),
225, 246
Cerda, Clarissa, 66
Chaldeans, 191
Chang, George, 271
Charitable Trust Section, 187
Chavez, Linda, 279
Chenowith, Helen, 123
Cheong Am America, Inc., 174, 182
Chicago Tribune, 194–95
Child Protective Services (CPS),
12, 15
China: Huang and, 180; human
rights abuses of, 178; Most
Favored Nation status for, 178,
197–98; U.S. satellite technol-
ogy and, 241–47, 260–62; U.S.
trade with, 175

China Aerospace, 244
China Great Wall Industry, 244
China Resources, 219–20
Chojnacki, Phillip, 19, 20, 25
Christ. *See* Jesus Christ
Christian Coalition, 214
Christopher, Warren, 245
Chung, Johnny, 217, 239–41
CIA. *See* Central Intelligence
Agency
Ciancio, Sam, 308
Ciresi, Michael, 54
Cisneros, Henry, xiii
Civil Rights Act of 1957, 275
Clark, Bonnie, 5
Clark, Marcia, 124
Clegg, Roger, 286–87
Cleveland Plain Dealer, 296
Clinger, William, 83, 89
Clinton, Bill: campaign finance
investigation and, 235, 249–51,
254–55, 257–58; campaign
finance reform and, 199; cam-
paign finance scandals and,
170–74, 188–90, 205–6, 220,
232, 239; character assassina-
tion by, xi, 112–13; clemency
offers of, 294–305; Dale's
acquittal and, 81; DNC
finances and, 172–73, 258;
Elian and, 313, 322, 331; executive privilege abuse of, 157,
158–67; Flynt and, 121–23;
Hillary's senatorial campaign
and, 294; Huang and, 177–78,
182; Ickes investigation and,
256; Indonesia policy of, 181;
Jones case and, 117; Justice
Department and, x–xii, 333–36;
Lee's appointment and, 275–76,
281–83, 291–92; Lewinsky
scandal and, 93–95, 98, 113;

Clinton, Bill (*cont.*)
Miami raid and, 323; Riadys and, 175; satellite exports investigation and, 242–43, 246–47; soft vs. hard money and, 172–73; Starr and, 111, 113–15, 130–31, 137–38; Tamraz and, 225–26; Teamsters and, 228–29; tobacco industry and, 39–42, 44, 46–47, 50, 52–58; Travelgate and, xi, 65–67, 71–74, 87–91; Waco and, xi, 34, 37; Whitewater and, 108–9; Willey and, 142. *See also* Clinton-Gore administration

Clinton, Hillary: abuse of power by, 86; campaign finance investigation and, 251; campaign finance scandals and, 170, 192; clemency offers and, 298–300; Clinton's clemency offers and, 305; executive privilege abuse and, 162; Lewinsky scandal and, 93, 96–98; senatorial campaign of, 294; Starr and, 95–96; Travelgate and, 65, 68, 82–91

Clinton-Gore administration: abuses of power of, ix; campaign finance scandals and, 169; civil rights and, 275; corruption of, x; crimes of, ix; Justice Department and, ix; law enforcement and, xi; rule of law and, x; satellite exports investigation and, 245; scandals in, xiii; tobacco companies and, 62–63; Tripp and, 139–40, 154–55; Waco raid and, 20. *See also* Clinton, Bill

Clinton-Reno Justice Department. *See* Justice Department

Cochran, Thad, 216

Coffey, Kendall, 322, 328
Cohen, William, 150, 151–53
Collins, Susan, 219
Commerce Department: Huang and, 177, 193, 219; Lippo Group and, 179; satellite exports investigation and, 246
Commerce, Justice, State, and Judiciary Appropriations Subcommittee, 61
Common Cause, 193
Congress: campaign finance reform and, 200; Democrats and, 190; Lee's appointment and, 282; Reno's blocking of, xii; Republicans and, 190; tobacco industry and, 54; tobacco regulation and, 40, 47, 50; Travelgate and, 74
Congressional Research Service, 49, 285
Connor, Joseph, 295
Conrad, Robert J., Jr., 265, 267, 270–71
Constitution, ix–x, 305
Conway, George, 117
Conyers, John, 99, 289
Cornelius, Catherine, 66–68, 70, 78
Coulter, Ann, 117
Cox, Archibald, 124
Cox, Christopher, 247, 260
Cox Report, 247, 260–62
CPS. *See* Child Protective Services
Craig, Gregory, 112, 318, 322
Crown, Henry, 302
Cuba, 307
Current Affair, A, 12
Currie, Betty, 159
Cutler, Lloyd, 159

Dale, Billy, 74, 75; acquittal of, 81; character assassination of, 86–88;

political prosecution of, 77–82, 91; Travelgate and, 67–68; Watkins memo and, 86–87

Dale, Blanche, 79, 82

Dalrymple, Donato, 308, 322

Danforth, John, 35–36

Danou, Julie, 191

Daschle, Tom, 201

Davis, Gilbert, 108, 116

Davis, Lanny, 103, 219, 232

DeBruin, David, 213

Defense Daily, 148

Defense Department, 53, 61, 146

DeGuerin, Dick, 22, 29, 30

Democratic National Committee (DNC): auditing of, 200; Buddhist Temple fund-raiser and, 223; campaign finance investigation and, 205, 212–13; campaign finance reform and, 199; campaign finance scandals and, 170, 171, 189–91, 192–95; Chung and, 240; Clinton's control of finances of, 172–73, 258; Hip Hing Holdings and, 217–18; Huang and, 178–80, 220; illegal foreign contributions and, 180–88, 216; pre-election campaign finance report of, 187–88; return of contributions by, 174, 192, 193–94; Starr and, 94–95; Tamraz and, 224–26; Teamsters and, 227–30; Victory Fund of, 217–18

Democratic Senatorial Campaign Committee (DSCC), 176, 199–200

Dershowitz, Alan, 324

DeSarno, James, 269

Devroy, Ann, 75

Diallo, Amadou, 289

Diamond Walnut Company, 255

Diringer, Elliot, 291

DNA Plant Technology Corporation, 45–46

DNC. *See* Democratic National Committee

Dodd, Christopher, 189

Dole, Bob, 184, 185, 229

Dole, Elizabeth, 261

Domenici, Peter, 126, 215

Donaldson, Sam, 80

Dorismond, Patrick, 289

Dozhier, Parker, 109

DSCC. *See* Democratic Senatorial Campaign Committee

Durbin, Richard, 50, 116

Earth in the Balance (Gore), 266

East Asian and Pacific Affairs Subcommittee, 196

Eastland, Terry, 233

Edelman, Peter, 333–34

Edson, Hiram, 3

Education and Information Project, 94

Eichenbaum, David, 174

Eisenhower, Dwight, 157

Elders, Joycelyn, 39, 40

Eller, Jeff, 65–66, 68, 69

Emanuel, Rahm, 50, 100; Lewinsky scandal and, 97

Emmick, Michael, 102

End Time prophecy, 6, 10, 11

Energy Department, 225

Environmental Protection Agency (EPA), 44

EPA. *See* Environmental Protection Agency

Ethics in Government Act. *See* Independent Counsel Act

executive privilege: Bush and, 158; Carter and, 158; Clinton and,

executive privilege (*cont.*)
157, 158–67; Eisenhower and,
157; Ford and, 158; Justice
Department and, 164–66;
Kennedy and, 157–58; Nixon
and, 158; OIC and, 163,
164–67; Reno and, 159; Starr
and, 160, 162–64, 167;
Supreme Court and, 158;
Whitewater and, 159

Fabiani, Mark, 182
FALN. *See* Armed Forces of
National Liberation
Farone, William A., 42
Farrow, Jeffrey, 303
FBI. *See* Federal Bureau of
Investigation
FDA. *See* Food and Drug
Administration
Federal Bureau of Investigation
(FBI): campaign finance investi-
gation and, 232–33; Clinton's
clemency offers and, 297, 298;
Huang and, 259; illegal foreign
contributions and, 197; Justice
Department vs., 232–33; leak
investigation and, 127–28;
Travelgate and, 68–73; Waco
and, 26–34, 34–36
Federal Election Commission:
Buddhist Temple fund-raiser
and, 183; campaign finance
scandals and, 187, 189, 198,
211; Hsia's defrauding of, 238
Federal Employee Health Benefits
Program, 53
Federal Medical Care Recovery Act
(1962), 51
Federal Rules of Criminal
Procedure, 98, 112
Federal Trade Commission, 40

Feingold, Russell, 191
Feinstein, Dianne, 196–97, 281
Fernandez, Alina, 317
First Amendment, 43, 104, 172
Florida, 45
Florida Department of Children
and Family, 309
Flynt, Larry, 94, 121–23
FOBs. *See* Friends of Bill
Fo Kuang Shan Buddhist Order,
183, 266
Foley, James, 310
Food and Drug Administration
(FDA), tobacco regulation and,
40, 41–44, 50–52
Ford, Gerald, 158
Foreign Relations Committee, 196
Formell, Juan-Carlos, 317
Fossell, Vito, 301
Foster, Vincent, 84; Travelgate and,
68, 69, 89–90; Tripp and, 139–40
Fourth Commandment, 3
Fowler, Donald, 182, 192–93, 220;
Tamraz-Clinton meeting and, 226
Frank, Barney, 116
Freedom of Information Act, 152
Freeh, Louis, 36, 235, 249, 253,
272, 304
Friedan, Betty, 85
Friedman, Paul, 238
Friends of Bill (FOBs), 76–77

Gallagher, Maggie, 140
Gallagher, Neil, 304
Gandhi, Mahatma, 185
Gandhi, Yogesh, 185–87
Gandhi Memorial International
Foundation, 187
GAO. *See* General Accounting
Office
General Accounting Office (GAO), 76
General Motors, 107, 134

Gephardt, Richard, 201
Geragos, Mark J., 129
Gertz, Bill, 245
"ghoul defense," 49
Gilman, Benjamin, 204
Gingrich, Newt, 181, 184, 191;
    Lee's appointment and, 279;
    satellite exports investigation
    and, 243
Ginsburg, William, 107
Glenn, John, 215, 249
Goldberg, Lucianne, 117, 140–42
Gonzalez, Elian: asylum application
    of, 311–14, 319–21, 328–31;
    Castro and, 309–10; Justice
    Department and, 318; Miami
    raid and, 322–26; O'Laughlin
    and, 314–16; rescue of, 307–8;
    State Department and, 310;
    surrendering of, 319–20; visita-
    tion of, 326–27
Gonzalez, Elizabeth, 328–31
Gonzalez, Juan Miguel, 307, 311,
    317–18, 323
Gonzalez, Lazaro, 308–9, 311–13,
    319, 322, 329
Gonzalez, Marisleysis, 309, 312,
    314, 317, 327
Gore, Al, xii; Buddhist Temple
    fund-raiser and, 183, 223–24;
    campaign finance investigation
    and, 235, 249–51, 253–55,
    265–72; campaign finance
    reform and, 199; campaign
    finance scandals and, 170, 181,
    185, 189, 190, 205–8, 222–24,
    231–32, 239; Clinton's
    clemency offers and, 304–5;
    foreign affairs and, 190; Hsia's
    conviction and, 238; Huang
    and, 176, 179; illegal foreign
    contributions and, 272; missing

e-mails and, 263–64; phone
    solicitations of, 222–23; presi-
    dential campaign of, 272–73; as
    "solicitor-in-chief," 205–8;
    suing for presidency by, 333;
    tobacco industry and, 44,
    51–52; Travelgate and, 70
government: rule of law and, ix–x;
    support of smoking by, 48–49
Graham, Bob, 51, 323, 326
Gramm, Phil, 299, 301
The Great Controversy (White), 3
Great Disappointment, 3
Great Tribulation, 9
Grobmeyer, Mark, 34
Grossman, Steven, 199
Guinier, Lani, 280
Gutierrez, Armando, 319

Haas, Robert, 263
Hale, David, 108–9
Hamilton, James, 89–90
Hamilton, William, 228
Hampson, Thomas, 219–20
hard money, 172, 222
Hartman, Robert, 80
Hartnett, Dan, 24–25
Hatch, Orrin, 55, 74; Clinton's
    clemency offers and, 295;
    Justice Department leaks and,
    126–27; Lee's appointment and,
    276–78, 280–81, 283–84, 285;
    Reno and, 208–9, 258
Headline, Bill, 75
Health and Human Services, 61
Healthy Buildings International, 44
Hernreich, Nancy, 159
Heslin, Sheila, 225–26
Higgins, Stephen, 15
Hip Hing Holdings, 217–18
Hodgkiss, Anita, 290
Hoekstra, Peter, 255

Hoffa, Jimmy, Jr., 227
Hoffman, Abbie, 138
Holder, Eric, Jr., 108, 127, 166, 298
Hotung, Eric, 218–19
Hotung, Patricia, 219
House Appropriations
  Subcommittee, 61
House Banking Committee, 85
House Government Reform and
  Oversight Committee, 68, 83,
  84, 126, 175–76, 235, 252; cam-
  paign finance scandals and, 195;
  Chung and, 240; Elian and,
  313; Huang and, 259; White
  House e-mails and, 263–64
"House of David," 10
House Rules Committee, 196
Houteff, Florence, 4–5
Houteff, Victor, 4–5
Howell, Bobby, 5
Howell, Vernon. *See* Koresh, David
Hsia, Maria L.: Buddhist Temple
  fund-raiser and, 184, 224, 238;
  Gore and, 266; Huang and,
  259; indictment and conviction
  of, 237–39; PLC and, 267
Hsi Lai Buddhist Temple, 183
Huang, John, 34; Buddhist Temple
  fund-raiser and, 183–84, 223,
  224; campaign finance investi-
  gation and, 215, 220, 259–60;
  campaign finance scandals and,
  176–80, 194, 216–17, 218–20;
  China and, 180; Clinton and,
  177–78, 182; Commerce
  Department and, 177, 193, 219;
  Democratic Party and, 182;
  DNC and, 178–80, 220; FBI
  investigation of, 203; Gore and,
  179; Hsia's conviction and, 238;
  illegal foreign contributions
  and, 174, 179, 181–82, 186;

Lippo Group and, 174, 177,
  178; PLC and, 267; Riady and,
  176, 259–60
Hubbell, Webster, 118, 175
Hughes Electronics, 241, 242,
  245–47, 260
Humphrey, Hubert H., III, 45
Hunger, Frank, 51–52
Hustler, 94
Hyde, Henry, 119, 123, 209, 304

Ickes, Harold, 147; campaign
  finance investigation and, 251;
  campaign finance scandals,
  205–6; investigation of, 255–57;
  labor unions and, 228;
  Lewinsky scandal and, 97
Immigration and Naturalization
  Service (INS): Elian's asylum
  application and, 311–12,
  320–21, 328–30; Lazaro and,
  308–9; Miami raid and, 324;
  upholding of decisions of, 318
Independent Counsel Act, 35, 105,
  165–66; campaign finance
  investigation and, 250–51; OIC
  investigation and, 127; Reno's
  interpretation of, 209, 233, 250;
  Starr and, 124; Starr's impeach-
  ment referral and, 114
Indian health services, 53
Indonesia, 181
Ingersoll, Laura, 231
Inhofe, James, 151–52
INS. *See* Immigration and
  Naturalization Service
Internal Revenue Service (IRS):
  Justice Department and, xiii;
  Travelgate and, 72–73
Investigative Group, Inc., 101
Iran, 244
Iraq, 191, 192

Iraqi Christian minority, 191
IRS. *See* Internal Revenue Service
Isikoff, Michael, 140–41

Jamar, Jeffrey, 23, 26, 30–32
Jesus Christ: coming of, 2–5, 8;
    Kingdom of God and, 4; Seven
    Seals and, 9–10
Ji Shengde, 241
Joe Camel, 40
Johnson, Norma Holloway: execu-
    tive privilege and, 160; leak
    allegations and, 111–12, 128;
    Starr's exoneration and, 130,
    131, 135
Jones, David, 18
Jones, Michelle, 10
Jones, Paula, 95, 113
Jones, Perry, 18
Jones, Rachel, 7
Jones, Walter, 47
Jordan, Vernon, 118, 119–20
Josten, Bruce, 56
Judicial Watch, 263
Justice Department: breast implant
    manufacturers and, 63; cam-
    paign finance investigation and,
    213–14, 232–37, 241, 247–55;
    campaign finance scandals and,
    169, 175–76, 188, 193, 195–97,
    208–10; checks and balances
    and, x; Clinton and, x–xii, 296,
    298, 333–36; Clinton-Gore
    administration and, ix, xiii; cor-
    ruption in, ix; Danforth investi-
    gation and, 35–36; Elian and,
    318; executive privilege abuse
    and, 164–66; FBI vs., 232–33;
    Gore's phone solicitations and,
    222; Healthy Buildings
    International and, 44; Huang
    and, 259–60; IRS and, xiii; Lee

and, 333; Miami raid and,
    327–28; missing e-mails and,
    264; OIC and, 165; politiciza-
    tion of, ix; satellite exports
    investigation and, 241–47;
    Sonntag v. McConnell and, 285;
    Starr and, 95, 106–8, 123–27,
    136–37; tobacco industry and,
    39–41, 44–47, 50–57, 58, 60;
    Travelgate and, 74, 79, 91;
    Tripp's right to privacy and,
    151–52; Waco and, 32–34;
    Waco investigations and, 24–25,
    35–36. *See also* Reno, Janet

Kanchanalak, Pauline, 194, 201;
    campaign finance investigation
    and, 220; FBI investigation of,
    203; indictment of, 247–48
Kane, Dan, 309
Kantor, Mickey, 97, 255
Kendall, David: Hale and, 109–10;
    Lewinsky scandal and, 97; Starr
    and, 95–96, 98, 100, 114, 119,
    120, 123–24
Kennedy, John F., 157–58
Kennedy, William, 68, 73, 89
Kern, John W., III, 112, 127, 135
Kessler, David, 42, 43–44
Kessler, Gladys, 60–61
King, Coretta Scott, 294
Kirkland & Ellis, 117
Kirtley, Jane, 104
Klein, Joe, 281
Kopel, David, 22–23, 25–26
Koresh, David: ATF warrant for,
    13–15; Branch Davidians and,
    6–7; life of, 2, 5–6; name change
    of, 8–9; Roden and, 7–8;
    SDA and, 6; as Seventh
    Messenger, 4, 5, 7, 9; sexual
    proclivities of, 9, 10–11; surrender

Koresh, David (*cont.*)
   pledge of, 29; theology of, 2, 6, 9, 10; treatment of children by, 11–12; Waco and, 26–27, 33; Waco raid and, 1, 2, 17–20, 22, 23
Kornblum, Carole Ritts, 187
Kronenberg, Duangnet, 247, 248
Krovisky, Joe, 47

La Bella, Charles: campaign finance investigation and, 231, 233–34, 249–53, 269; campaign finance scandals and, xii, 169–70; Independent Counsel Act and, 250–52, 256–57, 258; punishment of, 252–53; satellite exports investigation and, 246–47
labor unions, 190, 227
Lader, Philip, 77
Lake, Anthony, 245
Lamberth, Royce, 147
Lambuth, Betty, 263–64
Lance, Bert, 121
Landmark Legal Foundation, 123, 127
Larry King Live, 80
Late Edition, 100
LaTourette, Steven, 205
Leach, Jim, 84–85
Leahy, Patrick, 103, 291–92, 301
Lee, Bill Lann: advocacy record of, 276; appointment of, 275; consent decrees and, 276; Florida election and, 333; opposition to, 277–81, 283–85; Proposition 209 and, 277–78; quotas and, 276–77; racial preferences and, 288–91; as recess appointment, 281–83; Republicans and, 278–80
Lee, John H. K., 174, 182

Lee, Wen Ho, 261
Legal Defense Fund, 275, 276
Lehane, Chris, 270
Lenzner, Terry, 101–2
Levin, Carl, 215
Levin, Mark, 127
Lewinsky, Monica: grand jury testimony of, 115; Jordan and, 119–20; Starr's handling of, 108, 110, 115–16; Tripp and, 140–42, 142–43
Lewinsky scandal: Clinton and, 93–95, 113; executive privilege and, 158–59; Hillary and, 93, 96–98; Justice and, xiii; right of privacy and, 104–5; Starr and, 104–5
Lewis, Ann, 97
Lewis, Marcia, 115–16
Lichtman, Judith, 85
Lieberman, Joseph, 114; campaign finance investigation and, 203–4, 218; Tamraz-Clinton meeting and, 226
Lindsay, Mark, 263, 264
Lindsey, Bruce: executive privilege abuse and, 159–62; Lewinsky scandal and, 97
Lippo Group: campaign finance scandals and, 218; Commerce Department and, 179; founding of, 174–75; Huang and, 174, 177, 178; Hubbell and, 175; Trie and, 221
Lippo Ltd., 174
Litt, Robert, 267
Little, Greg, 56
Liu Chao-ying, 239, 241, 244, 260–61
Liu Huaqing, 239, 260–61
Livingston, Robert, 122–23
Lockhart, Joe, 122; campaign finance scandals and, 185, 191;

Clinton's clemency offers and,
295; Lee's appointment and,
291; Starr and, 103
Loral Space and Communications,
241–44, 247, 260
Lorenzo, Orestes, 312
Los Angeles Times, 104; campaign
finance scandals and, 174, 180,
182, 186–87, 239
Lott, Trent: campaign finance
scandals and, 203–4; Lee's
appointment and, 279; Reno
and, 209; satellite exports inves-
tigation and, 243
Loutchansky, Grigory, 191–92
Lowell, Abbe, 119
Lum, Gene and Nora, 194–95
Luque, Nancy, 129, 132
Luu, Robert, 241
Lynch, Larry, 24

Macheteros, 293, 294
Mack, Connie, 323
Madigan, Michael, 214
Madison, James, ix
Madison Guaranty Savings and
Loan, 84, 85
Mandanici, Frank, 106–7, 132, 133
Mann, Caryn, 109
Mansfield, Steven, 271
Mapili, Maria, 237
Marcus, Jerome, 117, 118
Marine, Frank, 59–60
Marshall, Brad, 268
Marshall, Thurgood, 276
Martens, Darnell, 67–68, 70
Martin, Douglas Wayne, 24
Maughan, Ralph T., 70
Mayer, Jane, 145, 146, 147, 149
McBride, Ann, 235
McConnell, Mitch, 62
McCurry, Michael, 50, 197; allega-

tions against Starr and, 95, 178;
campaign finance reform and,
199–200; Gore's phone solicita-
tions and, 207; Lee's appoint-
ment and, 280, 282; satellite
exports investigation and, 243
McDougal, Susan, 106, 128–29
McGrory, Mary, 143–44
McHale, Paul, 112–13
McHugh, John, 205
McLarty, Thomas F. "Mack," 76,
83, 84; executive privilege
abuse and, 162; Tamraz-
Clinton meeting and, 225–26
McMahon, Henry, 16
McManus, Doyle, 104
MCRA. *See* Medical Care
Recovery Act
McSweeney, John, 88
Medicaid, 47, 49
Medical Care Recovery Act
(MCRA), 47, 58, 63
Medicare, 47, 49, 52, 53, 55
Medicare Secondary Payer Act
(MSP), 58, 63
Meehan, Martin, 40, 41
Meese, Edwin, III, 164
Meet the Press, 96, 100, 185
Meyerhoff, Robert, 232
Miami Herald, 316
Middleton, Mark, 193
Mikva, Abner, 207
Miller, William, 2–3, 4
Millerism, 2–3
Milley, Kevin, 145
Mills, Cheryl, 97, 162
Minnesota Supreme Court, 45
Mississippi, 45
Monicagate. *See* Lewinsky scandal
Montanarelli, Stephen, 143
Moody, James, 118, 142, 145
Moore, Michael, 41, 50, 317, 325

Morris, Dick, 148; campaign finance scandals and, 170, 171; Lewinsky scandal and, 93–94
Morrison, Toni, 121
Moynihan, Daniel Patrick, 301
MSP. *See* Medicare Secondary Payer Act
Murray, Alan, 104
Myers, Dee Dee, 69–70, 73–74, 75

Nadler, Jerrold, 108
Nangle, John F., 132–34
Naraski, Karen, 281
National Economic Council, 245
National Firearms Act, 13
National Policy Forum, 211
National Public Radio, 103
National Rifle Association, 214
National Security Council, 225–26
"New Light" revelation, 11
New Mount Carmel, 5
Newsweek, 86, 125
New Yorker, 145
New York Post, 126
New York Times, 107, 127–28, 146
Ng Lap Seng, 220, 221, 236
Nicholson, Jim, 123, 211–12, 238–39, 273
Ning, Hashaim, 181, 182
Nixon, Richard, 121, 158
Noble, Ron, 24
Nolan, Beth, 76
No More Wacos (Kopel and Blackman), 22, 25
Nordex, 192
North Korea, 192
Northrop Grumman, 263–64
Novak, Robert, 237
Nuccio, Richard, 310
Nussbaum, Bernard, 89, 139–40, 333–34

O'Connor, John Cardinal, 294
O'Laughlin, Jeanne, 314–16
Office of Professional Responsibility, 125, 127
Office of the Independent Counsel (OIC): attacks on, 100; executive privilege abuse and, 163, 164–67; Justice Department and, 125–27, 165; leak allegations against, 99, 110–11, 128; Reno's undermining of, 95; Travelgate and, 83; Tripp tapes and, 118. *See also* Starr, Kenneth
Office of the Surgeon General, 49
Ogden, David W., 54
OIC. *See* Office of the Independent Counsel
Olson, Ted, x–xi
"Operation Trojan Horse." *See* Waco raid
Osteen, William L., 43

Pacific Leadership Conference (PLC), 267
Packwood, Bob, 99
Pakistan, 244
Pandolfi, Ronald, 246
Panetta, Leon, 77; campaign finance scandals and, 184–85, 268
Parkinson, Larry, 269
Pascarella, Rocco, 295
Passportgate, 150
Pastorella, Richard, 295
Patrick, Deval L., 275, 280
Peat Marwick, 69, 87
Pelosi, Nancy, 244
Penelas, Alex, 326
Pepperdine University, 106
Perloff, Susan, 144
Philip Morris, 42–43, 56

Pinzler, Isabelle, 285
PLC. *See* Pacific Leadership Conference
Podesta, John, 78, 97
Popular Boricua Army. *See* Macheteros
Porter, Richard W., 117, 120
Posse Comitatus Act, 21
Post, Markie, 76
Privacy Act, 152, 153
Proposition 209, 277–78
Puerto Rico, 293–94

Quigley, Craig, 152–53

Racketeer Influenced and Corrupt Organizations Act (RICO), 58–61
Radek, Lee J., 134, 271–72
Rand, Josh, 109
Ray, Robert W., 90
Reagan, Ronald, 233
Rebozo, Bebe, 121
Rendell, Ed, 273
Renfrew, Charles, 135
Reno, Janet: campaign finance investigation and, 214, 230, 233–36, 253–58, 269–72; campaign finance scandals and, xii, 193, 208–10, 231–32; Clinton's crimes and abuses of power and, x–xi; conflicts of interest of, 233–34; in contempt of Congress, 252; Elian and, 313, 315, 318, 331; executive privilege abuse and, 159, 167; firing of U.S. attorneys and, xi; Gore investigation of, 222, 265; Independent Counsel Act and, 209, 233, 250; Koresh's surrender pledge and, 31; Koresh's treatment of children and, 12;
Lee's appointment and, 282, 283–84; Miami raid and, 323, 325; OIC and, 95; Starr and, 99, 111, 116–17, 123–27, 137; stonewalling by, xii; tobacco industry and, xi, 40–41, 47, 51, 53–57, 61–63; Travelgate and, 72; Tripp's right to privacy and, 152; Waco and, xi, 30–35, 37. *See also* Justice Department
Reporters Committee for Freedom of the Press, 104
Republican National Committee (RNC), 188; campaign finance scandals and, 210–12
Republicans: Congress and, 190; DNC's foreign fund-raising activities and, 184; Lee and, 278–80
Riady, James, 34; campaign finance scandals and, 174; Clinton meeting with, 175; Huang and, 176, 259–60; illegal foreign contributions and, 216; indictment of, 262–63; PLC and, 267
Riady, Mochtar, 174–75, 181
Ricks, Bob, 30
RICO. *See* Racketeer Influenced and Corrupt Organizations Act
right of privacy, 104–5
Rivera, Geraldo, 107, 112, 124
Rivera Live, 107, 112, 124
Robbins, Steve, 315
Roberts, Cokie, 122
Robinson, James K., 269
Roden, Ben, 5
Roden, George, 7–8, 22
Roden, Lois, 5, 6, 7
Rodriguez, Mary, 325
Rodriguez, Raquel, 314
Rodriguez, Robert, 15–16, 18–20
Rodriguez, Rosa, 313

Rogers, Harold, 61–62
Rohrabacher, Dana, 122
Roll Call, 47
Romer, Roy, 200, 212–13
Rose Law Firm, 68, 84
Rosen, Marvin, 178
Rosenzweig, Paul, 117–19
Ruff, Charles F. C., 160–61; campaign finance investigation and, 205; Clinton's clemency offers and, 294; Lewinsky scandal and, 97
rule of law, ix–x
Russia, 190
Ruth, Henry, 252
Ryrie, Charles, 9

Sacramento Bee, 182
Safire, William, xii, xiii, 85, 102
Sample, Penny, 70–71
Sandler, Joseph, 211
Sarabyn, Charles, 19–20, 25
Scaife, Richard Mellon, 106, 108–9, 132
Schippers, David, 167
Schmidt, Susan, 102, 124, 166
Schneider, Steve, 22, 26, 28, 29
Schwartz, Bernard, 241–43, 246
Schwartz, Jonathan, 166
Scruggs, Richard, 50
Sculimbrene, Dennis, 68–69, 78
SDA. *See* Seventh-Day Adventist Church
Second Coming, 6, 8, 9
Secret Service, 78, 86; executive privilege abuse and, 162–65; Treasury Department and, 163
Seligman, Nicole, 102
Senate Ethics Committee, 99
Senate Governmental Affairs Committee, 137, 171, 178, 236; campaign finance investigation

and, 203–4; Clinton and, 258; Ickes and, 255; labor unions and, 227
Senate Judiciary Committee, 285; Elian and, 317; tobacco industry and, 47
Senate Rules Committee, 203
Serrano, Jose, 300
Seven Messengers, 4
Seven Seals, 9–10
Seventh-Day Adventist Church (SDA): Branch Davidians and, 2; Christ's coming and, 2–5; formation of, 2–3; Koresh and, 6
Shaheen, Michael E., Jr., 110, 134
Sherburne, Jane, 101
Shotgun News, 15
"Showtime" raid. *See* Waco raid
Silberman, Lawrence, 165–66
Simon, Donald, 193
60 Minutes, 16
Smeal, Eleanor, 281
Smith, Stephen A., 132, 133
Social Security, 49
soft money, 172, 222
Solomon, Gerald, 146, 196
Sonntag, William, 285–86
Sonntag v. McConnell, 285
Sosnik, Doug, 97
Spearing, Mary C., 44–45
Specter, Arlen, 240, 265
Spielberg, Steven, 240
"Sputnik." *See* Koresh, David
Starr, Kenneth: attacks on, 113–15; attacks on staff of, 101–4; character assassination of, xi, 94–100; Clinton and, 111, 137–38; conflicts of interest of, 107, 116–17, 119–20, 132; DNC and, 94–95; executive privilege abuse and, 160, 162–64, 167; exoneration of,

130–37; formal complaints against, 105–8; General Motors case and, 107; impeachment referral of, 114–15; Jones case and, 141; Justice Department and, 95; leak allegations against, 98–101, 110–12, 127–28; Lewinsky and, 104–5, 108, 110, 115–16; McDougal's attack on, 128–29; prosecutorial zeal of, 105; Reno and, 111, 116–17, 123–27, 137; Travelgate and, 83, 89; Tripp and, 117–19, 124, 142, 144; Watkins memo and, 83. *See also* Office of the Independent Counsel

State Department, 310

Steele, Julie Hiatt, 129, 132, 133

Stent, Anthony, 295

Stephanopoulos, George, 71, 74; executive privilege and, 159

Stern, Mark, 60

Stone, Alan, 26, 33–34

Strauss, David, 253

Suharto, 181

Sullivan, Richard, 216–17

Supreme Court: campaign finance laws and, 172; executive privilege and, 158

Surface, Tom, 146

Susler, Jan, 296–97

Tabackman, Steven C., 78–79, 81–82, 86

Tabor, James, 26–27

Taiwan, 176

Tamraz, Roger, 224–26

Teamsters, 227–30

Terry, Luther, 48–49

Thailand, 194

Thibodeau, David, 10–12, 29

Thomason, Harry: Lewinsky scandal and, 93; Travelgate and, 67–68, 76–77, 84

Thomason, Richland & Martens Inc. (TRM), 67, 70, 77

Thomasson, Patsy, 66, 68, 78

Thompson, Fred, 249; campaign finance investigation and, 203–4, 212–16, 218–19; campaign finance scandals and, 211; China Plan and, 239–40; Huang and, 218; Independent Counsel Act and, 256; Red Chinese and, 219; Vacancies Act and, 285

Thornberry, B. J., 189–90

Thornburgh, Dick, 164

Tilley, Kimberly, 223

Time magazine, 191; campaign finance scandals and, 210

Timmerman, Kenneth R., 266–67

Timperlake, Edward, 34

tobacco industry: civil action against, 46–52; Clinton and, 39–42, 44, 46–47, 50, 52–58; Clinton-Gore administration and, 57–59, 61–62, 62–63; congressional regulation of, 40, 47, 50; FDA and, 40, 41–44, 50, 51; Gore and, 44, 51–52; Justice Department and, 39, 40–41, 45–47, 50–58, 60; regulation of, 40, 41–44, 50; Reno and, xi, 40–41, 47, 51, 53–57, 61–63; RICO and, 58–61; second-hand smoke and, 44–45; settlement with, 46; state action against, 45, 52–53; war against, xiii; war on, xi; weakness of case against, 59–60

Tobe, Amy Weiss, 186, 194, 195; campaign finance scandals and, 222

Today show, 282

Tom, Maeley, 215–16
Totenberg, Nina, 103–4
Travelgate: aftermath of, 88–91; Clinton's character assassination and, xi; Clinton and, 65–67, 71–74; Congress and, 74; Dale's trial and, 77–82; FBI and, 68–73; firing of employees and, 66, 68–74; FOBs and, 76–77; Gore and, 70; Hillary and, 65, 68, 82–86; investigation of, 88–91; IRS and, 72–73; Justice Department and, xiii, 74, 79, 91; Kennedy and, 89; Reno and, 72; Starr and, 83, 89; television networks and, 74–75; trials resulting from, 77–82; Watkins memo and, 82–86, 86–87, 90–91; World Wide Travel and, 65, 66
Treasury Department: Secret Service and, 163; Waco investigation and, 24–26; Waco raid and, 20; Waco report of, 13, 14
Tribe, Lawrence, 324–25
Trie, Charles Yah Lin, 195–96, 201; campaign finance investigation and, 220–21; campaign finance scandals and, 236–37; FBI investigation of, 203; Huang and, 221; indictment of, 236–37; Lippo Group and, 221
Triplett, William, 34
Tripp, Linda: arrest of, 146–48; attacks on, 142–51; character assassination of, xi; Clinton-Gore administration scandals and, 139–40; importance of, 154–55; Lewinsky and, 140–42, 142–43; Lewinsky scandal and, 117; media attack of, 143–44; right to privacy of, 148–55;

Starr's handling of, 104, 108, 117–19, 124, 144; Willey and, 140–41, 142
TRM. See Thomason, Richland & Martens Inc.
Truth at Any Cost (Schmidt and Weisskopf), 102, 166
Turley, Jonathan, 57
Tutu, Desmond, 294
Tyson, Laura D'Andrea, 245

Udolf, Bruce, 102
UltraAir, 72
United Charter School, 290
United States Chamber of Commerce, 55
United States v. Nixon, 158
Unlimited Access (Aldrich), 140
Urborn, Warren K., 132
USA Today, 121
U.S. National Council of Churches, 314
Utomo, Juliana, 218
Uydess, Ian L., 42–43

Vacancies Act, 284–85
Van Eimeren, Robert, 70
Veterans Affairs, 61, 62
veterans programs, 49
Vietnam, 181
Viscusi, W. Kip, 49
Voles, Lorraine, 207
Voting Rights Act, 275, 289

Wachtell, Herbert, 59
Waco: ATF warrants and, 14–16; children at, 31; Clinton and, xi; culpability in, 37; FBI and, 26–34; fires at, 32–33; government and, 37–38; investigations of, 14; Justice and, xiii; possession of property at, 7–8; Reno

and, xi, 30, 31, 32–34; U.S. government and, 1–2. *See also* Waco raid

Waco raid: ATF and, 1, 8, 16–26; Branch Davidians and, 21, 22; casualties of, 1, 2, 18, 20; Clinton-Gore administration and, 20; element of surprise and, 19–21; government's plan of attack and, 23–24; Koresh and, 2, 17–20, 22, 23; Treasury Department and, 20, 24–26; who fired first in, 22–23. *See also* Waco

Waco Tribune-Herald, 16, 23

Wall Street Journal, 42, 54, 104, 287

Wang Jun, 195

Washington Post, 71, 75, 81, 104; campaign finance scandals and, 183, 196; Hillary and, 86; Tripp and Lewinsky and, 144

Washington Times, 149

Watkins, David, 69; memo written by, 82–86, 86–87, 90; Travelgate and, 65, 66–67

Waxman, Henry, 40, 41

Weiner, Robert, 144

Weingarten, Reid H., 236

Weisskopf, Michael, 102, 124, 166

Wertheimer, Fred, 189

Wheeler, Sharon, 17

White, Ellen G., 3–4, 6

White, Frank, 311

White House Travel Office. *See* Travelgate

Whitewater, 108–9, 159

Whitworth, Wendy Walker, 80

Wiersbe, Warren, 9

Wilhelm, David, 216

Will, George, 284

Willey, Kathleen, 129, 140–41, 142

Williams, Maggie, 217

Williams, Scott, 49

Williams & Connolly, 101

Wiriadinata, Arief, 180–82, 270

Wiriadinata, Soraya, 180–82

Woodward, Bob, 196

Woolsey, R. James, 192

Wootton, Jim, 55

World Wide Travel, Inc., 65, 66, 70, 71

Worthen Banking Group, 176

Wright, Susan Webber, 106, 132

Wu, Mr. *See* Ng Lap Seng

York, Byron, 136

Young Brothers Development, 211

Zaccagnini, Anthony J., 143

Zappa, Frank, 232

Zeifman, Jerome, 190–91

Zhan, Keshi, 201

Zimmerman, Jack, 22

Zumbado, Tony, 328